1 (frontispiece) Reculver

ROGER HIGHAM

KENT

B. T. Batsford Ltd
London

CONTENTS

LIST OF ILLUSTRATIONS

ACKNOWLEDGMENTS

I should like to express my grateful thanks to Mr Frank Jenkins, MA, FSA, for his help in reading through the typescript and making suggestions for its improvement; also to Mr M. W. Powell of Wilmington, Mr & Mrs D. W. Higham of Trottiscliffe, Mr & Mrs Andrew Gemmill of Cowden, and Mr & Mrs Graham Waters of East Farleigh, for their hospitality. Most of all, I should like to thank my wife for her constant support, encouragement, and practical help.

The Author and Publishers would like to thank the following for permission to use photographs in this book: J. Allan Cash (Pls 3, 18); Noel Habgood (Pl. 15); A. F. Kersting (Pls 4, 5, 9, 10, 12–14, 19–21, 28, 29); Kenneth Scowen (Pls 6, 8, 22, 26, 31, 33); the late Edwin Smith (Pls 1, 2, 7, 11, 16, 17, 24, 25, 27, 32, 34); Spectrum Colour (Pl. 30). The map is by Patrick Leeson.

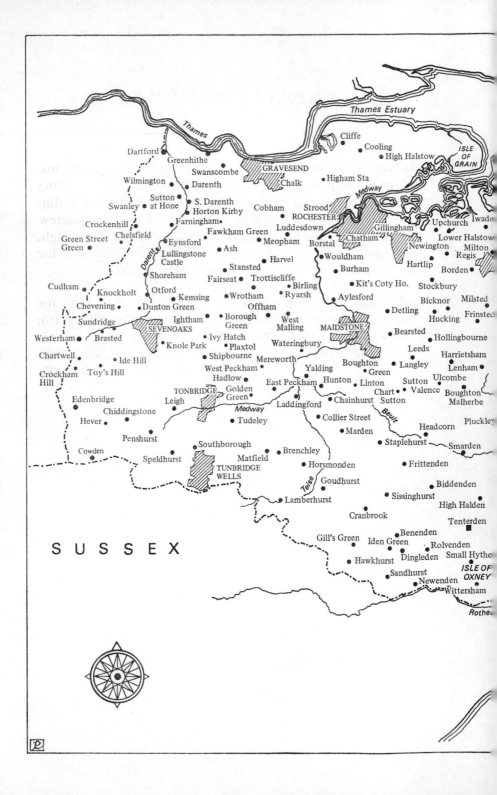

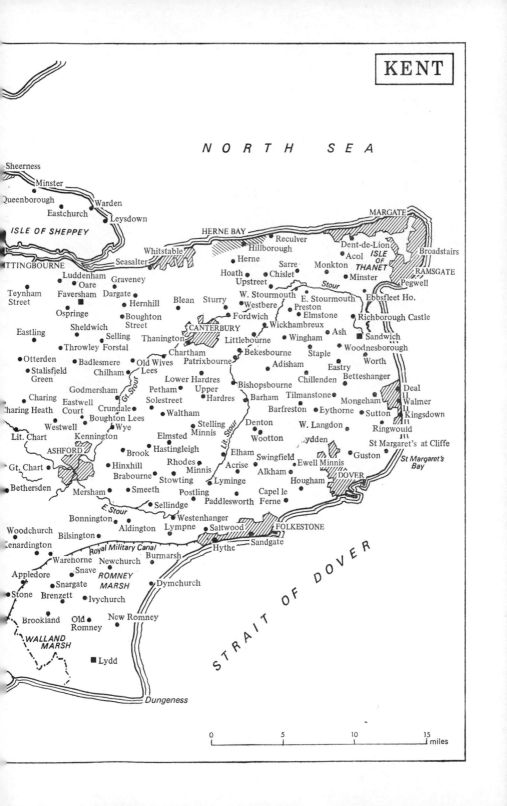

KENT

NORTH SEA

Sheerness
Minster
Queenborough
Eastchurch
Warden
Leysdown
ISLE OF SHEPPEY
TTINGBOURNE
Seasalter
Whitstable
HERNE BAY
Reculver
Hillborough
Herne
Dent-de-Lion
Acol ISLE
OF
THANET
MARGATE
Broadstairs
RAMSGATE
Pegwell
Luddenham
Oare
Graveney
Dargate
Sarre
Hoath
Chislet
Monkton
Minster
Teynham
Street
Faversham
Ospringe
Hernhill
Blean
Sturry
Upstreet
W. Stourmouth
Westbere
Stour
E. Stourmouth
Preston
Ebbsfleet Ho.
Sheldwich
Boughton
Street
Fordwich
Elmstone
Richborough Castle
Eastling
Selling
Thanington
CANTERBURY
Wickhambreux
Ash
Sandwich
Throwley Forstal
Littlebourne
Wingham
Woodnesborough
Otterden
Badlesmere
Old Wives
Lees
Chartham
Patrixbourne
Bekesbourne
Staple
Worth
Stalisfield
Green
Chilham
Adisham
Eastry
Betteshanger
Godmersham
Charing
Eastwell
Court
Petham
Lower Hardres
Upper
Hardres
Bishopsbourne
Chillenden
Deal
Charing Heath
Crundale
Solestreet
Barham
Tilmanstone
Mongeham
Walmer
Boughton Lees
Waltham
Barfreston
Eythorne
Sutton
Kingsdown
Westwell
Wye
Stelling
Minnis
Denton
W. Langdon
Ringwould
Lit. Chart
Kennington
Elmsted
Wootton
ydden
St Margaret's at Cliffe
ASHFORD
Brook
Hastingleigh
Elham
Swingfield
Guston
St Margaret's
Bay
Gt. Chart
Hinxhill
Rhodes
Minnis
Acrise
Ewell Minnis
Brabourne
Alkham
DOVER
Bethersden
Mersham
Smeeth
Stowting
Lyminge
Hougham
Postling
Paddlesworth
Capel le
Ferne
Sellindge
Bonnington
Aldington
Westenhanger
Lympne
Saltwood
FOLKESTONE
Woodchurch
Bilsington
Cenardington
Royal Military Canal
Hythe
Sandgate
Warehorne
Newchurch
Burmarsh
Appledore
Snave
ROMNEY
Snargate
MARSH
Dymchurch
Stone
Brenzett
Ivychurch
Brookland
Old
Romney
New Romney
WALLAND
MARSH
Lydd
STRAIT OF DOVER
Dungeness

Westbere
Eastling

0	5	10	15

miles

Introduction

There are at least three good reasons why Kent makes a fit literary and photographic subject: firstly, it is large, secondly, it is diverse and thirdly, it is accessible.

A fourth reason, perhaps transcending the first three, could be suggested: its importance. Size, diversity and accessibility do not necessitate this, but three others factors do: one, its geographical situation at the extreme south-eastern tip of England and the nearest of all counties to France and consequently to the Continent of Europe; it has been, is and clearly will be the connecting link between Britain and Europe. Secondly, it is near to London, the capital city of Great Britain. London has, admittedly, captured a large north-western part of Kent, but it has contributed also to the third factor, the high population, nearly 4 per cent of the population of England.

Despite the latter factor and mainly because of successive Town and Country Planning Acts since 1947, Kent has remained mainly agricultural, considerably horticultural, has extensive woodlands and clean rivers, and has an astonishingly diverse range of *flora* and *fauna*. Because of the high population which, in comparative figures, has been consistent throughout its history, to embellish its natural diversity of physical features it has as attractive and complete a range of architectural features as anywhere else in the kingdom: standing and subterranean Roman buildings, examples of ecclesiastical architecture from the Roman chapel at Lullingstone through all the changing scenes to the most modern, palaces, houses and cottages from all phases from the middle ages to the present day.

Until some 200 years ago it was impossible to support a large population, however extensive a county's acreage, without fertile soil capable of high food production, and the kind of climate to ensure it. Kent has had both these essentials, and in their turn they have enabled the remarkably wide range of habitats for *flora* and *fauna*, in which, with the exception of mountain types, Kent is one of the richest of counties in the British Isles. Fortunately much interest is taken in these aspects and as a result nature conservation is represented in Kent by several strong groups: there are Nature Reserves, National Trust sites and walks protected by the Forestry Commission numbering over 50.

The fertility of the soil, aided by the climate, has in the past produced for Kent the title of 'Garden of England': recent sneers, partly justified by the spread of urban and industrial activities and their unsightly accessories, have altered this to the 'Backyard of England', but nevertheless it can be pointed out that within the county can be found nearly half the orchards, half the hops and over one-fifth of the soft fruit grown in England and Wales. In addition to this and other market-garden produce, Kent can also show a wide diversity of crops and livestock. Even so, there is still room for 109,000 acres of woodland, occupying about 12 per cent of the total area, making Kent one of the most wooded counties in England.

There are not many rivers, but interest in their well-being in recent years and concern for the rate of pollution has resulted in sufficiently effective action by the Department of the Environment for them to be able to claim in 1971 that 92 per cent of the total length of rivers in the care of the Kent River Authority were now classed as unpolluted.

The same Department has been active too in maintaining an excavating important archaeological sites, with the result that the Roman work at Lullingstone, Reculver and Richborough can be seen and studied, the medieval remains at St Augustine's Abbey in Canterbury and at Dover, Eynsford and Rochester Castles, for example, are preserved, and early modern defence works like Upnor and Deal Castles are maintained and explained. The National Trust have cared for mansions and palaces like Knole, Sissinghurst and Chartwell, individual owners such as those of Penshurst and Hever have admitted the public to them, and to the enormously rich multiplicity of parish churches, with two great cathedrals, everyone is welcome, except that, for reasons of security, some are kept locked. There is also in Kent an excellent range of domestic buildings in most of the national styles, and a large number in the various vernacular types, depending on the material available locally: for cottages in the Downs, flint is used; for those on the ragstone and sandstone ridges, often a base of local stone. For the huge number in the Weald and woodland valleys and hills, timber predominates, and it is one of Kent's glories that there are still standing within its boundaries some 4000 timber-framed houses of the medieval and post-medieval stages. Thatch is rare because tiles have always been available, and as a result tile-hanging and painted weatherboarding are the commonest of Kentish vernacular styles. In an agricultural county farm buildings must be numerous, and although tumbledown barns and sheds, if picturesque, are not useful and therefore get replaced by less attractive concrete structures, there are nevertheless plenty of fine timbered barns, and that contribution to the rural landscape which has always been reckoned peculiarly Kentish, the cowled and steepled oast-kiln is still widely prevalent in hop-growing districts, although with the decline in the acreage of hops now required by brewers many of them have been converted for private use as houses.

In a county bordered by a narrow sea-passage on one side and by a great city on another, a stable indigenous population is unlikely to remain for long undisturbed; early ethnic distinctions between Jutish Men of Kent and Anglo-Saxon Kentish Men probably soon became only traditions, and although there still exists a hard core of long-established Kentish families, many of whom speak with a distinctively Kentish accent if not with a Kentish dialect, the proximity of London and the Continent has plentifully overlain these with a multitude of immigrants speaking nothing very distinctive at all. Under such conditions, Kentish dialect, where it survives, does so in rural areas and among farming communities, where a sickle is still a 'brish-hook', sandwiches for lunch are still 'progger', an easy job is a 'solomon' and a rough piece of land is a 'cant'.

Partisanship is nevertheless strong in Kent and soon seems to be implanted in even the newest arrivals from other parts of the kingdom, especially where sport is concerned, and particularly on the

Introduction

cricket field. Knowledge of and familiarity with the place in which one lives can produce a proportionately deep and lasting affection for it, and a corresponding desire to take care of it and protect it from all the potential devastations of modern developments, as generations of forerunners have protected Kent from invasion by foreign armies.

It is to be hoped, therefore, that in this book about a large, diverse, accessible and important county with traditions so strongly entrenched that they can be transmitted even to the latest newcomer from London or the 'shires', even so small a part of the stock will have been drawn from a vast storehouse to tempt the reader to look more closely at his surroundings, and penetrate more deeply, with even keener interest, into their structure.

2   The 'Pilgrims Way', near Wrotham

3 *The Gatehouse, Lullingstone Castle*

4 *Lees Court, Sheldwich*

CHAPTER ONE

Wantsum and Swale

From the high chalk hills between Ramsgate and Minster, in the Isle of Thanet, there projects a long, low ridge southwards to where the River Stour makes its great loop, flowing past the old port of Sandwich before meandering out to the sea. On the very end of this tongue of land there is a massive power station, which began generating electricity in 1963; its three cooling towers dominate the landscape and can be seen even from Canterbury, 12 miles away. Near by there is, on the western side of the ridge, a farmhouse called Ebbsfleet. Below it on either side of the slow river, the green flat meadows stretch away westward; there is nothing except the name of the farm to indicate that the nature of the place has changed, changed utterly during the 15 centuries since the ancestors of the Men of Kent landed here.

Thanet, of course, was an island, in the days when Britannia was a province of the Roman Empire (or, to be more accurate, four provinces) because the Stour and the Little Stour converged and emptied, near the place still called Stourmouth, into the Wantsum Channel, a broad tidal passage between Reculver in the north, and this ridge of Ebbsfleet in the east. The ridge, forming a natural protection against the perils of the English Channel, provided on its western side a haven, and became known by the name of a man, one of these early Men of Kent, who established his homestead there: the water was called the Fleet, the man, Ypped, the place, Ypped's fleet. In time, it became Ebbsfleet.

What it was called in the year A.D. 449 is not known; in fact hard evidence of the arrival at Ebbsfleet in that year of Hengist and Horsa and the first of the Jutes is similarly elusive. The very existence of two men called Hengist and Horsa, and the origins of the people called Jutes, are matters which are still debated: there are no certainties, only possibilities and probabilities. But the names Hengist and Horsa both mean horse (Hengist is a stallion, Horsa is any kind of of horse), and a white horse is the traditional badge of Kent; the Jutes, who quickly called themselves Kentings from the aboriginal name of the region, Cantium, were the creators of the Kingdom of Kent and the founders of its customs, culture and land-divisions, and the givers of names to most of its towns and villages.

The Venerable Bede and the Anglo-Saxon Chronicle both give 449 as the date of the landing, and Hengist and Horsa as the leaders. Hengist appears in a minstrel's saga of the Battle of Finnsburh, in Frisia, and Horsa is chronicled by Nennius in the ninth century as having been killed in the battle at Aylesford, so we can reasonably accept that they existed. Where they and their Jutes came from is equally hard to establish; it is often assumed that, in common with the Angles and Saxons, they inhabited the northern plains of Germany and in particular, Jutland, or Jute-land. But the contents of early Kentish burial sites reveal not only a culture far in advance of that found in Anglo-Saxon England but one remarkably similar to that of the Franks of the middle Rhine. Add to this the similarity of land distribution, in that a unit of land was reckoned not as a land measure but that which could be covered in a day's ploughing by a team of eight oxen, and the characteristic Rhineland district name of '*gau*': as Ruhrgau and Argau from the Ruhr and Ara, so in Kent Stour-geh (Sturry), and Lymin-geh (Lyminge) from Stour and Limen (the river which once flowed by the hill of Lympne); these hints seem to indicate that the Jutes might have been the Iuthungi, a Germanic tribe from the Upper Rhine and Danube, allied to the Alamanni who settled in what is now Alsace, after the turbulence and continuous movement of the fourth and fifth centuries. The Jutes seem to have arrived at the Rhine-mouth, beaten some Frisians at the Battle of Finnsburh, and been recruited by the chief magistrate of the sub-provincial region of Cantium, Vortigern, to help him repel the invading Picts (the painted men) from the north.

In 1949 some intrepid and lusty Danes built a long-ship and sailed it across the North Sea and up the Thames, to mark the fifteen-

5 Porch on the West Front, Cobham Hall

hundredth anniversary of what they thought was the arrival of their ancestors the Jutes of Jutland. The ship stands on dry land in Pegwell Bay, near Lloyd's Hoverport, with a plaque to say that Prince George of Denmark had attended the ceremony to mark the occasion. The ship, the *Hugin*, and the Hoverport, are north of the supposed landing-place at Ebbsfleet, and north also of the place where the next important arrival on this unpretentious piece of ground is supposed to have occurred: behind the sand-dune lining the Stour estuary is the A256, the road from Sandwich to Ramsgate, and on the landward side of this is St Augustine's Golf Club. Doubtless the holy Augustine would be surprised to find his name associated with a game more usually connected with St Andrew, but there are worse ways of marking a site, and the stone which is supposed to do this is much less easy to find. We have no less an authority than the Venerable Bede to tell us that it was to Thanet that Augustine, with his 40 monks, came, and the Wantsum was then about three furlongs wide. King Ethelbert, the King of Kent and at that time the most powerful in all England, had a Frankish wife, Bertha, who was already a Christian and had with her in Ethelbert's palace at Canterbury her chaplain, Liudhard: Ethelbert, while meeting Augustine in the open air in case of evil arts, very fairly permitted him to preach the word of God throughout his kingdom while reserving his judgment on something that was new to his subjects.

So, here at Ebbsfleet, within a space of 150 years, these two turning-points in the history of the county – and of the country – occurred: the Jutes came to Kent, and Christianity came to the Jutes.

At one end of the ridge of Ebbsfleet stands the huge power-station, and at the other, the Hoverport, where the still novel and unfamiliar hovercraft come roaring and swooshing out of the sea and across the level sands. Between power-station and Hoverport runs the busy road, for ever teeming with the omnipresent noise of motor traffic. In some parts of Kent, the past seems to live on, its memories still ineradicable; in others, the busy present, the rush and turmoil of the age, predominates; here at Ebbsfleet, past, present and future mingle: things began here, things are continuing now and show signs of continuing in some unknown shapes. I arrived at

6   *The Darent, ford and bridge at Eynsford*

Ebbsfleet on foot, from the train at Minster, and it is as a pedestrian that I shall view the County of Kent, and try to share with the reader the sights and sounds and thoughts of what has happened within its boundaries, what is happening now, and what might happen in the future. Walkers are not numerous in Kent, and in fact there is none of the kind of walking country where one can set off with pack, boots and stick for days on end and meet no one. Kent was thickly populated even when Julius Caesar saw it, and it has remained comparatively so ever since. And yet, even now, when the South-East of England generally and the London area in particular bears a colossal burden of population, there are tracts of country in Kent, of forest and farmland, which are either thinly populated or quite uninhabited, and it seems that full realisation of this can only come when one can go through them at the snail's pace of walking, by narrow lanes or by footpaths. There have been constant outcries in recent years, and rightly, against the urban and industrial debasement of what ought to be the Garden of England, and fears of what might happen to it should the threats be carried out of huge overspill cities built to accommodate the crowding hordes of London, or of the airport at Maplin Sands, across the Thames Estuary, whose noise would surely add to the present clamour, or of the awful uncertainties and possibilities of the Channel Tunnel, again being debated and this time seriously considered as a desired link with Europe. There is no denying that the fulfilment of all these projects would change radically certain aspects of certain parts of the county: change for the better for some, for the worse perhaps for many. But Kent is a large county, and I have walked something in the region of 900 miles to look at it, and then only partially; I think that, in this generation, much of it is likely to be subordinated to the country's general needs, but that, perhaps, a larger part, containing at least some of its topographical and architectural treasures, will survive into the next generation.

I began my tour of the county at Ebbsfleet in Thanet, and I continued it in regions roughly divided one from another by natural boundaries, such as hills and rivers, and sometimes by ancient roads like the Watling Street. These regions form the subjects for the chapters of this book, and the progress, again roughly, is anti-clockwise around the county. I hope that there will be something of interest in these regional chapters alike to visitors to Kent, to those large numbers of people who have come to live here from other parts of England and who want to know something of their new home, and perhaps even to Men of Kent and Kentishmen themselves, so many of whom know far more about their ancient Kingdom than I can ever tell them.

Minster, on the southern edge of the Isle of Thanet, is one of its oldest inhabited sites. It is now a small village with some mellow cottages, such as the row opposite the church marked 1710, and the one on the right up the street with a section of chequered stone and flint around its bow window; there is a tall and dignified Town Hall, still in use, but the principal interest lies, as appropriate in a place whose name derives from *monasterium*, in its ecclesiastical buildings. The church is the most obvious, a fine cruciform structure with some Roman bricks in the wall either side of the west door, in the tower, some flying buttresses, and what Walter Jerrold calls 'a trumpery spire', small, slim and shingled, on top of the tower. It has been much restored: its incumbent from 1644 to 1660, that revolutionary period when the English world turned upside down, was Richard Culmer, a hard-line Puritan iconoclast who smashed all the stained glass and ornaments in the church and defied all the efforts of his parishioners, who called him 'Blue-skin Dick' from his blue cloak, to get rid of him. The church probably incorporates parts of one of the churches of one of the monasteries, and since at various times there were three of these it is rather difficult to decide which was which.

Egbert, a seventh-century king of Kent, had connived at the murder of his kinsmen Ethelred and Ethelbert, at Eastry (Eastor-geh) where he had a palace. To expiate this crime he is said to have given land in Thanet to the boys' sister Domneva (alias Ermenburga, alias Eabba, further to confuse matters) for the foundation of a monastery. Domneva built it on the south side of the island near the water, the Wantsum, and was consecrated abbess by the Archbishop of Canterbury, Theodore. Her daughter Mildred succeeded her, ultimately becoming, with St Augustine, one of the most revered Kentish saints. Domneva's sister Ermengitha built the second monastery about a mile to the east, but this has vanished without trace. The successor of Mildred, Edburga, found the existing monastery too small and built the third near by, and moved Mildred's body there; it is said to have worked miracles. In the eighth century the Danish raids began, and since a monastery of nuns on the water's edge was to them ridiculously vulnerable, it was burnt and sacked several times. The last time was 1011, when the abbess Leofruna was captured by the Danish King Sweyn, and thereafter there were no more nuns.

There are, however, nuns there now. Along the road east of the church are the last surviving remains of the old abbey, in stone with round-headed windows, and in the yard between it and its farm buildings can be seen blue-clothed nuns at work: one, in a wide-brimmed straw hat and carrying a scythe, might look like an illustration for *The Canterbury Tales*, but another climbs aboard a brand-new red tractor and roars off to the fields. Minster is again a Benedictine convent, and its buildings are based on Edburga's second monastery.

A farm track leads off across the ancient shoreline (a house called Durlock is a reminder of the creeks and inlets that once were used for ships) to Ebbsfleet, and the road runs along the ridge by the sanddunes to Pegwell Bay and the Hoverport. In the bay, if the tide is out, tiny moving dots represent people digging in the time-honoured fashion for molluscs; the sands seem to stretch to France and it is safe to walk along the base of the chalk cliffs, which are scoured by the sea into sudden caves and gorges. It is possible, but not very comfortable, to walk to Ramsgate by this way: long before, there is a precarious ferroconcrete stairway which it is tempting to climb, and leads into the backyard of the Belle Vue inn. This is a good place from which to begin a tour of the Thanet coastal towns, beginning with Ramsgate.

Until the eighteenth century Ramsgate was no more than a fishing village with a handful of houses, but the increase of trade with the Continent brought it port traffic, wheat and malt to London, coal from Newcastle and passengers to the Netherlands, and consequent prosperity gave it new houses, built in the style which has seldom been rivalled for elegance before or since. There is the mighty crescent of the Regency Hotel, rows of iron-balustraded houses and other hotels in ordered ranks down to the harbour. Near the harbour is the astonishing Customs House, in terra-cotta advanced Byzantine with a green dome, and then beyond it a series of 'Pleasureamas' and 'Superamas' and numerous other attractions: the world of Frith's famous painting transformed to modern times. The harbour has two basins, divided between pleasure and business; in the inner basin a German ship is moored, unloading German motor-cars, a great stack of timber stands on another wharf, and at a third sand and gravel is being transferred from ship to shore. At the other end of the basin a mass of private pleasure-yachts are tied up to convenient jetties. The water in the outer basin is much rougher, as if to prepare week-end mariners for the perils of the open sea.

A clifftop road runs from Ramsgate to Dumpton Gap, a sudden break in the chalk cliffs, and on to Broadstairs, where Georgian houses cluster in terraces over the little bay: the crescent of sand is crowded, gay with colour, alive with sunbathers, donkeys, Punch and Judy and trampoline experts. On the northern arm of the bay is a plain house with a battlemented roof, Fort House, now called Bleak House because Charles Dickens once stayed there, and wrote (but not *Bleak House*). Dickens was often in Kent; he was born in Portsmouth, but his childhood began in Chatham, and his early ambition, to own Gadshill Place, was realised. Many are the reflections of Kent in his novels, and Dickens-lovers have frequently overstepped the mark of common sense in labelling with certainty houses and places which they think are identified in them. The writer, like many artists of the imagination, would take a name from one place, give it to a house from another and set it in a third place: the impression he gives is vivid, but the edges of the picture are blurred.

A steep little street passes beneath a flint archway, marked 1510, down to the harbour. Beyond the weatherboarded harbour-master's house the mole fends off the blustering sea from the boats in the small harbour, and a paved promenade at the cliff-foot leaves the northern arm of the bay and heads for the North Foreland. At the top there are large and luxurious mansions, now mostly hotels, schools and nursing-homes, all the way to the North Foreland Light.

On the next promontory beyond Joss Bay is Kingsgate Castle. The 'gate' or break in the cliffs beyond it was until 1683 called St Bartholomew's, or Bartlem, Gate, but Charles II happened to land there on a voyage from London to Dover and, apparently, renamed it. The Castle is one in a collection of 'follies' on the clifftop, in dark flint, and they were all built by Henry Fox, Lord Holland, in 1760, for his own residence and amusement. His reputation for venality elicited some lines of fierce satire from Gray, and it seems quite likely that the castle was built from funds which should have belonged to the Government. Lord Holland bequeathed his castle to his elder son; to his younger, Charles James, he seems to have left his liking for a way of life that was quite unlike the home life of Mr Pitt.

From the 'Captain Digby', an inn built from the same materials and in the same style as the castle, a road runs inland through several acres of cabbages at George Hill to considerably greater acreages of new housing at Northdown and the unattractive outskirts of Margate. In the middle of these is Salmestone Grange.

A grange was an outlying house, a manor farm, belonging to a monastery, in this case St Augustine's, Canterbury. The abbot, progressing round his abbey's estates, would stay there and receive tenants, their complaints and their rentals. In the early fourteenth century their complaints were evidently such that no abbot could assuage them: the tenants besieged the two resident monks for a fortnight, and perhaps burned some of the buildings, since a new chapel was dedicated in 1326. The chapel still stands, along with some of the remaining buildings, in flint ashlar, attached to a large old house. The chapel is apparently in use, by children from the nearby Catholic primary school.

Margate, whose town and suburbs fill the northern coast of Thanet, became in the eighteenth century one of the first of the seaside resorts, and it was a Margate man, a Quaker called Benjamin Beale, who invented the bathing machine. Successive generations of Londoners came by the current boat, from the Margate hoy to the Royal Sovereign, to enjoy its pleasures, and still they come, but today by road and train; they are not pleasures which appeal to everyone, so if Margate does not attract, then Margate can be shunned. If, like Eliot, 'On Margate sands, I can connect Nothing with nothing', then go somewhere else, for there are plenty of other places in Kent, to suit all tastes.

At Garlinge, the massed houses behind Westgate give place to farmland: a farm called Dent-de-Lion or Dandelyon, beside whose ordinary barns and sheds stands a fifteenth-century turreted gatehouse in alternate courses of flint and brick, preserves a name which was extinct even when the gatehouse was built. The family of that name flourished in the time of Edward I, and the last male heir died in 1445; the gatehouse is the remnant of the mansion which replaced the Dandelyons' manor house.

The lane from this farm leads straight into inland Thanet, and here can be seen the characteristic Thanet landscape: gently undulating, open country with very few trees, huge fields of corn and cabbages, and long-distance views of the hilltop roads, of aircraft at Manston Aerodrome, of the tops of the Ebbsfleet cooling towers. All the trees in the island seem to be massed around Quex Park, and from them there protrudes a metal Eiffel-like structure topped by a weather-vane and called Waterloo Tower. The village of Acol lies in a cunning fold of the hills, almost invisible from its approach road, and the long road trails on through the corn and cabbages; gulls, pigeons and lapwings swoop and cry, the troughs in the hills, the air and the light are like a seascape, quite different to any other Kentish scenery.

At the south-western tip of Thanet, where the Wantsum, when it was a channel three furlongs wide, changed its course from due south to nearly due east, is the village of Sarre. Its houses and cottages, many of them built by Flemish settlers in brick, in their characteristic gabled style in the seventeenth century, are sited, not along the road but at right-angles to it, facing a long-vanished waterfront. There was little enough of it left when they were built, for then Sarre was long past its hey-day; it had a centre some 100 yards east of the Crown inn, and a church on higher ground, and an Anglo-Saxon cemetery so full that it yielded a vast store of pottery, urns, amphorae, coloured beads, gold jewellery, weapons and coins, and even bone counters, with dice, for games. Tolls for the ferry were still collected in the time of Edward III, but the church of St Giles was exempted from the customary tenths in the time of Richard II:

the decline came from a decrease in population, and that from a loss of importance. Less shipping was using the Wantsum, because it was beginning to silt up. Eventually the Sarre Wall, which still carries the road to Thanet from the mainland, was built to stop the flow of the sea-tides and make the haven deeper, but soon the sea refused to come that far. The inhabitants of Sarre went to St Nicholas-at-Wade, on the healthier uplands, and the church of St Giles was abandoned. Now the Wantsum is no more than a drainage dyke, little different from the many others on these once tidal levels, and one crosses it into and out of Thanet almost without noticing it.

Islands which are not islands, seaports and naval bases miles inland, rivers of dry land and non-existent promontories: the vicissitudes of East Kentish geography are hard to understand. Three main causes contributed to the changes. Firstly, the slow-moving rivers, Stour, Little Stour, the stream called Sarre Penn and other tributary brooks, brought down silt which accumulated over a long period; secondly, the currents in the English Channel threw up an ever-increasing bank of shingle at the eastern end of the Wantsum, south of Ebbsfleet; thirdly, the soft clay cliffs of the northern coastline crumbled under attack by the sea, and the tides washed the debris into the Wantsum and gradually blocked the North Mouth. When they built their first fort on it, the Romans found Reculver a promontory, an ideal vantage point for guarding the northern entrance to the channel and even equipped with a haven on what is now its landward side. The minor road which they built out of Canterbury to serve it still forms the basis for the modern road: it ran from the river-port at Sturry, straight across country until it veered east along the promontory to the fort and camp at the end. Half the camp of Regulbium, some of whose walls are still visible, close by the King Ethelbert inn, is in the sea; Leland, in the sixteenth century, said that Reculver was a quarter of a mile from the sea. By 1708 Battely was writing that the waves had devastated the north face of the fort; in 1809 came the great storm which carried away half the fort and most of the churchyard.

According to the Anglo-Saxon Chronicle, in 669 King Egbert of Kent (the same who gave Thanet land to his niece Domneva for her abbey of Minster) gave 'Reculf' to Bass, his mass-priest, for another monastery, and ten years later his successor Lothair granted more land to its abbot. What happened to it is unknown, but by the time of Domesday the monastery and its possessions were held by the Archbishop of Canterbury. The twin-towered church, built almost entirely from Roman materials conveniently adjacent, survived as the parish church of Reculver. When the storm of 1809 threatened to wash it all away, the vicar and churchwardens dismantled it, leaving the towers, and built another church with the materials at Hillborough, a mile away and safely inland. Trinity House bought the remains, since the towers were a valuable landmark for shipping, and shored up the cliffs.

The old towers are still a landmark: approaching from Hillborough along the Romans' road, they can be seen standing out against the grey-blue sea and sky. The church at Hillborough, called Reculver Church, is the same as when it was built in 1809. The road slopes down past an untidy farm, across some cabbage fields and rises again to the remains of fort and church. There are very few other buildings, apart from the inn, but there are acres of caravans and a shanty-town of amusement arcades, bingo-halls and fish-and-chip shops. The church, whose towers have been much restored and strengthened, and is now in the care of the Ministry of Works, stands aloof, on the narrow remaining southern portion of the Roman fort, and faces the hungry sea. There is a surviving dark and slippery stone staircase in the northern tower, which leads up to the gallery between the two, and there are new stairs climbing higher still in the same tower, for those with strong constitutions and a head for heights. There are now strong groins below to keep the sea at bay, but it was a near thing: they and the sea are only a few feet from the base of this northern tower.

From Reculver there is a pleasant walk along the tops of the clay, grassy cliffs to Beltinge. They have no defences against a northerly gale, and every year the sea gobbles up a few more feet of them. Beltinge is in seaside bungalow country, always growing, and one feels that some of the bungalows are built rather optimistically near the edge of the cliffs. Herne Bay, a more sedate kind of resort than Margate, has a pier, and a signpost on the sea-front which points out, rightly, that there is nothing much between it and the North

Pole. The full significance of this is keenly felt by residents of Herne Bay in midwinter or in the teeth of one of the aforesaid northerly gales.

Inland from Beltinge and Herne Bay, across railway and Thanet Way, the main road which serves this part of north-east Kent, there are more enormous estates of new houses at Hunters Forstal, a hill previously distinguished only by a black windmill, which still looks as if it ought to be working. The housing continues to the village of Herne, the parent of the overgrown offspring at the Bay, where several cottages and a large and airy church demonstrate its venerable seniority. There is a memorial in the Church to Nicholas Ridley, who was vicar from 1538 to 1549. A Calvinistic puritan, as Bishop of London in 1550 he led the operation to remove 'relics of papery' from all London churches, particularly altars: a simple table was all that was needed. He paid for it, under Queen Mary, and Foxe recorded Bishop Latimer's famous comment to him as the flames scorched them; but the 'flame of remembrance' which Latimer and Ridley lit has too often become an excuse for ignorance, bigotry and hatred: the long shadows cast by it are still with us.

Starting from the churchyard at Herne, it is possible by taking footpaths and lanes to avoid the continuous line on the sea-coast of modern housing developments, and arrive in Chestfield. The whole of this distance is flanked on the hills to the south by the thick-set depths of the Forest of Blean which, since it is impossible to venture far in the country between Canterbury and Whitstable without encountering it, I shall mention again in this chapter. Chestfield, apparently all mixed up with its golf course, is full of expensive houses and unmade roads, which lead to the hills above Whitstable; from them on a clear day can be seen not only the sea and the Isle of Sheppey, but the coast of Essex as well. It is perhaps as well to bear this view in mind, because down in Whitstable itself there is rather less to gladden the eye. There are certainly some picturesque boat-sheds and old houses, mostly in weatherboard, along the sea-front, and the harbour still functions, with small coasters sitting on the mud (when the tide is out) being loaded with sand and cement. There are yacht clubs, and on a fine day the beach is crowded; but the fishing-fleet and the oyster-fleet are gone, the large brick storehouse of the Royal Native Oyster Company is dead, dusty and neglected, and the whole waterfront has the appearance of a town which has not yet decided how best to cope with the twentieth century.

In the 1830s Whitstable was one terminus of the first passenger railway. There was a considerable traffic of people sailing from London to Whitstable and going on by coach to Canterbury, and the railway, opened in 1830, was supposed to speed up the process. The hills, covered by the Forest of Blean, between Canterbury and the coast, were too much for the engine; winding-stations were substituted, then better engines in the 1840s, but the line never paid and has long been defunct. Much of the track, however, the rails themselves having been removed, remains, and provides an excellent means of penetrating the forest. A small industrial estate has been built at South Street, on the Whitstable end of the line, and soon in the woods the track can be found and followed for a mile or so. The forest is soundless, but for birdsong and the wind-waves in the tree-tops; it has that quality too of timelessness, to remind one that here is land which has never been inhabited, which has never been anything but forest, and whose dimensions, although cut back over the centuries by cultivation in the valleys, clearings round the roads and villages and occasionally wholesale felling and logging, nevertheless still measure ten miles by some three or four. Much of it has been replanted with standard Forestry Commission conifers, but plenty is left of traditional oak, ash and thorn.

The old railway track has been bought and blocked by a farm at Blean, and one has to follow the farm track, which emerges at the church of St Cosmos and St Damian in the Blean. It is a simple building of flint ashlar, with a timbered roof, standing on the site of a pre-Conquest church which no doubt served a small parish of foresters. The present village, called Blean, is on the main road from Whitstable to Canterbury, and is still the only village actually within the forest. There are hamlets, like Denstroude, consisting in a few cottages, one of which used to be an inn of character called the Church and State but is now a private house. There are many paths and tracks through the forest, and one of them leads up from Denstroude. It is easy to get lost, and just as easy to find the way again, following a little stream which in spring runs between wooded banks bright with bluebells, primroses, violets and fresh beech-leaves, to Fox's Cross, Thanet Way and the coastal marshes, and Seasalter.

There are not many reasons for going to Seasalter unless one is taking a holiday in one of the multitudinous caravans or holiday-chalets, except for the tiny church of St Alphege, which seems to be the chancel of a once larger building. A path follows the sea-wall westward, and across the East Swale channel can be seen the green eastern levels of Sheppey and the massed caravans of Leysdown, apparently continuing from where they left off at Seasalter. At an inn called The Old Sportsman, which looks like a nineteenth-century Guardroom or Officers' Mess standing alone among the sheep-pastures, a lane heads south across the marshes to Graveney. A line of pylons can be seen, like skeletal giants, for miles to westward, because the land is so level: in fact it was once an open bay, then tidal flats. A ship of King Alfred's time was discovered deep below the marsh's surface, still attached to its hawser of twisted withies.

The church at Graveney has a Norman chancel-arch, a good fifteenth-century screen and several brasses, the best of which shows Judge Martin, in his judicial robes, and his wife. He died in 1432, having built Graveney Court, the manor-house next to the church. Another good church-and-manor group is down the lane and across the railway at Goodnestone, and the other village in this district that certainly should be mentioned is Hernhill, on the edge of the forest. On a high hilltop four or five timbered houses including part of the manor-house and the Red Lion inn, and the large-towered grey-stone church stand around a pretty green.

For the exploration of the marsh country by Swale-side, west of Faversham Creek, it is best to start at Faversham itself. From the station, Preston Street leads down to the town's centre, the crossroads with market-place and town hall, a long chamber with a clock-tower, supported on wooden pillars. On either side are old town houses of varying periods, and in Court Street, north of the market-place, are more, mostly of the sixteenth and seventeenth centuries. Two breweries, one of them the sole surviving independent Kentish brewery, exude a prevalent yeasty, hoppy smell; beyond them the road continues as Abbey Street, with more houses which testify to

Faversham's prosperity in Tudor and Stuart times.

Situated at the head of a still navigable creek, Faversham has always been a port. It was of sufficient importance as early as the ninth century to be favoured with a royal residence, and by the time that King Stephen founded his abbey there, it had become prosperous enough soon to be linked with Dover as a Limb of the Cinque Port. As the Cinque Ports declined, so the wool trade picked up, and when that had ceased to be profitable, there was still boat-building and there was now gunpowder to be manufactured. Today there are the breweries and an assortment of other industries which crowd together towards Davington.

A large timbered house, No. 80, Abbey Street, is interesting for three reasons: one, for itself, a good example of a Tudor town house for a wealthy merchant, secondly that the latter was Thomas Arden who was murdered there by his wife and her lover in 1550, inspiring some 35 years later a work by an unknown dramatist called 'Arden of Feversham', and lastly because it has a stone wall which is one of the few remaining fragments of the abbey of St Saviour, founded in 1147 by King Stephen. It was colonised by an abbot and 12 monks from Bermondsey, thus coming under the sway of the great house of Cluny, in Burgundy, and was so esteemed by the unhappy king that he had his wife buried in its church in 1152, his son Eustace in 1153 and himself in 1154. Thereafter, reports on visitations made at intervals from 1275, when the archbishop deposed the abbot, to 1511, when he ordered more reform, usually seem to have found less than monastic conditions. In 1368 Archbishop Langham found that the monks were eating flesh, were not observing the rule of silence, were not showing the abbot their possessions, that one was quarrelsome and a producer of discord and that the house was £12 in debt. A porter was removed because 'he was the cause of access of dishonourable women'. It was nevertheless rich enough to escape the first dissolution of 1535, but none survived the second: the site was reverted to Sir Thomas Cheyne, the Treasurer, in 1540, and was subsequently bought by this same Thomas Arden.

Near the church, which is large, faced with dark flint ashlar and has an elegant tracery spire which is a landmark for miles around, is

35

a brand-new Queen Elizabeth Grammar School. Its one-time predecessor, hard by the churchyard, is a timbered building which
might have been about big enough to accommodate a couple of
dozen pupils.

Along West Street where houses as old as any in the town are in
less good repair, down to the watery, marshy valley at the head of
the creek and up the other side, the road comes to Davington, now
an extension of Faversham. Behind a high stone wall on the left of
the road at the top of the hill is the one-time priory church, serving a Benedictine nunnery established shortly after the house in
Faversham, in 1153 by one Fulk de Newenham. Many monastic
houses never really recovered from the effects of the Black Death:
the inquisition of 1535 found that the prioress had died earlier that
year, the last nun nine years before, and only a novice was left, so
it was dissolved. Surprisingly, the church is mainly intact, its high,
plain nave and Romanesque arches proving its twelfth-century origin.

Past the modern factories, on a ridge by an arm of Faversham
Creek, is Oare, whose name apparently is derived from a word for
seaweed. It has a faintly maritime air, and once controlled the road
to the defunct Harty Ferry, which is not so long gone that people
living cannot remember it working. West of it the low hills, repre-
senting the most northern part of the North Downs, give way to the
Swaleside marshes, which are green and fertile and thinly inhabited.
A circuitous lane leads to Luddenham Court, by which is a little
church with a brick tower. The incidence of a church without a
village does not necessarily mean that there once was one: in the
early years of medieval Christendom, before the eleventh-century extension of papal authority, the building of churches and appoint-
ment of priests was largely in lay hands. The lord of a manor would
naturally build his church near the manor-house, so that his tenants,
coming in from their far-flung holdings, could pay their dues and
attend church together. The fabric of buildings might have been re-
newed many times, but very often their sites have not been, as will
be seen in other parts of the county. Luddenham is a manor-house
with a variety of roofs and as long a lineage as any, but its church is
no longer in use.

The wandering lanes, through scattered hamlets, Elverton and Buckland, over and back across the railway, reveal a surprising number of timber-frame houses, some of which were probably built in the fifteenth century. At Teynham there are more, three in a street, surrounded by enough hop gardens and cherry orchards both to remind us of Dickens' Alfred Jingle's category of Kentish characteristics, and of Richard Harrys, fruiterer to Henry VIII, who cultivated the cherry in this same vicinity. The houses, perhaps, show how quickly the art of cherry-growing throve, for they may have been built in Harrys' time.

Orchards and hop gardens meet boats and gulls at Conyer, a small village by a narrow creek off the Swale: a few old barges squat on the mud in various stages of preservation, but boats in Conyer Creek are mainly small pleasure-yachts. As if to emphasise its change from a working wharf to a week-end-sailors' haven, facing one finger of the creek there have been built some very stylish houses, in weatherboard over their own garages, with balconies, and a yacht-club air. The boatyard, whose wharf is behind the inn, seems to be fully occupied; there is soon to be a modern marina.

A footpath from Conyer goes straight as a die between water-meadow and orchard to the railway, and a mile or so along the lane by its side is a pretty little millpond, whose eighteenth-century boarded mill is in use as a small factory. Overlooking the pond is the motte part of a Norman motte-and-bailey castle (the pond is on the site of the bailey) which could well have been founded on an earlier, Saxon earthwork. There is very little visible to show for this, just a hill with a derelict cottage and a clump of elms, and on the far side a ditch—the moat—filled with old rusty cars and other modern junk. A passenger in a train could pass it every day and never realise its ancient military significance as a guard to the vulnerable hinterland, so easily accessible from the Swale marshes to marauding seafarers. On the other side of the railway, up a small hill, is Tonge church, a still, silent place, built when the castle had decayed. Down on the levels again, a lane goes to Elmley Ferry, the other old way to Sheppey, longer dead than Harty. From it a path cuts across a strange marshy wilderness and woods choked with more dumped cars and rubbish of all sorts. At the end, near some cement works on the edge of Milton Creek, is a tiny ruined chapel, ivy-grown, roofless and quite derelict.

Sittingbourne, which can only be reached from the chapel through the paper-making and cement-works district of Murston, has achieved large dimensions and a reputation for drabness from these same two industries. Basically, it is a Watling Street town, and in the middle ages had a hospital for the accommodation of pilgrims to the shrine of St Thomas of Canterbury, and a hermitage, both at the western end. Later, the coaches would call, and like Faversham it benefited from being sited at the head of a creek deep enough for trading ships: there are still a number of good eighteenth-century houses in the Street, like the one with bow windows and pillared porch.

But for all its size now and medieval functions, Sittingbourne was small beer in the time of King Alfred, who gave his title to Milton Regis. Milton and his 'little town of Faversham' were important for their maritime position in an age when huge marauding armies of Danes were establishing camps in Thanet and Sheppey. A little tree-covered knoll called Castle Rough in front of the enormous Kemsley paper-mill, on the western bank of Milton Creek, is possibly the fortification built by the Danes' leader Haesten in 892, although it is too small to have accommodated his army. By shrewd manoeuvring of his army, King Alfred kept the Danes in a position of stalemate, until at last he was able to bring Haesten to terms, and the Danes withdrew.

Milton's continued pre-eminence over its neighbour until comparatively recent times shows in the remarkably well-preserved houses in its streets, converging on the market-place. Several examples survive from the fifteenth century onward: in the High Street, Nos. 75–77, for instance, is a Jacobean town-house, and Nos. 100–102 are in a timbered hall-house. In the market-place is the Court Hall, a long two-storeyed building, with lock-ups on the ground floor and a council-chamber upper room, of the mid-fifteenth century. The church is down the hill, on the edge of what evidently used to be part of the creek; parts of the original Saxon building are in the north wall, but it was restored after the Norman

7   *The staircase, Knole*

8 Ightham Mote

9 Quebec House, Westerham

10 The Study, Chartwell

11 Old Soar Manor, Plaxtol

Conquest and additions of an aisle and a chapel were made in later centuries. The tower, for example, was added in the fourteenth century, and is claimed as the largest in Kent (presumably among village churches: it could hardly compare with, say, Canterbury's Bell Harry). In the churchyard is a tombstone of a man, on the list of churchwardens, who was killed by a 'rockett' in 1696: of what kind or in what circumstances remain a mystery.

The main road to the Isle of Sheppey passes through Iwade, undistinguished and racked by noise from the traffic, and from it a lane mercifully permits the pedestrian to escape to the sheep-pastures and orchards on the last piece of rising ground before the Medway Estuary. An old anti-aircraft gun-site moulders away on the point from which a wide land- and seascape can be seen, from Queenborough and Sheerness on Sheppey, to the ships at anchor at the Isle of Grain jetties, round to the bulk of Kingsnorth Power Station. In the foreground is a wide, shallow inlet from the Medway, Stangate Creek, which opens to an even wider gulf called, at its farther end, Funton Creek, and at its nearer (from the vantage point on the hill), Bedlams Bottom. The latter name has its attractions for those with a whimsical turn of mind, and so does the bay, despite the derelict barges aground on the mudbanks and the quite unforgivable quantity of human junk deposited at its roadside fringe: it is devoid of other human manifestation, deserted by all but the numerous seabirds which wail in their plaintive and evocative fashion over the wind-ruffled water. Immediately inland, pear orchards cover the rising ground, and at Funton there is a brickworks. A brickworks might not perhaps be worthy of comment, were it not for the fact that there was one here, or hereabouts, in the vicinity of Lower Halstow and Upchurch, in the third and fourth centuries. Quantities of its products have been used by English church-builders, and the church of Lower Halstow itself is no exception: in fact it relies very heavily on Roman brick and tile for its materials.

Lower Halstow (spelt Halgastaw in *Domesday Monachorum*, meaning a holy place, but probably not a Christian holiness) is at the head of another creek. Its oldest houses cluster behind the church, practically on the water's edge, and it has a good jetty and mooring-place for small boats. A couple of Medway barges, rigged and ready for sailing, lie at anchor, and if the sun is shining and the tide in, the water blue and sparkling, larks singing and terns swooping, blue butterflies playing about the short grass, who could resist lingering there for a while?

Upchurch, on a hill across the gently undulating cornfields and orchards, is not quite so compelling; its church has a shingled steeple, in sections like a candle-snuffer, but the houses are plain and there is not the salt smell in the air, or whatever it is that elevates an equally plain waterside village. North of Upchurch were found large numbers of fragments of Roman pottery, evidently from pottery works, and on marshland which is now submerged in the estuary: another geographical change since Roman times. Several Roman villas have been discovered in this area, too: one at Boxted, south of Lower Halstow, another at Hartlip, beyond Watling Street, and a third at Sutton Baron, near Borden.

A path from Upchurch passes through a secluded valley which Gore Farm has to itself, a typically Kentish farmhouse sheltering among its fruit trees, with geese on its own reservoir. From the nearby hamlet of Breach it is not far to Newington, a Watling Street village spread along the road with, still, some 400-year-old houses. If the Street, the old Roman road from Canterbury to London, can be endured as far as Keycol Hill (which someone has ingeniously suggested must be derived from Caius Col, Caesar's Hill, for no known reason) then a lane can be found to Bobbing. This is a small village, with a small church, and must have been a poor living for the nefarious Titus Oates, perjurer extraordinary, who contrived to be its vicar for a mercifully short spell.

From Bobbing one can either walk to the Isle of Sheppey, or return to Sittingbourne and take the train: the latter is recommended for speed and comfort, and the excitement of crossing the Kingsferry Bridge and seeing the timber-ships moored at the Kemsley Paper Mill's dock. The train arrives at Queenborough, which on first inspection looks anything but exciting and even, if the factory near the station is emitting its customary appalling smell, distinctly off-putting.

East of the station is a vague grassy mound and a fenced-off ditch. On it there once stood a fine castle, the most modern that four-

teenth-century military planning could devise. King Edward III decreed it, to guard the western entrance to the Swale, Henry Yevele,
the architect, under Prior Chillenden, of the latest parts of Canterbury Cathedral, probably designed it, and Master John Box, mason
in the service of the same Prior and of the Crown, supervised the
works, which continued from 1361 to 1377 (the King's Works were
often a long time in building because the King's revenues were a long
time in coming). It was designed on a circular plan, with an outer
bailey, defended by a moat and wall, concentric with the circular
keep. It had a gateway in the west wall and a postern in the east,
and a passage between, connected with the keep, so that even if the
outer bailey were captured, the passages and the keep could be held.
The small village at the water's edge, called Bynnee, was renamed
Queenborough, after Edward's Queen Philippa (a fact recognised by
an inn near the station) and became a town of importance. But not
for long, because the castle decayed from neglect, and in 1629 was
pulled down, to the last stone.

The town also dwindled, but seems to have flourished again in the
eighteenth century, because its street is full of houses of that century and a fine Guildhall, with a pillared portico and a date, 1728.
Today it has its smelly factories and a waterfront full of small
boats.

It is a long, dull trudge to Sheerness, an approach through the
dreariest, most desolate street opposite the high dockyard wall, once
full of taverns but now in a ratio of two closed to every one still
open. At the end of the wall there is an eighteenth-century terrace
and church, once high-ranking officers' quarters, and a check-barrier
to the dockyard gate, which indicates that this once important
naval base is not entirely moribund. The sea-wall is lined with
jagged remains of the nineteenth-century fort and more recent concrete blockhouses; the road cuts through the fort's ramparts and
across its moat and enters the town of Sheerness, which now appears desperately seaside, but without the means to achieve the
transformation to another Margate. Two huge, gaunt cinemas, one
lingering on as a bingo-hall, the other dead, remind the town of its
missing ships' companies.

The sea-wall from Sheerness to Scrapsgate is newly rebuilt and provides a pleasant walk in the sunshine, with one eye on the ships in the Medway estuary, waiting for the tide. At Scrapsgate a road turns inland and uphill, past holiday camps and summer bungalows and through streets of modern houses to Minster, on the island's high central ridge. As in the case of Minster in Thanet, the name derives from *monasterium* and in *Domesday Monachorum* it is written as Sexburgamynster. Sexburga ruled Kent after her husband died, until her son Egbert (who has already appeared in this chapter) was old enough to take up his duties. In about 670 she founded and endowed a nunnery here in Sheppey, and settled there as prioress with 77 nuns. The monastery very probably suffered from the attack by the Danes in the ninth century, but it seems either to have survived or been revived, because it appears fairly regularly in records from 1186, when it was given tithes in Bobbing amounting to ten shillings a year, until Thomas Cromwell's investigation of 1535, when only the prioress and eight nuns were left and the value was found to be too low: it was dissolved there and then. The Abbey gate is still there, a four-square gatehouse, but not much else of the buildings except the fine church, which includes what was the Abbey chapel, called St Sexburga's, high-roofed with Romanesque windows and some Roman tiles in the walls. On the south side of the chancel is the tomb of Sir Robert Shurland, once Lord Warden of the Cinque Ports, whose family were great Sheppey landowners. By his right leg on the monument is a horse's head, which either commemorates or has elicited a legend, the crux of which was that he had been warned that his horse would be the death of him; to dispose of this he killed it, but years later he found its skull on the beach and contemptuously kicked it, a piece of bone pierced his foot and he died of blood-poisoning.

The Shurland lands were inherited by the Cheyne family, one of whom is also entombed here; and there is a stone knight in fifteenth-century armour which it is thought might be the Duke of Clarence, Edward IV's brother, the one who is supposed to have been drowned in a butt of Malmsey. There are quite a number of curiosities to examine within the church, and if long enough is spent on them the church clock might strike the hour: an interesting experience because it winds itself up with a tremendous whirring and clattering before each chime. Twelve of them provide a sure cure for melancholy.

Minster is on the highest point in the island, and of course there are horizon-raking views all around, to the north of the sea, to the south of the Swale and the Kentish hills. Descending from this eminence eastwards, a lane from Pigtail Corner runs into the only really rural part of Sheppey on the high ground, a gentle valley with farms and cornfields, and glimpses of the remains of Shurland Castle, a large, towered and turreted red-brick gatehouse, quite ruinous. Sir Thomas Cheyne (or Cheyney), who was Henry VIII's Lord Treasurer, was descended from Sir William who married the last of the old Shurland family in the early fourteenth century. He managed to acquire a disproportionately large amount of the dissolved monastery lands in Kent, became exceedingly rich, and built a huge mansion to replace the old Shurland manor-house, with nine quadrangles, stone walls and an area of several acres. The King and Ann Boleyn visited him there, but a mere 40 years elapsed before it was a dilapidated ruin: Sir Thomas's son moved elsewhere and spent his entire fortune.

The eastern end of Sheppey, from Warden Point to Leysdown, is caravan country. The cliffs of Warden Point are clay, like those of Reculver, and have suffered and are suffering the same fate: they used to extend very much farther out to the north. The main road which runs along the base of the ridge from Leysdown to Queenborough overlooks a wide sweep of low marshy country, including Sheppey's two other islands, Harty and Elmley. If the Harty Ferry were still running, it would be useful to the walker because he could see the lonely church and inn by the water there, and get across to Oare and then Faversham; as it is he has the prospect of walking four miles there and four back again, because there is no other way.

Eastchurch, near the remains of Shurland, is the only village on this side of the ridge. The good fifteenth-century church was rebuilt in 1431 through the generosity of an earlier Cheyne than the acquisitive Sir Thomas and his spendthrift son. He gave lands to the Cistercian abbey of Boxley for the purpose, and a Cistercian monk, William Nudds, was its first vicar. The church remains with hardly any alteration, a good example of the perpendicular style.

The only other hill on this side of the central ridge is occupied by the buildings of H.M. Prison. It is an open prison: the flat, desolate marshes, criss-crossed with watercourses and terminating in the wide and rapid Swale, are walls enough.

CHAPTER TWO

Downland

South of Watling Street a wide tract of country extends to the escarpment of the North Downs, constituting the longest unbroken line of the Downs in Kent. It used to be crossed by only two main roads, the one from Faversham to Ashford, and that from Sitting-bourne to Maidstone; now, the new motorway, M2, cuts a swathe through it from east of Faversham to its western extremity. Despite the constant activity on this road, the Downland remains among the loveliest, quietest and least inhabited country in the county.

Its northern slopes, running gently down to Watling Street, undulate mildly and bear every year a prodigious quantity of fruit, mainly cherries and hops. Farther south the hills are higher, the valleys deeper, and corn predominates. The mile or so to the steep escarpment is heavily wooded, the heads of the valleys are deep, silent ravines, and traffic is almost non-existent. There are no towns in all this area, but from Bredhurst north to Rainham and from Walderslade to Chatham, at its western end, the new housing estates spread for mile upon mile, and unless one happens actually to live among them, there is no longer any reason for going to those parts.

An exploration of the region on foot could start from Chilham railway station, and make off immediately uphill to Old Wives Lees which, despite its intriguing name, is a mostly modern village. There are hop gardens and orchards all about, and on the hills to the north are the dense greenwood heights of the extreme south-western peak of the Forest of Blean. Close beneath it, where the main railway line from Canterbury to Faversham runs deep in a cutting, there is a crossroads and a fine Elizabethan house at Rhodecourt Farm, timber-framed with a continuous jetty in front, oriel windows and brick chimneys. Across the railway, through a corner of the woods and the hamlet of Hickman's Green, the lane heads for Boughton Street, in the parish of Boughton-under-Blean. The Street is Watling Street, which here takes the traffic from the M2, whose entrance is a mile westward. The effect on the people of Boughton is traumatic, because not unnaturally they must endure perpetual din, danger to life and limb, and extreme difficulty in crossing from one side of the street to the other.

The houses in this harassed street, some standing on a bank slightly above the road, are handsome examples of all styles from the fifteenth century to the twentieth. One of them might have been the hospital for lepers, for the foundation and erection of which, in honour of the Holy Trinity but without licence, Thomas atte Herst (of 'Bocton atte Blee') was pardoned, in 1384, by King Richard II. Little more is known of it, not even whether it was in being when Chaucer made his pilgrims see the rascally Canon and his Yeoman catching up with them at the very spot.

Boughton church is more than a mile distant from the street by road, and in it is the alabaster tomb of Sir John Hawkins: not the seaman, who died in the disastrous expedition to Panama in 1595, but one of the Hawkinses of Nash Court, not far from Boughton Street (nor, now, far from the Brenley Corner roundabout), who was buried in 1587.

Boughton church is nearer to Selling station than is Selling itself; cherry orchards enclose the road tightly all the way up to this hilltop village, from which the sea is just visible. Opposite its inn there is a tiny one-storey brick cottage which looks as if it might have been a toll-house.

Sheldwich is on the A251 road from Faversham, and the approach from the direction of Selling, in high summer, is across a sea of barley which fills a plateau from end to end and shimmers aquatically in the heat and ripples in the breeze. The greater part of the village is at Sheldwich Lees, a little to the south on a side-lane, where cottages line a large and lush green. A drive from the lane serves Lees Court, which may have been designed by no less an architect than Inigo Jones and was the home of the old Civil War

Royalist Sir George Sondes, who had two sons: the younger murdered the elder and was hanged for it.

A footpath near this drive leads to Badlesmere Court, and it is
worth taking it, not so much for the Court, a good enough Georgian
manor-house, but for the little church close by it: the church and
court grouping again, the buildings replaced, the site the same. The
church is mentioned in *Domesday Monachorum* (at Baethdesmere)
and may have been the immediate predecessor of the present building, which has thirteenth-century lancets over the altar, a wooden
crown-post roof from the fourteenth century, and an interior
otherwise completely reorganised in the eighteenth century, the
chancel-arch removed, and a George I coat-of-arms over the door.
Manor and church once belonged to a family which had disappeared
as completely as the chapel which once stood on the northern side
of the church and housed their tombs. The best known of them is
Bartholomew de Badlesmere, an ambitious, flamboyant character
whose name is linked with two castles of Kent and a king and queen
of England.

Bartholomew, son and heir of Gunselm de Badlesmere, succeeded
his father in 1301 when he was 26. He appears to have been favoured by Edward II (who, as is well known, had some odd friends),
because he was granted Chilham Castle and manor in 1309 and became Lord Badlesmere. Later, he obtained the grant of Leeds Castle,
in addition. He served the king well in his struggles against the
Scots, but became more and more involved in politics, joining
Aymer de Valence, Earl of Pembroke, in a third party to mediate
between the Earl of Lancaster's and the king's parties. Eventually,
after an episode which had best be reserved for its connection with
Leeds Castle, Bartholomew joined Lancaster and Pembroke joined
the king. The Lancastrian party was defeated at Boroughbridge in
1322, Bartholomew was captured, attainted and hanged as a traitor
on Tyler Hill, Canterbury (apparently, on the present site of Darwin
College) and his head stuck on a pole in Burgate. His son, Giles, died
without issue, and that was the end of the family Badlesmere.

By another footpath, Badlesmere Green can be reached, back on
the Ashford road, and at Leaveland Court, a timbered manor-house
with, again, a little church close by, a lane dips into a large basin (in

the hills) of wheat, presided over by the high-towered church of Throwley. Throwley Forstal, at a distance from the basin of wheat and from the church, might serve as the archetypal English village green, fringed by white cottages, an inn, the post office and a farm; only the church is too far away to complete the picture. On a sunny day in summer, when, as now, no traffic troubles it except for trac- tors and tradesmen, it needs only the chorus of village maidens to make good the flight into fantasy, for that is where, normally, such a place only exists.

But this is the beginning of the wooded country on the edge of the escarpment, a region of winding, dipping and climbing lanes among the sudden steep valleys, of few farmsteads and fewer villages, of deep, undisturbed rustic calm. The lanes – there are several to choose from – run from the hill of Stalisfield Green down to the parkland of Otterden and up to Otterden Place, a brick Tudor manor-house largely rebuilt in the eighteenth century when its little church was also newly fashioned. There is hardly a village of Otter- den at all, and yet, like Luddenham, the manor and church have existed in some form since before the Conquest, when the Normans' surveyors marked it as Ottrindaenne.

A choice of roads leads back to Faversham: at the corner of the Otterden estate a crossroads tempts one either to the farther valley and Doddington and Newnham, or to the hilltop and Eastling. Both are rewarding, for Doddington has a basically Norman but mainly thirteenth-century church and some fine gardens, and Eastling, from which the tree-fringed tops of the Doddington valley are visible, has a beautiful timbered Elizabethan house with oriel windows, a per- fect country house for a squire of small pretensions. It is neverthe- less a long way to Painters Forstal, a bridge over the M2, and Ospringe.

The church of Ospringe, the first part of the village visible from this direction, has a curious gabled tower and looks wholly Vic- torian, but is a Norman church, heavily restored. Two major items of interest concerning Ospringe must be mentioned, one above ground, the other beneath it. That on our level is the surviving half of the Maison Dieu, or Domus Dei, which is said to have been founded by King Henry III, who granted land for its upkeep in 1239. In a house on the north side of Watling Street a Master, three regular brothers and two secular clerks were to entertain poor and needy pilgrims and travellers, and also to look after lepers, for whom the second house was built on the south side of the street. It is this second house which still stands, on the corner of the lane from the church; lepers evidently became less numerous, because only a hundred years later a room was furnished and kept in it for the king, should he chance to travel that way. He used it, as the chronicler Jean Froissart records, in 1395: '. . . when the King (Richard II) had had his sleep, I went back to the Archbishop's palace in which he was staying and found Sir Thomas Percy giving orders to his people to move off, for the King had decided to go back for the night to Ospringe, from which he had come that morning.' This Camera Regis can be seen, because the Maison Dieu is in the care of the Ministry of Works and open to the public.

The second and invisible point to remember about Ospringe is that beneath it, stretching from Judd's Hill, west of the church, all the way to Faversham church, are foundations of buildings, cemeteries, pottery and other relics of a Roman town, with their road of Watling Street running diagonally across it. Coin series found in various parts of the site last to the end of the fourth century, but a large Jutish cemetery found east of Ospringe could indicate a continuity of occupation in early post-Roman times. Stone chapel, on the site, was a Roman mausoleum converted to a church at about the time of Augustine. The town may, or may not, be the *Durolevum* of the rather vague Antonine Itinerary, which refers to places by name but gives impossible distances from known towns and so has caused a good many antiquarian headaches. At all events Ospringe, for a small Watling Street village, has a surprisingly momentous past.

Sittingbourne is a good starting-point for another dip into this Downland area; the houses now stretch all the way to Tunstall, but there is a lane, turning off by the hospital, which avoids them, passing through strawberry fields and cherry orchards and the small hamlet of Highsted, up a long valley and under the M2 to Milstead. Here at a crossroads, with the church on one side and the cricket field on the other, there is a very good Elizabethan manor-house, bigger than but similar in style to the one at Eastling; it is timber-framed, with continuous jetties (the characteristic overhangs of timbered houses) and a clock-tower. A small thatched barn is in the grounds. On the other side of the road next to the churchyard there is a hall-house, with a dated eighteenth-century chimney and bricked-up ends. According to Mr Kenneth Gravett, a well-known authority on Kentish timbered buildings, the style of the hall-house, otherwise known as the Wealden, or Yeoman's house, was well established by the end of the fourteenth century. It consisted of a central hall, open to the rafters, with both ends two-storeyed and jettied laterally, and a single hipped roof. The timbers were widely spaced, with prominent and symmetrical braces in the wings. This was known as Kentish framing: it is typified by the curved arch-braces supporting the eaves wall-plate where it crosses the hall in front, between the two projecting upper storeys. Towards the end of the fifteenth century, around 1470, the Kentish framing was re-placed by close-set upright timbers, called close-studding. After 1500, the arch-braces disappeared and a longer horizontal beam permitted a continuous jetty along the front; but the most impor-tant changes in the sixteenth century were the abandonment of the open central hall and its replacement by brick chimneys (previously the smoke from the fire had escaped through a louvre in the roof), which enabled flooring to cover the whole upper storey. Houses built after 1500 were fully equipped with chimneys, two storeys and a continuous jetty. Porches began to be added in the early seven-teenth century. There was never any real practical reason for the jetties, except perhaps to add a little space to the upper rooms; they seem merely to have been an aesthetic embellishment. The most surprising thing about these timber-framed houses, to my mind, is that so many of them have survived into modern times, consider-ing the uninsurably combustible nature of their materials.

The lane from Milstead turns its (or rather, the traveller's) back on the M2 and begins to lose itself in the deep Downland peace on the way to Frinsted. Most of the cottages in Frinsted appear to have been replaced in the 1860s by a consistent Tudor-cum-Jacobean style in patterned brick; the village hall and the monstrous inn, like a railway station, are also of this period. There was in fact a burst of building activity in rural Kent in the 1850s and 1860s, because this was the period of greatest prosperity and stability in the agricultural world. The removal of the Corn Laws in 1846 had not had the disastrous effect that everyone feared, Britain was far ahead of the rest of the world industrially, and the cheap wheat which would eventually wreck the whole scene had not yet begun to flood in from America. These were the years of equipoise, the age of Palmerston, peace and prosperity. No wonder that landowners felt confident enough to rehouse their tenants in modern cottages, build inns and halls and new farmhouses, barns and sheds. It was not until the mid-1870s that it all changed, when a succession of disastrous harvests brought the imported wheat in by the ton, and English agriculture crashed, and stayed on the floor, until the war of 1939–45.

Between the villages of Frinsted, Wormshill, Bicknor and Hucking (the last two are more like districts than villages) there are a number of steep little dry valleys, the heads of the long Downland valleys that run south to north, at this end mostly uninhabited save for the occasional small cottage. High, cool beechwoods hem them in, their bottoms are grass where cows and sheep graze undisturbed, and there are no intrusions from the high-speed commercial world. There are orchards between the woods and forestry plantations, and after the lonely inn at Hucking called the Hook and Hatchet and a couple more vales, near the escarpment of the Downs there is a peculiar structure on the hilltop at Coldblow which looks like four giant dustbin-lids on end. Paths through the woods take one away from this possibly electronic device to the top of the hill at Thurnham, where there is an overgrown high embankment. Known as Goddard's Castle, for no certain reason, this hill is in fact a relic of a Norman castle, consisting in a mount and courtyard, once encircled by stone walls. Some parts of the walls are still there, but so obscured by the all-enveloping vegetation that a visitor could hardly be blamed for doubting their existence. The choice of site is obviously good: standing on the mount, which has been severely cut about by quarrying on one side and the road on the other, the intrepid castle-climber can see something of what the garrison could see, and that is an enormous distance, over the ragstone hills east of Maidstone and beyond to the Weald.

There is another castle at Thurnham, called Binbury Castle, but it is in the private grounds of a farmhouse and therefore inaccessible. It is said to be similar in plan to the first, but could hardly be better positioned.

Most of Thurnham is below the Pilgrims Way, which runs along the foot of the Downs; it has a church which has a fine timber roof with crown-posts, and no chancel arch, and in the churchyard is the grave of the great Kent cricketer Alfred Mynn, born in Goudhurst, died in 1861, the 'Champion of English cricketers'. He was formidable with both bat and ball and also extremely popular it would seem, since '400 persons have united to erect this tombstone'. The Pilgrims Way is traceable along most of its length throughout Kent from the western border with Surrey at Titsey, to about Folkestone. It was no doubt used by pilgrims to the shrine of St Thomas at Canterbury in the middle ages, but predates them by at least 1500 years, since it was probably one of the trade routes used by the Celtic population of Britain in the dim centuries before the Roman invasion of A.D. 43. The name Pilgrims Way has nevertheless stuck, and been enshrined by Ordnance Survey in Old English script on their maps, so doubtless it will stay.

A short walk along it westward from Thurnham brings one to Detling, where there are some interesting cottages and, on the right-hand corner of the old Way, the small Tudor gateway, in rather eroded mellow brick, of East Court. Detling once suffered in the way that Boughton still suffers, from heavy traffic through its street, grinding up the steep hill which takes its name. Now there is a by-pass and a new road to take the uphill traffic, while the old Detling Hill road takes the Maidstone-bound lane. Detling people may now cross the road without becoming an instant insurance risk, but they will never get rid of the noise.

At the top of the hill (Thurnham and Detling are the only two villages south of the Downs that I shall mention in this chapter) the road goes off in the direction of Sittingbourne and on the left of it a narrow lane allows one to creep behind the Kent County Agricultural Showground, which occupies an old R.A.F. airfield, out of earshot of the traffic-noise, in thick woods. The woods along this heavily screened lane, in fact, have rather alarming names: Murrain

Wood, Scragged Oak and Stockings Wood (the latter hinting perhaps of a nasty murder), but on the far side of them is a sparsely
inhabited dale of arable and pasture-land, within a mile and a half
either way of a main road but so oblivious to both that it might be
in a different county. At its northern end is a farmhouse called by
the map Yelsted but labelled Guildstead, and a switchback mile or so
eastward from it another idyllic village green at Stockbury. Its
church, a quarter-mile farther on, is close by the remains of another
Norman motte-and-bailey castle, quite small and therefore possibly
the stronghold of the lord of the manor. Its moat is still quite deep,
and its site is clearly defensible, on the edge of a steep slope. The
Maidstone road is at the bottom, but it can be crossed at once.

Stockbury is only a couple of miles from Hartlip, a village on a
ridge in the middle of orchard country, which in spring, for a brief
spell, is a sight worth going to see, which is more than Dr Johnson
could say for the Giant's Causeway. The ridge is high and breezy
and full of prosperous houses, many of which are new and possibly
unconnected with cherry-growing. The large church has a high and
solid tower, which on its northern side has steps leading down to a
door and a tiny slit window: a cell once occupied by an anchorite, a
hermit who, in return for a meagre ration supplied by parishioners,
would spend his life in prayer for intercession for remission of all
their manifold sins.

The M2 crosses the Maidstone road, the A249, near Stockbury,
with one of those complicated systems of lead-in roads, and from
the junction a humble lane leads to Oad Street, where a decent
Tudor timbered house bears the irresponsible title of 'The Olde
House', and Sutton Baron or Barne, one of those farmhouses which
has been growing gradually for centuries, as can be seen more easily
from the back. The Roman villa which was found beneath an
orchard opposite the house is once more interred. Borden, to the
north, is distinguished by a remarkable number of timbered cottages.

The difficulty with this route, for the walker, is that it is hard to
work in a visit to Bredgar without missing somewhere else. It would
be worth it because there are some good cottages there and the remains of a small college, for which Richard II in 1392 granted a
licence to Robert de Bradegare and others to establish one chaplain

and two clerk scholars to serve God and celebrate divine service in the parish church: which, no doubt, they did, to everyone's satisfaction, for we hear no more about them. The college now forms part of a private house.

Rochester, Chatham and Gillingham, although they are at the western end of this Downland, properly belong to the Medway, and will therefore have to wait for another chapter.

12　*The Long Gallery, Penshurst Place*

13　*Penshurst Place*

CHAPTER THREE

Thames-side

Thames-side Kent has been cut in half. At the risk of offending the people of Greenwich, Eltham, Chislehurst, Bromley, Orpington and Beckenham, for example, I am going to point out that, although they might feel that these places should still be treated as part of Kent, in spirit and now in administrative fact they are all within the bounds of Greater London. The boundary runs up the Darent from the Thames, and then the Cray; Bexley is in Greater London, even Chelsfield, even Cudham and even Downe. In point of fact, I shall trespass on these in the next chapter, because they are still demonstrably rural, but here I shall only creep across the border into Bexley. 'Troynovant is now no more a city', wrote Dekker, meaning London. 'O great pity! is't not pity?' Unintentionally prophetically, he was right: London is now a conurbation, and includes chunks of Essex and Hertfordshire, all of Middlesex, the northern half of Surrey and this triangle of north-western Kent. The boundary of Greater London is only official recognition of a fact.

One way to get out of Strood, which is a Medway town and will scrape a mention in a later chapter, is to climb up to Frindsbury, whose houses, admittedly, adjoin those of Strood, but whose church stands aloof on the extreme edge of a cliff, overlooking the river. It used not to be a cliff, but the chalk has been quarried away to make it one. The church has a tall spire, which makes it a well-known landmark, a fair amount of original Norman work remaining, such as the round-headed chancel arch, and some Roman brick and tile used among the flint in the walls. Keeping to the lane past the church, both the sprawl of houses and the A289 road to the Isle of Grain can be avoided, and it is not far to the wooded heights of Tower Hill and the sharp descent to the attractive little High Street of Upper Upnor. At the bottom is a path to the river-front (the river is of course the Medway, not the Thames: we are still on the southern side of the Hundred of Hoo) and another through the gateway of Upnor Castle.

The dockyard at Chatham had been established in the last years of Henry VIII, but there was no fortification in the Medway estuary to protect it, other than the decayed castle at Queenborough. In Queen Elizabeth's first year, 1559, therefore, work began on one of her very few military constructions; a good strong bastion was built of stone with a moat on the landward side and the riverside foundations in the water. A triangular bastion was added some 40 years later (of limited use because the guns on it could not be moved and could only fire in one direction), but it was still the only Medway defence when the Dutch fleet sailed in and created havoc in 1667. This occasion appears to have been the only time the castle was in action, and its efficacy is symbolised by the display outside it of some guns from English ships sunk, and inside of some Dutch cannon-balls. The raid inspired the well-known stable-door-shutting technique, when the castle was improved and other Medway defences built. By 1693 the castle looked much as it does now. Until 1960 it was still in use as a naval munitions store, but is now, in excellent condition, cared for by the Department of the Environment (ex-Ministry of Works).

The peninsula between Medway and Thames called the Hundred of Hoo, and the Isle of Grain at its blunt point, together used to comprise one of the least-visited territories in Kent. The state of affairs described by Walter Jerrold, in 1908, when he had 'zig-zagged over it without seeing anyone beyond villagers and field-labourers' remained very much like that until fairly recently, when Kingsnorth Power Station was built near Hoo, and on the Isle of Grain a colossal oil refinery arose on the lonely marshes. Hoo has spread its houses up to the main road from Strood, and that is as busy as any arterial thoroughfare. Beyond it, however, the scenery has changed little.

The villages are humble and unpretentious and several, Hoo St Werburgh, St Mary's Hoo, All Hallows, have come to be known by the names of their churches. A high ridge of land runs along the middle of the peninsula, on either side sloping to mud-flats, saltings, marshes, wide open acres of vegetables and grazing cattle and sheep. From, for example, Beacon Hill, above Lower Upnor where the training-ship *Arethusa* lies at moorings, there is an excellent view of the Medway as it winds out to sea, with perhaps a frigate of the Royal Navy steaming up to Chatham, and below, the spire of Hoo St Werburgh above its house-roofs, and the masts of the Medway barges in their 'retirement colony' on Hoo Flats. From High Halstow, where there is a timbered cottage with a single-storey wing, on the road, which is what its name implies, the Old Forge House, the prospect to the north is equally good. Once clear of a high wooded hill (trees are uncommon in the Hundred as a general rule) which is Northwood Hill Nature Reserve, there is an unimpeded panorama of the long open fields of corn, potatoes, beans and cabbages, with dots of occasional farmsteads, down to the green levels studded with cattle, then the river, bearing a constant traffic of passing ships (up or down, depending on the tide) and beyond that the unsightly industrial clutter on the Essex coast. On a fine, sunny day, there is much to see and much to admire, but for what perhaps is its truer atmosphere, nine-tenths of the year, it is necessary to follow the winding lane down to a cluster of trees on the edge of the levels, a small village and a gaunt-towered church, and imagine a small boy who 'found out for certain, that this bleak place overgrown with nettles was the churchyard; ... and that the dark flat wilderness beyond the churchyard, intersected with dykes and mounds and gates, with scattered cattle feeding on it, was the marshes; and that the lower leaden line beyond was the river; and that the distant savage lair from which the wind was rushing, was the sea ...' Cooling is best of the several candidates for Pip's village, in, of course, Dickens' *Great Expectations*, not only because of the little stone lozenges in the churchyard (not merely five, as in the book, but no less than 13, as the Comport family died 'en masse' in the 1770s) but also because it is on the very brink of the 'marsh country, down by the river', and Dickens' words linger in the mind there, even on a sunny day. The church itself is interesting, apart from its fictional connections, because although it was rebuilt in the 1380s, when the nearby castle was built, it has a blocked-in doorway in the north

wall, which still has its original wooden door, of the previous century, on the inside, performing for nearly 600 years no useful function at all. There are also half a dozen old oak pews at the west end
which are supposed to have been made in the twelfth century, and
a stone font from the same period.

Cooling Castle is near the church so was probably the original
manor-house, but was strengthened and crenellated as part of the
defences against the French in the late fourteenth century (more
stable-door-shutting, as the French had raided parts of the coast
with impunity in the 1370s) by the lord of the manor, Lord (or Sir
John) Cobham. It then became the property of Sir John Oldcastle,
who was one of Lord Cobham's granddaughter's five husbands, and
earned himself a place in the history books by leading a Lollard rebellion against his erstwhile friend, now King Henry V, in 1414. The
Lollards, much influenced by the teachings of Wycliffe, were a curious mixture of genuine heretic and mere protestant, of intellectual
and rabble, knights and commons. The king was strictly orthodox
and also decisive in action: the rebellion soon collapsed. Oldcastle
was caught, escaped, was caught again and executed. In the next
century the castle was besieged by Wyatt, trying to raise a protestant standard against Queen Mary's Catholic husband, the King of
Spain, but the Lord of Cooling, then a Lord Cobham of a new family, resisted strongly.

The castle appears curiously like two castles, because the heavily
machicolated gatehouse stands on the edge of the old motte, with a
few crumbled walls and towers, and an elegant house and a huge
barn, and the bailey stands apart, in its own (dry) moat, encircled by
curtain walls, with no apparent connection. The round towers on
the corners and the high stone walls conceal what is evidently a
pleasant garden within, planted with, of all things, palm trees. The
well-known enamelled plaque on the right-hand tower of the gatehouse was evidently put there when it was built; it says:

> *Knoweth that beth and shall be,*
> *That I am made in help of the contre,*
> *In knowing of which thing,*
> *This is Chartre and witnessing.*

That the castle was only in action during civil disturbances should not be held against whoever it was devised the rhyme: in fact it is now very chipped and hard to read.

A circuitous lane makes two miles out of one to Cliffe, which is also on the edge of the marshes but is larger and less atmospheric, perhaps because a great many new houses have been added to it. The church is also larger than Cooling's, mainly thirteenth-century work with a carved screen, some wall-paintings and chevron shapes on the pillars of the arcading in the nave. It is dedicated to St Helen, who was the mother of the first Christian emperor, Constantine I: she is reputed to have been a barmaid, and for some reason was a favourite with the Anglo-Saxon kingdom of Mercia which, in the eighth century, conquered the kingdom of Kent. The village, in which Mercian councils were sometimes held, was then called Cloveshoo.

The High Street of Cliffe, lined with old weatherboard cottages, descends to the levels and stops. A farm track crosses at the end, and followed westward can take one, if lucky, round the base of the chalk cliffs and quarries to a cement works and a path across the marshes to Lower Higham church and the site of Lillechurch Priory. If not lucky, or if one's attention is distracted by the passage of ships on the river or the plovers on the marshes, it can take one two miles the wrong way along the side of a series of lagoons full of wildfowl, by some incredibly isolated coastguard cottages, to the river-bank, and back another two miles by the side of Cliffe Creek to the same cement works. If time is no object, this excursion can be warmly recommended; if limited, the sight of Cliffe church tower within a mile and a half, after an hour's walking, can be frustrating, especially as all signs of the path to Lower Higham church seem to have vanished.

This isolated church, advanced by Donald Maxwell as yet another candidate for Pip's in *Our Village* (Dickens no doubt took features of several to combine into his imaginary village) was called Lillechurch and was granted to Mary, the daughter of King Stephen, as a conventual priory and was colonised by nuns from Stratford-at-Bow in about 1148. It was never very big, seldom exceeding the 16 with whom it began. Investigated in 1521, it was found to have had for many years only three or four, and now only three, two of whom were 'convicted of gross immorality by several witnesses'. The priory was forthwith suppressed.

The church and its cluster of houses, Church Street, are near the railway, a single track line that once served the Hundred of Hoo with a celebrated tank engine known as 'the Gravesend Flier'. The main part of Lower Higham is grouped around the station on the main line to Strood, at the end of the famous tunnel which was excavated to transmit a canal from Gravesend to Strood, intended to shorten a barge's journey from Thames to Medway. It never paid, because by the time it was finished the barge trade was losing to the railways anyway, and it was bought by the London, Chatham and Dover Railway Company and converted to rail-carrying: it was opened in 1846.

The countryside in this area is almost treeless except for the windbreak lines of poplars, a heavy rolling sea of cornfields, waving gently down from the wooded hills to the south, down to the river. On the crest of one of the bigger waves is the tiny village of Chalk, whose church, at the highest point, has some curious sculptures on the porch gable: above a trefoil-shaped niche is the lower half of a grinning face and a hand holding a beer-pot, and below it is a frog holding a jug.

Modern Chalk is a sprawling mass of houses half a mile along the A226 road, which joins Denton and Milton in a chain of streets and habitations all the way to Gravesend.

Walter Jerrold's comment on Gravesend, 'The old part of the town has a certain picturesqueness in its narrow ways, but it has not much to hold the attention of visitors', can still judiciously be applied. The High Street, which is not the main road with all the shops and buses, but a narrow street that comes up from the riverside, is certainly attractive, and there is always a tinge of excitement about maritime places like this, as if one might encounter at any moment a Dickensian 'waterfront character', but much of Gravesend nowadays, and there is very much of it, is unfortunately rather dull. The fort, which was originally built as part of Henry VIII's defence system, was entirely reconstructed, under General Gordon, in the 1860s. Gordon himself took a great interest in social welfare, and worked hard to help and encourage poor and ragged boys to find their feet in a much less sympathetic world than today's.

The story of Pocohontas, the Indian princess who married one of the first Virginian tobacco planters, clings to Gravesend. She returned to England with her husband, John Rolfe, but fell ill, and was being taken back to Virginia when she died. She was taken ashore at Gravesend and buried, according to the parish register, in the chancel. The church was subsequently demolished and replaced in the eighteenth century, and no memorial stone survived. In 1907 a skeleton was found in the churchyard which was thought to be that of a Red Indian woman, but there is no way of being sure it was Pocohontas.

The ferry business once brought great prosperity to Gravesend: in the early part of the nineteenth century the long ferry, as it was called, brought passengers from London on their way to the Medway towns. By 1816 there were 26 sailing boats on the run, and even when these were replaced by temperamental steam-boats, the traffic continued and by 1840 more than a million passengers a year were being ferried back and forth. They were met at Gravesend by a fleet of omnibuses. The railways, of course, killed that livelihood, just as the Dartford Tunnel has killed the car-ferry to Tilbury. There are still river pilots in Gravesend, but other river traffic seems to have declined.

The riverside country between Gravesend and Dartford is cut up by ancient and modern chalk-quarrying, built over with rows of drab houses and sprawling cement works, and overlain with dirty grey cement dust. Northfleet and Swanscombe converge along the road but are otherwise separated by water-filled chalk quarries. It is possible that there might be something in the legend that Swanscombe derives its name from Sweyn the Danish king who invaded England: in Domesday Book the village is called Swinescamp, only some 80 years after Sweyn is supposed to have wintered his warriors there. There is little actual evidence of Danish presence, but there is at Springhead, between Northfleet and Southfleet near Watling Street, considerable evidence of another Roman town. In 1814 the foundations of some baths were discovered under a cottage, and subsequently a temple area and many other walls and building remains, together with tombs in stone and lead, cinerary urns, coins of all emperors from Augustus to Gratian (late fourth century) and a pair of shoes in purple leather, an openwork pattern, ornamented with gold thread. The town might have been Vagniacae, but the usual trouble arises with the Antonine Itinerary : Vagniacae is mentioned as nine miles on the London side of Rochester, which is perfectly correct, only between Vagniacae and London comes another town, Noviomagus, which is supposed to be ten miles from London and 18 from Vagniacae; since Springhead itself is 18 miles from London there seems to be an indirect route involved somewhere, and one simply cannot be certain.

Watling Street leads off towards Dartford, and nowadays a new stretch of motorway departs from it by Swanscombe Park, cuts through Darenth Wood and by-passes the earlier by-pass of Dartford. Darenth Wood has been severely treated by this intrusion, for the motorway traffic has filled it with noise, and between the bridge over it and the old A2, others have filled it with piles of rubbish. On the river side of the A2, Watling Street, fresh endeavours are being made to excavate every last available square inch of chalk. A hideous moonscape has been opened up, a nightmare of chalk and dust in which monstrous wheeled scavengers gobble up yet more particles of Kent and deliver them to the cement-makers.

On the Gravesend road at the XVIIIth milestone from London (for so it is still inscribed) a road dips behind the walls of Ingress Abbey, which is the Merchant Navy College, to Greenhithe, a pleasant waterside village with some good Georgian houses and a green embankment where one can sit and watch the river and see, riding at anchor near by, the old *Worcester*, which is used as part of the College. There are boatyards and slipways, and the celebrated yards and wharfs of Everards, the coastal shipping line. 'Waterfront characters' abound.

Odd footpaths, through cement-dusty backyards and works and by the railway, sunk deep in a cutting, lead to the church of St Mary, Stone, which stands marooned on a height, the hills all around cut away by chalk-quarrying. It is sometimes known as 'the lantern of Kent', perhaps because, lit up at night, it provides a landmark for navigators of the Thames. It was rebuilt in the thirteenth century, with a high chancel similar in style to work in the contemporary Westminster Abbey. According to Edward Hasted, in his great work on Kent, on 14 January 1638 the church was struck by lightning, and 'the roof and steeple were burnt, and, as tradition reports, the heat was so intense the bells melted as they hung'. Perhaps the lantern nickname began then. Flying buttresses were added in the fourteenth century to strengthen the tower, but the steeple has never been replaced.

The Gravesend road meets Watling Street at the Brent, and running down the steep East Hill enters Dartford. This ford of the Darent has long attracted occupation, from the Stone Age to this day; the Romans' '*via strata*' to London, later called the Watling Street, crossed the ford, and sufficient remains have been found to indicate a small settlement here in the days of the great Empire. The ford, the river being shallow, was considered quite adequate until at least the fourteenth century. When the Earl of Woodstock, the son of Edward I, died in 1330, having held the manor of Dartford, an inquisition was held, and it was found that, there being no bridge, the passage over the river was worth 13s. 4d. in yearly rent to the manor, and that the ford was kept by a hermit who had a cell on the eastern bank, with a chapel which was supported by the alms of pilgrims who used the road. The chapel has long since disappeared, and so has the leper hospital which gave Spital Street its name, but an almshouse on West Hill still occupies its site.

The contribution of Edward III to Dartford was the only house in England of Dominican nuns, or 'Sisters of the Order of St Augustine according to the institutes and under the care of the Friars Preachers', who were Dominican friars. His grandmother Queen Eleanor thought of establishing the house, and his father Edward II obtained sanction from the Pope for it, but was deposed before effecting it. Edward III carried it out, choosing Dartford for the site and aided by financial support from one William Clapitus, a vintner and sheriff of London. In 1356 the first nuns arrived, and by 1361 the work was finished. In its 200 years of existence, strict discipline and plain living were observed by the nuns throughout. Even when it was dissolved, in 1539, there were still 26 good nuns. Henry VIII eventually granted the priory and manor to his ex-wife Anne of Cleves; after her death, under the Catholic Queen Mary, the nuns returned, but only for two years. Elizabeth I closed it again and the nuns went to the Netherlands whence they first came.

Not much remains of the priory buildings, just a piece of wall on the premises of Messrs J. and E. Hall, and that probably dates from the time of Prioress Elizabeth Cressener, who ruled the house from 1488 to 1537. Dartford, in fact, has covered its medieval past with the necessities of its more recent industrial past and engineering present. A German named Spielman set up the first paper-mill in Queen Elizabeth's reign, and was soon employing 600 men, and in the same reign the first iron-slitting mill was erected. In 1792 a millwright named Hall established a factory and iron foundry employing 300 men; paper, engineering and cement works further developed in the nineteenth century and, together with chemical products, still form the basis of Dartford's industry today.

The Grammar School, founded in 1576 in the room over the market-place (which has also disappeared long since), has stood on the same site on West Hill since the last century and can be seen if one takes the way across the Heath to Bexley. The motorway by-pass, which makes the outlying village of Wilmington rather noisier to live in than before, has demolished part of the southern side of the Heath, but it is still possible to walk the old paths across much of it, and it seems not to have changed a great deal on account of the road.

The motorway rejoins the old Rochester Way in the Cray valley near Hall Place, a fine Tudor mansion with walls in a pattern of chequered stone and flint. Its medieval predecessor is supposed to have entertained the Black Prince at some uncertain period, to remind us of which legend the large and unprepossessing tavern across the way is named after him. Bexley, which is now in Greater London, has lost every vestige of village atmosphere. It once had a large white weatherboard mill on the Cray, but it was burnt down some years ago, and has been replaced by a modern replica designed as a hotel. The streets are so full of traffic that it takes a long time to cross the road, and only the little church, which has a shingled candle-snuffer spire, preserves an element of rustic peace.

The Cray, for a stretch along North Cray Road, runs through

trees and meadows, but at Foots Cray and then St Paul's Cray is swallowed up by the houses and factories. Walter Jerrold in 1908 wrote that 'Orpington—where the Cray starts on its eight-mile flow to the Darent—is an old village the centre of an extensive fruit and hop-growing district which spreads far into the surrounding parishes'. That description, so apt for a village of Kent, no longer applies: Orpington, rightly, is in Greater London.

CHAPTER FOUR

Darent

In addition to the Darent valley, which provides this chapter's heading, from the village of Darenth south to Dunton Green, I shall examine also the Downland to west and east of it. To the west, reversing the previous chapter's observations on Orpington, there are large tracts of land which are still palpably Kentish in appearance, so I shall trespass on Greater London territory in order to describe them. To the east, mainly to the south of the main railway line from Victoria to Chatham, except for Cobham, there is a wide area of comparatively unspoilt Downs country crossed by only two main roads, the A20 from Farningham to Wrotham, and the A227 from Gravesend to the same village.

By cunning ways out of Wilmington or southern Dartford one can creep past the bulk of the housing estates, which line the hills to the west like an invading army, and climb the steep lane to Old Swanley, an agreeable village with a Victorian church: its clocktower, like a corporation Jubilee memorial, crowns the wooded hill. Swanley Junction, a railway town, swarms across the old main road, filling the loop of land made by the new one. But the new road stops it short and the country, with a footpath to Petham Court Farm, begins again at once. Crockenhill has spread, but is still recognisably a Kentish village, and from the lane going south from it, part of which is actually the boundary of Kent and Greater London, on the heights of Skeet Hill, one can see a strip of farmland and woods, and then suddenly the massed houses and blocks of high-rise flats begin, and that is London, stretching away north-westward as far as one can see. The art will be to flirt with its fringes, and extract from them all that seems still to belong to Kent.

From Well Hill, where there is a large white Victorian house with a square observatory on top, a lane dips into a valley, past a kind of land-locked Noah's Ark called the 'Chelsfield Farm Animal and Bird Farm', and climbs up to Chelsfield, a pretty village with weather-boarded and flint cottages and, on the other side of one of the several main roads which intersect this area, a thirteenth-century church with a tall spire and three long lancet windows in the chancel's east wall, with remnants of round-headed windows above them. A lane from the church crosses a railway and passes the Chelsfield Riding School which is in a former farm called Julian Brimstone, of all names, and then there are discreet rows of Green-belt kinds of houses all the way downhill to Green Street Green. This is the outer fringe.

A steep climb through thick woods provides the escape route from the main-road village last named, for which Street Green Street would give a better indication and ratio to its properties; it turns into a descent into the Vale of Keston, a shallow valley at the end of which is the steep hill of Holwood Park. A footpath crosses it but the Park is, as it always has been, private, and offers no more than a glimpse through the trees of Caesar's Camp. Like several other sites so called, it had nothing to do with Caesar but predated him by a couple of hundred years, being a Celtic Iron Age fort. Certainly, near by at Warbank, there are the sites of some Roman buildings, but they date from 200 or 300 years after Caesar. What then can be seen in Holwood Park, after trudging up the steep banks? Looking back, there are hiking parties on the road, picnic parties on the grass, Scout and Guide camps among the trees, and overhead a con-stant stream of small private aircraft out from Biggin Hill (if this is a Sunday in high summer), none of which could be described as ex-citing. Neither is the stone bench by the pathside on the hilltop, but it is at least interesting, because it is inscribed: 'From Mr Wilber-force's Diary, 1788: "I well remember after a conversation with Mr Pitt in the open air at the root of an old tree at Holwood just above the steep descent into the vale of Keston I resolved to give notice on a fit occasion in the House of Commons of my intention to bring forward the abolition of the slave trade." Erected by Earl Stanhope 1862.'

Opposite the bench, railed off, is the stump of an aged oak, with a new young tree springing from it; the railings are old and rusty, so presumably this is the same tree.

Pitt was born at Hayes Place, not far away, the home of his father Lord Chatham, and in later life lived at Holwood. He had a passion for planting trees—many of those growing there today must have been planted by him—which is certainly more constructive than Gladstone's passion for cutting them down.

From Holwood Farm to Downe the conurbation can be left behind, for these are the western parts of the Kentish North Downs and soon the county boundary will be crossed again. At Downe, a hilly village where at the crossroads at the top, with an elm tree, benched all round, two inns and a spired thirteenth-century church face one another, Charles Darwin lived; he studied here, in a field near his house, such creatures, apparently, as earthworms.

The way to Cudham is extremely precipitous, alternating between thinly inhabited vales and heavily wooded hills. At the top of one of the steepest and highest of the hills is Cudham church, which, like those at Downe and Chelsfield, is of flint, has a spire and was built in the thirteenth century; in addition it has a colossal and venerable yew tree in the churchyard, with a girth rivalling the famous one at Selborne. Along the lane is a flint-walled, slate-roofed, single-storey Forge, whose anvil stands outside, but which seems to be a workshop of some description. Still more alpine scenery, becoming ever higher, brings the perspiring traveller to Knockholt, which also has a small church, and whose name over the centuries has come by its preceeding *Kn* after an origin as Acholt, or oakwood. The name is ever apt, since the whole place is thickly wooded, and none more so than Chevening Park, into which a footpath entices one from the road.

There are beautiful oaks and beeches in the park, of great age and majestic stature; they provide a preparation for the view when the path emerges from among them: below a grassy meadow, and framed against a wide, panoramic background is Chevening House. It looks like the best example of the early eighteenth-century, Queen Anne style of country house, in rosy pink brick, graceful and symmetrical, but that is a façade built on to what might have been less grand but possibly even more graceful, a house probably designed 100 years before by Inigo Jones. It was for about 250 years the home of the Earls Stanhope; the first earl, after a highly adventurous and distinguished career in the army, mostly in Spain, during which he rose by merit to the rank of general, returned home after the war in 1712 and became immersed in politics. He was at his best in foreign affairs, diplomacy and negotiation, and would probably have been more prominent in English history, perhaps at the expense of Sir Robert Walpole, had he not died at the early age of 48. His wife was a Pitt, and a strong intermingling of Pitts and Stanhopes ran throughout the eighteenth century. The 3rd Earl married William Pitt's sister Hester, who died at Chevening, aged 25: Stanhope thereafter was at odds with Pitt over the French Revolution—he became known as 'Citizen' Stanhope because he sympathised, like Charles James Fox, with the revolutionaries—and seceded from the House of Lords over it. He was a great inventor, was always developing some new project, and in fact worked hard for the public good, whether in politics or science. His daughter Lady Hester restored the Pitt alliance by becoming her uncle's confidante, until he died, after which she went to the Levant, earned a reputation as an eccentric and died out there in 1839.

It was the 5th Earl, the founder of the National Portrait Gallery, who had the stone seat placed in Holwood Park: he wrote a life of Pitt which became a standard work for historians. The last earl, having no heir, has bequeathed Chevening to the nation as a country home for a Minister, and it has now been decided that the Lord Chancellor should have it.

By the entrance gates there is a little village, also in rosy brick, and Chevening church, which precedes all the Stanhopes since it was built in 1262. It has a Stanhope chapel, and a pitifully lifelike marble effigy, by Chantrey, of a Lady Frederica Stanhope and her baby, who both died in 1825, when she was 25.

Chevening, and Dunton Green, which one reaches (if one must) across a maze of motorway fly-overs, are at the southern end of the Darent valley: Chevening is on the escarpment of the Downs. I shall return to the Dartford, northern, end of the valley and begin its exploration at Darenth.

There is a large modern extension of Darenth at Lane End, below the woods, but the old village on the river, just two miles upstream from the ford at Dartford, has been left alone. Below the church a little bridge crosses the clear, shallow Darent, and despite the modern proliferation of motor traffic, not much has changed in 20 years at least. The church is a rarity, a pre-Conquest foundation with some of the original structure, including some Roman tiles forming quoins, and claims to have been built in 940, the time of King Athelstan. The blocked-in Romanesque arches could be from this date, and perhaps the remarkable little vaulted sanctuary, with three little round-headed windows. The main part of the fabric is flint. There is a good Norman font, perhaps from King Stephen's time (1135–54), with carved stone figures in eight arcades. The church today is evidently very lively in Darenth: it has added to its southern side a well-constructed meeting-hall, is running fêtes and flower-shows, and generally bears all the hallmarks of a vigorous and active incumbent.

Half a mile upstream from the bridge is a rectangle of trees and scrub above a pool of the river, where small boys fish for tiddlers; beneath its surface is a large series of foundations built by the Roman settlers. Starting in the first century, a house received subsequent additions until it was a stylish villa, centre of an agricultural estate. Not many coins have been found on the site, but they range throughout the building's life, from the first to the fourth centuries.

A footpath crosses the bubbling Darent and a patch of wilderness and arrives at what was once a preceptory of the Knights Hospitallers of St John at Sutton-at-Hone. A flint chapel with lancet windows remains, attached to a graceful Georgian house set in lovely grounds. Geoffrey fitz Peter, Earl of Essex, granted to William de Wrotham, archdeacon of Taunton, all his land in 'Sutton de la Hane' to make a hospital for the maintenance of 13 poor men and three chaplains, and this was confirmed by King John in 1199. Later the Hospitallers, one of the two religious orders of knights founded to help protect the Latin Kingdom of Jerusalem, acquired it, and the hospital passed to their care. It was broken up by 1338.

The road at Sutton-at-Hone is the busy valley road from Dartford to Farningham, known (or at least it used to be known) as Five-Mile Lane. It bears a heavy load of traffic, and old houses with jetties

15   East Farleigh Bridge

16 Detail of Henry IV's tomb,
    Canterbury Cathedral

17 Corbel in the south-east choir,
    Rochester Cathedral

which overhang the road, such as the one opposite the school, are likely to be severely smitten. Farther along the road, opposite the entrance to the house of St John of Jerusalem, is a row of alms-houses in dark red brick, with mullioned windows. Above the centre house's door is a coat of arms and an inscription: 'Katherine Wrote widdow, wife of Robert Wrote Esquier, anno 1597.' Whether or not this was the Wrote of Wrotham, I could not say.

At South Darenth the river flows past the paper-mills, and the way, passing beneath the great arched railway bridge, is beside hop gardens to Horton Kirby, a village of pretty flint and weather-boarded cottages, and a thirteenth-century church with a modern brick tower. A screen of mighty beech trees effectively hides the fine stone Elizabethan manor-house, Franks, from the traveller along the little lane back to the main road.

Farningham, at the end of Five-Mile Lane, owes its preservation as a village to the by-pass which has for a long time now channelled the ever-increasing A20 traffic in an arc away from it. The village evidently flourished in the eighteenth century, since many of its houses and cottages are of that period. There is much use of white-painted weatherboard, as in the Mill House and the cottages near it, and several stout brick houses, like the White House, dated 1743. Downstream from the bridge there is an old brick arcade which looks like the remains of an earlier bridge, but is a screen which protected the ford, before there was a bridge. In the church, which was restored in the last century, there is an interesting stone font of the fifteenth century, carved in eight panels with figures showing the seven sacraments, with the Mass to make up the number.

There must have been a comparatively dense population in the Darent valley in Roman times, judging by the number of foundations discovered; in addition to the villa at Darenth, there are others above and below Farningham, and another has recently been found in the field by the river, opposite the Manor House. Then there is Lullingstone, but we shall come to that.

Sparepenny Lane runs along the valleyside above the river at Eynsford. Close by the river, among the green meadows, there stand the crumbled grey-stone walls of a small Norman castle. It was built by William de Eynsford, son of Ralph, who was given permission to fortify his manor-house by his lord, Archbishop Lanfranc, because his land was an island of Lanfranc's estate in a sea of his unruly and ambitious neighbour, Odo, who was both Bishop of Bayeux and Earl of Kent. William rebuilt the castle, which consists of a roughly pentagonal stone curtain wall, in about 1100, and his male descendants, all called William, held it for a further six generations.

Much work has recently been carried out by the Ministry of Works in excavating the undercrofts of the great hall and solar, and all is neatly turfed, gravelled and labelled so that it is easy to grasp the shape of the buildings and imagine how they once looked.

Where a lane branches off to mount the valleyside, by the war memorial, there is a group of weatherboarded cottages, one that looks like a former hall-house of the fifteenth century, another a peculiar shape, called Windmill Cottage; there are many more of equal interest in this charming village, and particularly those in the lane to the ford, opposite the church, which has a Norman round-headed doorway and an apsidal sanctuary of the thirteenth century with three lancets. A slim spire surmounts the tower, and what with that, and the ancient bridge standing close by the still usable ford across the river, and the timbered, gabled house on the far side, the picture would be perfect, were it not so frequently supplemented by the bulking, gleaming motor-coaches which, visitor-laden, creep along the narrow but busy Sevenoaks road through the village, looking desperately for somewhere to park.

A short walk from Eynsford, under the railway bridge, by the side of the shining Darent where it flows, at its best, in a soft green valley of pastures, fields and wooded hills, would be worth ten times the distance in order to see the Roman villa of Lullingstone. Unlike most other Roman sites, which once excavated, examined, scoured for movable relics and measured, are usually filled in again, this one has been encased in an air-conditioned building with timber walls and a perspex roof: the reason is not hard to find, for not only are there mosaics, one showing Bellerophon slaying the Chimera, but wall-paintings as well, some probably pagan, but some quite definitely Christian, with figures praying, hands outstretched, and fragments of the *chi-rho* symbol.

The villa was begun in the first century A.D., in the half-century following the Roman invasion and occupation of Britannia, and developed and enlarged in the second and third centuries. Britain actually benefited from the critical difficulties which beset the Empire in the third century, because whereas the colonists tended to import from the Continent far more than they exported, when the imperial in-fighting, followed by Barbarian invasions, cut short the avenues of trade, the Britons began to do things for themselves. They started to make their own pottery, for example, drink more beer than wine and improve their agriculture until it was possible, when at last the frontiers of the Empire were restored under Aurelian and consolidated under Diocletian, and Britain brought back into the fold after its brief autonomy under the bold Carausius by Constantius, to export corn and other farm products. These included wool, and the farms of Kent no doubt shared in the very considerable woollen cloth industry which had developed. The Emperor Diocletian, in his famous Price Edict of A.D. 301, assigned the maximum permitted price to British woollen products, naming two of them, the *Birrus Britannicus*, a hooded waterproof cloak, and the *Tapete Britannicum*, a rug for saddles or couches.

Villas such as Lullingstone grew in prosperity and size: the fourth century saw them at their peak of luxury, but there was a sharp interlude in the 360s when, according to the historian Ammianus Marcellinus, 'as if the trumpets were sounding the war-note throughout the whole Roman World, the most savage peoples roused themselves and poured across the nearest frontiers. At the same time the Alamanni were devastating Gaul . . . the Picts, Saxons, Scots and Attacotti were harassing the Britons with constant disasters.' It was probably a raiding party of Saxons who burnt down the villa of Lullingstone in 367.

The peace was restored by the firm measures of Count Theodosius, and eventually the villa was rebuilt. At some time after 385, when Christianity was nearing its zenith in the Roman world, a Christian chapel was built into the villa, or a room converted for its use; at the same time, it appears that pagan worship continued in another room. This was not unusual: in many leading Roman families, for several generations the women would be fervent Christians, like St Jerome's pupils and correspondents, while the men, like good

Roman senators, would continue the old traditions of the gods. Britain, being a remote province cut off from the mainstream of ideas and thoughts, fostered a surprising diversity of pagan cultures, and Christianity made small headway until the 380s, then to be practised, often enough, only in private houses such as this.

There is a good example of a bath-house attached to the villa, and among the many objects found among the débris are two portrait busts of the second century, of men who were probably the resident family, the bones of a man in a lead coffin and skeletons of sacrificed geese, a hunting dog and a baby.

Lullingstone Castle, on the days when it is not open to the public, must be inspected from the outside with care and decorum, because it is in private land and the lane to it from the villa is private. It is not a castle in the sense Eynsford is: the lovely ruddy brick house was built in the sixteenth century, and although its castellated gatehouse remains it was never intended for warlike purposes. Within its precinct is the little church of St Botolph, and a notice in the gatehouse forbidding entry precludes, to all intents, a visit to the church as well; although greatly restored in the reign of Edward III it contains much Norman material, and also the tombs of generations of the family who occupied the manor, if not the house, from the fourteenth century to the present day. From the London merchant John Peche who bought the estate, the descent came to Sir John Peche, Henry VII's champion, who broke 14 spears against contenders in the lists at a tournament in 1494, to Sir Percyvall Hart his grandson, to Sir Thomas Dyke who married the last Hart and to the present Hart-Dykes.

Castle Farm almost certainly predates the Castle: on a mound moated by the river, a timbered farmhouse based on what could be an early hall-house occupies one of those sites which have had a continuous succession of habitations since 'time out of mind', as they say. Shoreham, near which there is another Roman site, has the advantage over Eynsford in lying off the main road, and is correspondingly more restful. The Darent bubbles around, through and under parts of the village, forming a garden boundary here, a roadside splash there and a centrepiece as it hurries under the bridge. There are many attractive cottages and houses, a row of Tudor brick almshouses refurbished by the mother of Dudley Greenwood, R.A.F., who was killed in 1943; attached to the King's Arms there is a low flint ostler's box in which the ostler would lurk, waiting for care of the customers' horses; the church has a brick tower, but is built of flint and stone and originated mostly in the fifteenth century; its fine timbered porch is of this date, and within there is a great rood-screen. The church, like many others nowadays, is kept locked; in our retrogression from civilisation we have reared too many who will profane, smash and steal beautiful things wherever they may find them.

From Shoreham there is a footpath which goes through the park-land of Filston Hall, near the railway, and emerges in Otford. De-spite being, like Eynsford, straddled across the main Sevenoaks road, and having a large modern addition to its western parts, across the river, Otford maintains its character; the duckpond around which the traffic must go, the green space in front of the church, the re-mains of the palace in a rough field, all contribute to this, as do the old timbered houses like the Bull inn, and the one called Pickmoss, which has coats of arms in coloured glass in its long window and carved on its wooden door.

The manor of Otford belonged to the Archbishop of Canterbury. After the great battle fought at Ottanford, in 774, between the Men of Kent and those of Mercia, when Kent lost the fight and their autonomy, King Offa of Mercia granted the battlefield to Christ-church Priory, Canterbury, whose abbot was the Archbishop. Lan-franc, the brilliant Italian scholar of Bec, when he held this office under William I, appropriated Otford to his see, and the manor be-came an archiepiscopal residence. William Lambarde, the Eliza-bethan historian, tells two dubious stories about Thomas Becket: one that, while meditating on his devotions in the grounds of the manor he was so disturbed by the song of a nightingale that he 'in-joined that from henceforth no byrde of that kynde shoulde be so bolde as to sing thereaboutes'. The other is that, to improve the manor's water supply, Becket struck the ground with his staff and lo, a spring of water gushed forth. The water supply was further improved when Archbishop Warham rebuilt the manor-house as a sumptuous palace, between 1510 and 1520: they are the fragments of his work which exist now, a row of cottages with, at one end, a tower intact but empty, and at the other, one cut down but roofed and inhabited. The acquisitive Henry VIII took it from Warham's successor Cranmer, but, according to his secretary Morice, despised it because it 'standeth low, and is Rheumatick, like unto Croiden, where I could never be without Sickness'. If he happened to want to be in this district, this peerless prince decreed that he would stay at Knole, which 'standeth on a sound, perfect, wholesome Ground'. But the rest of his retinue could stay at rheumaticky Otford.

At Otford the so-called Pilgrims Way crosses the Darent, which, near the head of its valley, has turned north after running eastward from its source near Westerham. Having arrived at the end of the great gully that this apparently puny river has cut in the chalk Downs, we shall neglect it in favour of the old way. Close by the site of yet another stylish Roman villa, whose wall-paintings attest to the education and wealth of its owner, it hugs the escarpment of the Downs in its characteristic fashion and takes the traveller eastward, clear of the spreading streets of houses between Otford and Kemsing.

The Way passes north of the great house of St Clere and reaches Wrotham, at the foot of the famous hill of the same name which sidles down from the heights of the Downs, carrying the A20 on its way to Maidstone. The church of St George in Wrotham is large and airy, and is distinguished, apart from the good fifteenth- and sixteenth-century brasses and fine Perpendicular windows, by a vaulted passage under the tower, at the western end: this was built as a processional way, in order to avoid bearing the symbolic holy cross along unconsecrated ground. The manor of Wrotham was another of those which had belonged to the church since pre-Conquest times, and to the east of the churchyard there was another archiepiscopal palace, until the 1350s, when Archbishop Simon Islip had it pulled down and the material taken to Maidstone, to finish the palace there, begun by his predecessor John Ufford. There seems to be nothing now to indicate that the Wrotham palace ever existed.

Blacksole Field, west of Wrotham, by which a somewhat overgrown footpath runs from the road to the Pilgrims Way, is the site of one of the skirmishes during Wyatt's rebellion; Sir Thomas

Wyatt of Allington, claiming that Queen Mary, in marrying the King of Spain, would not only return England to Popery but would subject her to Spain into the bargain, raised an army of Men of Kent. A detachment of these were routed here by the Queen's men under the Sheriff, Sir Robert Southwell, and Lord Abergavenny.

From the Way near this somewhat unmemorable battle a steep lane permits a climb up Exedown Hill and a brief expedition into a sparsely inhabited triangular tract of Downland between the Darent valley and the A20. Normally this country is exceptionally quiet, because the A20 removes all passing traffic and channels it away down Wrotham Hill. There are occasions when an accident on the main road blocks it for an hour or two, and then the lanes are overfilled with cars and lorries trying to find a way round the blockage. The scenery is of high, dense woods, interspersed with cornfields. At Knockmill a steep lane runs down to Knatt's Valley, one of those Downland gorges which, at this southern end, is full of an astonishing proliferation of little modern cottages, some of substantial brick and tile, others of asbestos and corrugated iron, most of one storey and a few of about the size of beach-huts. The valley is steep-sided and deep, and sequestered by tall trees on either hillside; farther north the valley opens out and there are broad sloping cornfields on either side. At Maplescombe there are some more cardboard cottages, some farms and houses and the remains, up a steep valleyside lane, of a little chapel, screened from the road by a large new chicken-house.

The A20 can be reached by a lane which might perhaps be a few degrees out of the perpendicular, diagonally up the valleyside past a cunningly concealed and wonderfully chosen camping site. The unfortunate populace of West Kingsdown, at the top, not only have to endure the endless turmoil and roar of the main-road traffic but are obliged to do so in caravans or bungalows which have as much to recommend them architecturally as the Knatt's Valley beach-huts. A footpath into the woods permits escape from all this, and furthermore it takes one to Kingsdown church, a small Norman building with a little tower; some round-headed windows can be seen blocked in the walls.

From Kingsdown, north-east to the railway-line at Longfield and the A227 from Meopham to Wrotham, there is another wide extent of Downland which repays closer investigation. At Hartley, and north of the railway at Longfield and Istead Rise there is a large spread of modern housing, about which one cannot say the same. I regret that I have been unable to visit Southfleet.

To the left of the lane which goes north from Kingsdown lies the Brands Hatch motor-racing track, and a little farther on is the hamlet of Fawkham Green. Even in 1953, in the days of the Half-Litre Club, they complained about the noise from Brands Hatch; a bigger race-track, with more powerful cars, in the natural order of things must mean a bigger and more powerful noise to buffet the ears of the Fawkham Green residents. Little else has changed there except for some additional houses and an extension to the Rising Sun. The Green is at the head of a valley which runs down to Longfield; to West Yoke and Ash there is a steeply climbing lane back up to the high Downs. The church and manor at Ash are detached from the rest of the village in the familiar grouping. The manor-house is Caroline, dated 1637, in red brick with gables, and the church tower has been strengthened, also in brick, perhaps at the same date. In the church is a rather engaging memorial to 'James Fletcher, Esquire, of Rands House in this Parish, who having served his country for several years by sea and land retired from the gay world in a bad state of health in the 47th year of his age to this the place of his birth where it pleased a gracious providence to bestow upon him a comfortable state of health and all the other blessings that he could wish for. He departed this life on the 28th day of December, 1853, aged 88 years.' In the north aisle chapel there are tombs and memorials of seven or more eighteenth-century Hodsolls of South Ash Manor; two miles away to the east there is a hamlet called Hodsoll Street, doubtless from the same source.

Ridley, the adjacent parish, is a very small group of church, manor-house and a few cottages. The church is a simple nave and chancel, in flint, with a little white belfry; opposite the churchyard gate is Bowdler's Well, with a good thatched cover and dated 1810, but blocked with concrete. At Berry's Maple, in the dip between Ridley and Ash, the journey begins up a quiet, mostly uninhabited valley, not deep but lush with grass, crops and woods and pleasingly rustic, to Stansted, tucked into the end of it. By an elaborately statuesque war memorial a chestnut-lined lane leads to the churchyard, in which is a yew tree of formidable proportions, said to be 1000 years old. The church is of the fourteenth century, but a chapel was mentioned in the twelfth-century *Textus Roffensis*, the Rochester Priory rent-roll, and a lump of ivy-covered masonry near the yew tree could be it. If the tree really is 1000 years old, it might have been planted when the chapel (in, say, 973) was built.

Up out of Stansted's valley and on the tops again is Fairseat, where a muddy pond with ducks and moorhens faces across the road a small modern brick church and a large classically styled brick house with Grecian urns in stone poised on the squared front. Half a mile from it is the A227, the Vigo inn and a precipitous hill down the escarpment to Trottiscliffe.

Kent is full of idiosyncratic pronunciations: in this area there are three outstanding examples. Wrotham ('Root-ham') and Meopham ('Mep-ham') are fairly well known; Trottiscliffe ('Trosley') is something of a classic. The steep Vigo Hill meets the Pilgrims Way and turns sharply down the more gentle foot-slopes of the Downs; there are houses along the Way and most of the lane down to the village, which is distributed about a triangle of roads with some pretty flint-and-stone cottages, a couple of converted oasts and a white weatherboarded house which is the home of the painter, Mr Graham Sutherland. The church and manor-house are a short way to the east of the village; King Offa, after his victory at Otford, magnanimously granted the manor to St Andrew's church and priory, Rochester, and the manor-house subsequently became a residence of the bishops of Rochester. The wide-jointed masonry at the east end of the chancel suggests that a part, at least, of the church is of pre-Conquest origin. Bishop Hamo de Hethe was fond of the place and used it frequently, effecting repairs and alterations to manor-house and church when he spent all of 1342 there. He also stayed in the manor during the grim years of the Black Death (1348–9) and lost 32 of his household from it. Parts of the medieval house survive, but from the front it looks a simple, plain Georgian farmhouse.

The church is small and equally simple, but has a startlingly elaborate pulpit, with sounding-board above and delicately railed staircase, which was apparently brought from Westminster Abbey in 1824; it contrasts oddly with the plain box pews, and near the organ the instruments of the old church orchestra. In a glass case on a chest under the west window are some of the bones of 22 people who were found at Coldrum; since that is the best example in Kent of a Neolithic burial chamber, the bones are anything up to 4000 years old.

The Coldrum Megalithic Burial Chamber is half a mile east of the church, and accessible by a footpath. It stands on the edge of a terrace of chalk, the mound encircled by 24 stones in their original positions, 12 more at its foot and 5 more at the south-east corner (including one huge slab that might have been the capstone of the chamber). The chamber, at the eastern end, is 13 feet long and is made from five huge sandstone slabs. It is the best of the remnant of what must have been a vast Neolithic necropolis in the middle Medway valley, on both sides of the river: on the western side, Coldrum and two groups at Addington, on the eastern, several groups around the famous Kits Coty, which will be encountered in the chapter on the Medway.

The two groups of sarsen stones at Addington are rather hard to find now, because the Ordnance map has not been able to keep pace with the changing aspect of the landscape: another new road, a part of the A20, has cut through north of Addington and confused the issue. They are, or were, in Addington Park, a long barrow with 22 stones, the chamber having fallen, and a group known as the Chestnuts, 14 large stones comprising another collapsed chamber.

The villages on these southern slopes of the Downs, Addington, Ryarsh and Birling, are within earshot of the new road; they are otherwise comparatively untroubled. In Ryarsh are some good-looking eighteenth-century brick cottages; in Birling, in a dip, with the church standing up on a sudden rise at its northern end, is a large, ugly tavern, currently in pink and maroon, called the Nevill Bull, a reference to the arms of the Nevill family, which used to own Birling Place. Although it is now just a farmhouse, it is plain to see that Birling Place has been something more in the past; it stands on a high mound at the foot of the Downs, with a stone perimeter wall. It was a manor of Richard Beauchamp, Earl of Warwick and Lord

Abergavenny, and came with all the other Beauchamp lands to the Nevill family by inheritance. It is interesting to note that John Speed, in his map of Kent of about 1600, has marked in the vicinity of Birling Place a large manor and park called Comford, a name which seems to have disappeared.

Birling is not far from the Medwayside, cement-works country of Snodland; one need not advance any farther towards it than the group of buildings at the end of a farm track called Paddlesworth. By a huge angled barn, some extensive farm buildings and a rather decrepit Georgian manor-house, is a tiny chapel, of stone and flint, newly tiled and restored here and there, with a round-headed window in the north wall of the chancel and a pointed lancet in the east wall, and therefore possibly of twelfth-century origin.

A long climb up Birling Hill arrives at Holly Hill, from which one can pause, breathe again and look back at the wide prospect, to the cement-country, the hills on the far side of the Medway and even, on the far horizon, the unmistakable shape of Kingsnorth Power Station. In the woodland way by Holly Hill there is peace, a rural peace compounded of distant sounds of chaffinches, pigeons, cocks and hens, and the wind in the trees: the only noise to intrude on this, since even the rare roads are traffic-free, is that of aircraft.

This is the way to Dowde, a vanished village which has been replaced by one more modern called Great Buckland. It is at the head of another of those long fingers of valleys that probe into the heart of the Downs, a silent, remote place; the only reminder that here was a medieval village is the little chapel, similar in construction to Paddlesworth so probably also early twelfth century. The plaque on the wall says that the church 'fell into disuse about the period of the pestilence known as the Black Death, A.D. 1349', and was restored in 1905–6. As Dudesland, independent from neighbouring Luddesdown, Dowde about the year 975 was one of those places answerable for the cost of maintaining the King's Pier of Rochester Bridge.

At the northern, more open, corn-growing end of the little vale, across the meadows can be seen the church, manor-house, barns and cottages of Luddesdown, among the barley and wooded hills: a kind of essence, a thumbnail representation, of Kent, of England.

Approaching from the direction of Luddesdown, a view of the

great Tudor mansion of Cobham Hall may be obtained by passing under the railway by the path that leads to Lodge Farm, and turning right. The Lords of Cobham who built it were the family Brooke, who came to a sticky end on a charge of high treason under James I, and were replaced as lords of the manor by the king's cousins the Stuarts, Dukes of Lennox and Earls of Darnley. Their descendants held it until fairly recently, but it is now a school. It is hard to find a rival, among the houses of Kent, of its grace and elegance: the mellowed brick, the long windows, the four spired turrets are perfectly set amid the mighty cedars, beeches and oaks in the Park.

The importance of Cobham in the thirteenth to sixteenth centuries, apart from the noble occupants of the Hall, can be seen from the ecclesiastical buildings; the church, of the former period, is large and well-proportioned; on its northern side are some almshouses in flint and brick, and attached to its southern side is Cobham College, originally a college of priests who were to serve the surrounding parish churches, but refounded, also mainly in flint, in 1598 as more almshouses. In the church, in the wide chancel, is the elaborate and highly ornamented family tomb of the Brokes or Brookes. On the floor, there are 15 large brasses of Brokes and their predecessors the Cobhams, from the thirteenth to sixteenth centuries. The Earls of Darnley, on the other hand, all seem to be outside the church, recorded on stones on the south side of the chancel wall. Opposite the churchyard is the timbered inn, the Leather Bottle, which still leans heavily on Dickens' use of it in his *Pickwick Papers*, and a short way past this, in a new road off Battle Street called *Sarsens Close*, there are three large and several small lumps of sarsen, cunningly disguised as rock-gardens, which are the scattered remains of another Neolithic burial chamber.

At a bend in the road at the western end of the village is a large and gracious Georgian brick house called Owlets, which is now National Trust property and open to the public.

Between Cobham and Nurstead is a landscape typical of the northern slopes of the North Downs: high, airy and open, growing wheat and potatoes, beset by lines of electricity pylons and with splendid views of the distant Gravesend chimneys. Nurstead is another non-village, made up principally of the church-and-court group and little else. The fourteenth-century church, in flint, is a simple structure of nave and tower, with no chancel; the Court conceals behind a Tudor exterior of stone, a half-aisled hall of the thirteenth century. The family who occupied it between the seventeenth and nineteenth centuries, the Edmeades, fill the church floor with their tombstones.

Meopham extends along the A227 for some two miles; there is a mile from the station to the church, and another from the church, which, curiously, has a sarsen stone near its gate and another just outside it, to the Green, a large triangular expanse with cricket pitch and pavilion, flanked by two inns and a black weatherboarded windmill, its sails partly intact. But from the apex of the green a footpath at once leaves what appears to be advanced suburbia and dips into a hay-making, woody valley that might be 50 miles from the A227: when this can happen, even suburbia can still be called the country, since no one is far from it.

The footpath brings one to Harvel, and a lane to a totally new development in the woods above Trottiscliffe called Vigo Village. Here an attempt has been made to create a village: the houses are in squares with their fronts facing outwards instead of inwards, there are shops and there are signs that there might soon be a hall or a church; there is a school, there are playing fields, and a great deal of trouble has been taken to leave plenty of the original woodland trees and rough patches untouched. It is probably too extensive to be a coherent village, but it is a good try.

CHAPTER FIVE

The Green Hills

The hills of this chapter heading are those which run from Westerham to the Medway, between the North Downs and the Weald,
broken only by the little River Bourne which rises near Wrotham
and joins the Medway at East Peckham. They are sometimes re-
ferred to as the Lower Greensand Ridge, which is rather like Voltaire's famous observation on the Holy Roman Empire, since they
are not made of sand, which is not green, and they are not notice-
ably low. They are in effect green, however, because of the copious
quantity of forestation which they support, so my title is a compromise.

A convenient place from which a walker may begin his exploration of them is Sevenoaks, but it must be admitted that the early
stages involve a lot of main-road walking, which cannot be helped
since neither lanes nor footpaths go in the right direction. From
Sevenoaks station to Riverhead the road must be used, but by the
grounds of what used to be Montreal, a house named by Sir Jeffrey
Amherst, who captured the town in 1760, and now 'developed',
there is a comparatively peaceful lane to Bessels Green, across another motorway (the A21 to Tonbridge) and a footpath into the hills
and woods. It emerges at Dryhill, a sudden dip made by a little
stream, where the handsome stone and timbered houses and farm
buildings, sheltered by high woods all around, seem to be oblivious
of the modern world, dreaming over their lawns and gardens. The
footpath continues (after a fashion: little-used footpaths are invariably overgrown and often impassable) as far as Sundridge Place,
which must have been the original manor since it is close by the
church and certainly, from its stone-walled barns and sheds, looks
as permanent as the hills. The main part of Sundridge is down on

the main road, which regrettably must be endured all the way to Westerham. On the north side of the road is some parkland through which the Darent runs, and on rising ground appear the roofs of Combe Bank, which incongruously enough was a seat of the Dukes of Argyll in the nineteenth century: the great Whig family Campbell must be within reach of the House of Lords. The house is now in use as a convent.

On the left of the road to Brasted is a late hall-house, of the early sixteenth century, called Old Hall, which is an antique shop. Brasted Place, also on the left, is a classically styled mansion, built by Robert Adam, in a setting of approved parkland trees, such as chestnuts and cedars; it was once occupied by the exiled Emperor Napoleon III. Brasted has what would under quieter circumstances be a wide street, lined with pleasing houses of the seventeenth and eighteenth centuries, but which is made inadequate by the thunderous A25 traffic. It is no wider for the rest of its extent to Westerham, and some of the lorries are those from the Continent now known in England as 'juggernauts'. A by-pass is, however, under construction. When completed, perhaps the pressure on these unfortunate villages will be eased.

At the bottom of Westerham's hill is an upstanding, gabled brick Elizabethan house called Quebec House; it was called Spiers when General James Wolfe lived there, but it is now National Trust property and open to the public for its own interest and as a Wolfe museum. The ailing, unprepossessing youth who fought and conquered his disabilities is justifiably remembered for that as much as for his military achievements, and since he was born in Westerham vicarage and baptised in Westerham church, was brought up and lived in Westerham, he is recalled prominently as a local man. On the little green, up in the town, are two statues: one of Wolfe, the other, mounted on a block of stone given, oddly, by President Tito of Yugoslavia, of another local resident, Sir Winston Churchill.

The green is lined with attractive houses and cottages, and at its top end is the churchyard; the church is large and well-lit, its two big aisles giving a spacious effect. The subjects of both the statues are remembered, Wolfe in a table recording his baptism, and Churchill, in the lamp he gave to hang before the altar in the south aisle, over the brasses, and in his signature witnessing his grandchild's baptism.

The old George and Dragon inn, beyond the green, records that Wolfe stayed there in 1758 during his last visit to Westerham. Down the hill, going west, near a white weatherboarded inn called, in case he should be forgotten, the General Wolfe, is an ancient cottage claiming thirteenth-century origin (but shored up with much brick) called Pitt's Cottage. Near by a lane at last permits release from the A25, and one passes the gate to Squerryes Court, a late seventeenth-century house in the classical style, in red brick, slate-roofed, like a miniature Hampton Court. Wolfe was friendly with the Wardes, the family who owned it, and it was while he was in the grounds that he received his first commission: the actual spot is marked by a memorial. Also in the parkland of Squerryes Court are the source of the River Darent and a fortification made by the Celts of the Iron Age, about the third century B.C. The latter is on the verge of a wood called Goodley Stock, on the upper slopes of the ridge. Emerging from the trees on the far side, at Kent Hatch (perilously near the border of Surrey) one can enjoy the first of the long, rolling panoramic prospects of the Weald.

Crockham Hill is better known for its neighbour at Chartwell than for itself, but in its Victorian church is buried Octavia Hill, a lady who deserves to be remembered by anyone who today enjoys walking in heath and woodland, or in visiting the great houses and estates which are preserved for us by the National Trust, because she was one of the prime movers in founding it. Below the piece of Common preserved in her name, on a spur of the hills, is a group of expensive and beautiful houses, including a farmhouse called Frog-hole, and beyond it, set high up on a re-entrant made by a stream, is a red-brick Tudor house, with crow-stepped gables, called Chartwell. The National Trust own and care for it, and even without the many relics of and associations with the incomparable Sir Winston, the visitors would still come because the gardens, in terraces and with little lakes made from the stream, are as perfectly delightful as an English garden, well-tended, on a sunny afternoon in midsummer, can be.

A footpath through Chartwell's farm leads into the thinly in-

18 *The Old Cloth Hall, Smarden*

19   *Church of King Charles the Martyr, Tunbridge Wells*

20   *Mereworth Castle*

habited region of the foothills of the ridge, where a couple of cottages on a slope merit the name of Puddledock. Beneath the lee of the high woods, the lane climbs sharply up to Toys Hill, where I am sorry to report that the Tally Ho inn is now merely a private house. A terrace close by has been paved, around an old well, and seats provided from which the weary hill-climber can revive his spirits by contemplating the fair Vale of Eden all spread out below him. The hilltop woods on either side of the road across Toys Hill are in National Trust care (with particular reference to Octavia Hill); a footpath takes one through the cool shades of Scords Wood, into another re-entrant made by another stream: here in busy West Kent, within three miles of that hectic A25, is the essence of solitude, of restfulness to the senses. There is no rest to the traveller who wants to go to Ide Hill, however, because the way up to it by this same footpath is stern and hard.

Ide Hill is the third of the peaks of these Green Hills, and it too is well served, with a war-memorial park from which the Wealden carpet can be appreciated. Behind the hill is a sloping green with a small spired Victorian church at one end and some good eighteenth-century houses, and two inns, at the other. Beyond it a lane courses through the woods on the edge of the hills, crosses a bridge over the new A21 which by-passes Sevenoaks and takes one to the Sevenoaks side-streets. Immediately opposite the end of the lane on the old Tonbridge road are the grey-stone, slate-roofed buildings of Sevenoaks School, founded by the town's first known hero.

An orphan found in Sevenoaks in the days of Edward III and called, for want of a name at all, William Sevenoak or Sennocke, was apprenticed to a grocer in London, developed a sound business sense and became so prominent in the City as to serve a term as Lord Mayor, the immediate predecessor of Sir Richard Whittington. When over 40 he is said to have accompanied Henry V to France and fought at Agincourt, and when he died in 1432 endowed a 'Grammar School in some Convenient House within the said town' (Sevenoaks) where poor children could be taught for no fee. The school was refounded in 1560 as the Grammar School of Queen Elizabeth, and has an impressive list of celebrated pupils.

The church of Sevenoaks is near by, and contains the tomb of

William Lambarde, the Elizabethan historian and author of the *Perambulation of Kent*; it is he who recounts the story of Sir William Sennocke.

Opposite the church is the drive which leads into the grounds of Knole; if Sevenoaks itself has no more than its normal ration of historical and architectural interest, and perhaps a little less, Knole more than compensates for it on both scores.

It is hard to know how to describe Knole, and do it anything like justice, in the limited space permitted here : whole books have been written about it, like Vita Sackville-West's *Knole and the Sackvilles* which would be hard to better. Perhaps, if it will encourage readers to go there and see it all for themselves, a brief sketch of the house and its background would be permissible.

The house stands on a knoll, whence its name, which has been occupied by some habitation or another since, perhaps, Roman times. The present building was begun in the 1470s by Archbishop Bourchier as his country seat, and continued in use by successive primates until Henry VIII 'acquired' it, like Otford, from Cranmer. The Sackville possession began with Sir Thomas, who like a number of prominent Elizabethans was a practitioner of more than one art : in his youth he was co-author of the play *Gorboduc* and other works, and in his maturity, in the stern political world, as Lord Buckhurst, succeeded Burghley as Queen Elizabeth's Lord Treasurer. The Queen gave him Knole (he was her uncle as well as Treasurer, being related to the Boleyns) in 1603, and James I bestowed on him the title of Earl of Dorset. In 1605 he extended the house, leaving it with the appearance it has today : the whole long front and square battlemented gatehouse were his work, and the lead drainpipes in the courtyard are stamped with the date.

The Sackvilles, having achieved eminence and this great house's ownership, retained both; despite the 3rd Earl's support for Charles I in the Civil War they survived, and in the next century became Dukes of Dorset. Disaster came when the 4th Duke, a handsome and well-endowed youth of 21, died after a hunting accident soon after his birthday-party. The 5th Duke was an uncle, the next heir a girl, the boy's sister, who married a West, Earl de la Warr, and the family became Sackville-West, Barons Sackville, and still are, and still hold Knole, although National Trust have it in their care. The Sack-villes and their associates, like Lady Betty Germaine, who had a suite of rooms and lived her life in them, or Giannetta Baccelli—'Miss Shelley' to the staff—whose charms, evident from her mar-moreal likeness at the foot of the staircase, caused the 3rd Duke to add her to his acquisitions in Italy, or Catherine Fitzgerald, Coun-tess of Desmond, who lived for 104 years; all these people are vital to the house as it is now: they are not ghosts, their portraits, by Reynolds, Hoppner, Romney and others, do not accuse, they quiz. The things in the house, lovely as they are, the old ornamented sil-ver, the Carolean billiard table, the high and sumptuous beds of James II kept in readiness for him, the spy-hole from the secret room above the ballroom, the furniture, the glass, even the family mementoes, are only incidentals. The house lives through its per-sonalities, and despite the fair share of tragedies which they experi-enced, despite the long galleries and corridors, the creaking stairs, the rows of portraits, it exudes a sense of warmth, of friendliness: the guide told me that even his lady colleagues never minded going about, locking up and tidying, after dark.

The house is a village of its own: within its walls are the work-shops of carpenters, joiners and plumbers, and once even glass-makers. Its park is famous for its deer and majestic oaks and beeches, and more recently for its golf-course. Within these grounds, among the trees and grey-stone walls, there is something, some spirit of the continuity of past, present and future, which if indefinable is infinitely precious, for once destroyed it cannot be re-built.

Sevenoaks has spread in recent years, from the gravel-dug lakes about Dunton Green southwards to the very edge of the ridge. A convenient place from which to begin a tour of the eastern part of the Green Hills is Borough Green, which although it grew up around its railway station in the nineteenth century has cottages of the time when it was the hamlet of Barrow Green. It is surrounded by sand-pits (demonstrating that the stratum of sand found on the edges of this ridge is not green but reddish) through which one weaves a hazardous trail to get to Ightham, on the northern slope of the ridge. In its long street are several brick-and-timber houses of the sixteenth century, including the George and Dragon and the house at right angles to it, opposite, on the bend. The church stands a little apart from the village, on a knoll, now surrounded by roads on all sides. At the western end of the village is a brick house called Old Forge, with an anvil outside and a hop-bine growing over its walls. Near it, across the A25, a track leads steadily uphill, past Old Bury Hall, a modernised hall-house, to the thick woods crowning Oldbury Hill.

The trees conceal evidence of two different stages in our ancient history: they hide in their depths rock shelters, or caves, in which in the last century Benjamin Harrison found hundreds of flint implements, some so sharp they had apparently never been used; the caves were habitations of man in the Middle Stone Age, perhaps 4000 years B.C. It is also quite difficult to see among the woods the strong earthen ramparts that the Iron Age Celts threw up as a defence against a new wave of invaders from the Continent, about the third century B.C. Oldbury—whose name suggests that the early English settlers recognised its function—was made into a hill-fortress, to guard the approaches to the Kentish Weald.

The footpath around the forest, even in dry weather, tends to get churned up by horses, so that one is actually relieved to reach the lane at the western end. This returns to the A25, but it can soon be crossed, and the lane through the woods of Ightham Common comes to Ivy Hatch, a charming crossroads hamlet with houses and an inn in ruddy ragstone and tile; this is the entrance to some of the most perfectly rural country in the district. On the southern slopes of the ridge, and just on the southern side of a wooded hill called the Mount is a house which, again to paraphrase Voltaire, if it did not exist, would have to be invented.

Ightham Mote is a moated manor-house, founded in the mid-fourteenth century, and extensively rebuilt in the sixteenth, from which era the ragstone gatehouse and the timbered upper storeys originate. The continuity of possession was often broken, but did belong to one family, the Selbys, for some 300 years, until the late nineteenth century. One of them, Dame Dorothy, wife of a Sir William Selby, deciphered a coded message, warned Lord Mounteagle and so blew up, so to speak, the Gunpowder Plot. The house is now owned by an American gentleman who so loves it that, although he is only occasionally able to occupy the suite of rooms he keeps in it, insists on its preservation, for posterity, in its proper condition.

There is no doubt that this is being faithfully carried out: the moat, which is fed by a little stream called the Shode, is full of gold-fish, the gardens stretch out behind with level lawns, roses bloom-ing, fountains playing; the sun warms the old lichen-covered grey walls, reflects them in the moat, inducing in the visitor the feeling that so perfectly romantic a place can only be imaginary.

The gently sloping, heavily timbered country between the Mote and Shipbourne is quiet to the point where the traveller, already be-witched by the former vision, begins to wonder if some accident of time has transferred him, Wells-fashion, into some bygone century. All he can hear is birdsong, no cars, not even a tractor—until he comes to Shipbourne, and that is on the A227 to Tonbridge. Ship-bourne, on a rise with a few cottages and an inn by a Victorian stone church, faces a pleasingly wide expanse of grassland and com-mon; along the road a mile to the north another stretch of much smoother grass, lined with stately elms, leads the eye to the fitly named Fairlawne, a two-storey house in the classic style, built mostly in the seventeenth century. Then, it was the home of the Vane family, the best known of whom was that Sir Henry who was an ardent Republican and associate of Oliver Cromwell. Not many of his former opposition were executed when Charles II was re-stored to the throne: Vane was one. The justice of the case was questionable, and Vane, who met his end in a thoroughly dignified manner, was heard to say, 'It is a bad cause that cannot bear the words of a dying man.' And yet, some 20 years earlier, this same Sir Henry was instrumental in another travesty of justice: the attempt to impeach Thomas Wentworth, Earl of Strafford. Vane produced a document, of doubtful authenticity, which purported to substan-tiate his father's hearsay evidence that Strafford had suggested to Charles I that he could use the Irish army to subdue the discon-tented anti-Royalists of England; Strafford insisted, and won his case, that he had said that the king might use it in Scotland, which was in revolt. Although the impeachment failed, Pym organised a Bill of Attainder in the House of Commons, carried it and secured

Strafford's execution. If Vane's execution was unjust, so was Strafford's: the seventeenth century was one of the ugliest periods in English history.

On the eastern side of Fairlawne, reached by a lane from the main road, is Plaxtol, which has a stone church with no patron saint, being the only Cromwellian, completely seventeenth-century church in Kent. It had been a chapel, had begun to be rebuilt by Archbishop Laud, and finished in 1649 as the parish church. It has a fine hammer-beam roof, and in the chapel of the south-east transept, a simple carved wooden altar which is contemporary. The village cottages are mainly in white weatherboard or ragstone, and an inn on the corner of the street rejoices in the name of the Rorty Crankle, which apparently means happy corner.

A lane through the lower part of Plaxtol, by a wrought-iron foundry attached to an old twisted-roofed cottage, crosses the little River Bourne and rises to Old Soar Manor which, surprisingly, is a surviving part of a thirteenth-century manor-house. The hall part has been replaced by a Georgian house in brick, but the Solar, the lord's private room, with its attached chapel-cum-study and bedroom-cum-privy, and undercroft beneath, remain in extremely good condition and are open to the public. It belonged originally to a branch of the ubiquitous Culpepper family, which will be encountered in other parts of Kent.

The lane from Old Soar Manor runs along the outer fringe of Mereworth Woods and comes to the orchard country about West Peckham. The latter is one of those villages which can be gone to, but not through, since its lane ends in a wide green, its cottages, inn and church around it. The church has an eleventh-century Norman tower and in an aisle, a little upper room which was built as the private pew for the Geary family of Oxenhoath, who also owned Old Soar after the Culpeppers. A little way along the road to Mereworth is an ancient hall-house, behind a high yew hedge, called Duke's Place, which might, if it is old enough, have been the manor-house of the Knights Hospitallers, who once owned the manor. Nearer Mereworth, on the left of the road, is Yotes Court, which at a distance looks perfectly new but was actually built in 1658: the style is similar, but the proportions better than Squerryes Court.

Mereworth stands on the southern slopes of the ridge, just clear of the huge expanse of woodland which bears its name. Its church, in dark ragstone, has a tall stone spire, and was built by an eighteenth-century Earl of Westmorland, because the original church was too near his sixteenth-century castle, which he wanted to replace with a mansion on the lines of Palladio's Villa Capra at Vicenza. Horace Walpole, visiting, damned it with faint praise, and observed that 'though it has cost an hundred thousand pounds, it is still only a fine villa'. It is perhaps more interesting now than it was to Walpole, since only two other villas adapted from Villa Capra were built in England, and one of those, at Foot's Cray, was burned down. The church is in a basilica style, with Doric columns painted to resemble marble, and a painted roof. A semicircular window over the altar is filled with coloured heraldic glass from the old castle, and gives a yellowy-orange light.

The village, with several other less pretentious houses of the Earl of Westmorland's time, winds up the street to the woods, and a remarkably straight footpath enters them, to emerge surprisingly soon at a clear example of an assart, a tract of ground cleared from the woods for agriculture. In it, in a clump of trees on the right of the path, are the remains of a chapel. On the northern side of the woods the path arrives at Offham, where on the green is a white-painted post which is the remains of a quintain. A plaque on a stone beside it describes its purpose: 'The pastime—a Roman exercise—was for the youth on horseback to run at it as fast as possible and hit the broad part in his career with much force. He that by chance hit it not at all was treated with loud peals of derision'; and he that, by chance, neglected to get out of the way quickly enough, would get the sandbag attached to the other end swinging round and catching him in the back of the neck.

Bishop Gundulph of Rochester, the castle-building prelate of the late eleventh century, built a tower to protect his manor of West Malling, where he had also built a monastery. His protective tower, called St Leonard's, can be seen from the footpath which leads from the Offham lane to the A228 road. His abbey tower, at the other end of the fine wide High Street of West Malling, is locked away from public gaze behind a gatehouse since it is private property.

Quite close to West Malling, but rather hag-ridden by a nest of main roads, is Leybourne which, in addition to a large hospital, has the remains of a castle, a gatehouse, attached to a later house, of about 1300, with a slot like a letter-box above the gateway for pouring water on fires lit by putative attackers wishing to burn down the gate. It is, as can be expected, near the church like so many other manor-houses. In the church is a heart-shrine; Sir Roger de Leyburn, lord of the manor, died while on Crusade in the Holy Land, and desired his heart to be brought back to his manor's church. He had sailed with Prince Edward in 1268, on King Louis IX of France's abortive expedition to Tunis, to which he had contributed 1000 marks (£666 13s. 4d.). Years later, Edward I as he now was, and his Queen Eleanor, visited Sir Roger's son William, who later became the king's Lord Admiral, and gave votive crowns to the church. They are still there.

Eden and Medway

The River Eden becomes a Kentish river, after acting for a short distance as the county boundary with Surrey, about a mile south-west of Edenbridge, the derivation of whose name is obvious. Before joining the Medway near Penshurst, it flows through a part of the Kentish country west of Tonbridge and Tunbridge Wells, and south of the Green Hills. From the latter hills, Crockham Hill, Toys Hill, Ide Hill, of the ridge, the country slopes gently to the Eden. South of the river, a range of confused hills and valleys, steep and sudden, and broken through only by the Medway, extends to Tunbridge Wells. The whole region is well-endowed with trees and supports a great deal of animal husbandry with a preponderance of dairy farming. It also has a heavy, if scattered, population, because it is two desirable things: an attractive stretch of country and within reasonable reach of London. Geography is often an important factor in determining the course of events: would the Sidneys, a family of responsible servants of the Crown, have made Penshurst so exquisite a place if it had been farther from the focus of their work? Would Henry VIII have paid so much attention to either of the Boleyn sisters, with such consequences to English history, if their father's manor had been in, say, Dorset?

Accessibility from London has not only been the cause of the loss to Kent of the north-western triangle of the county: it is quite possibly the underlying basis of the ancient differentiation, which puzzles people from 'the shires', between Kentish Men and Men of Kent. The reason for this discrimination is still debated; the geographical dividing line is generally accepted as the River Medway. Those born east of it are Men of Kent, those born west of it, Kentish Men. What follows here is theory, unsubstantiated but presented for what it is worth: it seems at least possible that the origin of the difference is racial and legal. The main settlement of Kent in the wake of the post-Roman invasions was by the Jutes, who may have been a tribe from the Rhineland but in any case had a different level of culture and different laws and customs to their neighbours in Sussex and the shires, known as Angles and Saxons. The latter occupied the London area, northern Surrey, Essex, Middlesex, Hertfordshire. If they moved from London south-eastwards into Kent they came into contact with a people who had customs and legal entitlements denied to them. The Jutes, who quickly called themselves Kentings, were the Men of Kent, who were careful to make a special representation to William the Conqueror to safeguard their ancient customs. Those who had moved into the western part of the former kingdom of Kent, and were excluded from these customs (such as gavelkind, the division among sons of property when a landowner died intestate), were merely Kentish Men.

The distinction has persisted, although racial factors are long-forgotten and one law unites all England: it is still more probable that inhabitants of the eastern parts of Kent are descended from a line of ancestors born there, and that those of Kent north-west of the Medway have one, two or perhaps no Kentish generations before them. The theory rests in that Men of Kent are men of the county, for a number of generations, and that Kentish Men are immigrant settlers.

It is surprisingly easy to leave Tonbridge, now a town with enormous suburban-type development to north and south, on foot and arrive in the open country of this Vale of Eden. There is a footpath which leaves the Castle and crosses the water-meadows of the Medway, where tributary streams join it here and there, passes beneath the railway-line to Sevenoaks and joins the lane serving a minor industrial estate by a side-branch of the river; the name of Old Powdermill House offers a clue that it has been the site of an industrial estate for a very long time, and that the Medway's water has probably supplied the power for it. The lane, on its way to Leigh, takes one past a formidable thatched barn at Ramhurst Manor, over a motorway by-pass of Tonbridge, and by another venerable manor-house, a farmhouse in the tile-hung Wealden style called Great

Barnetts which is now near neighbour of a brand-new Moat Farm-house in a sensibly similar style.

The new motorway crosses both the railway (the dead-straight line that continues from Tonbridge to Reigate) and a smooth grassy trench called the Straight Mile, which was intended in the great canal-building days to extend Medway navigation to Penshurst. The reasons for doing this possibly appeared obscure even at the time, since the scheme was never completed: the railways put a permanent stop to any further canals.

Leigh (which is usually pronounced Lye) is mainly grouped around a large green, but has been extended greatly in recent years. Some of its cottages are genuinely elderly, and some in simulated Jacobean timber and stone were built in the last century; possibly they were the work of the architect of the wildly fanciful and romantic Hall Place: even the lodge-house looks like an illustration from Grimm's Fairy Tales. A long line of houses follows the road to Penshurst as far as the railway, but thereafter dense woods crowd in on either side. Names like Cinder Hill and Steamhammer Lodge recall the iron industry of 300 and 400 years ago, possibly in connection with Chiddingstone, as we shall see.

Penshurst is a place of three junctions: that of the roads, offering routes to Surrey, Sussex and eastward to the rest of Kent; that of the rivers Eden and Medway; and that of the modern and middle ages.

The latter junction took place in 1552, when Sir William Sidney was granted the manor by young Edward VI; since 1338, when Sir John de Pulteney, merchant, four times Lord Mayor of London, bought the manor from the surviving descendants of Sir Stephen de Penchester, Lord Warden of the Cinque Ports under Edward I in the late thirteenth century, the possession had passed through a variety of hands, including the Dukes of Bedford and Gloucester, brothers of Henry V, three unfortunate (or unwise) Dukes of Buckingham and the Crown. Pulteney had demolished whatever buildings that had satisfied the Penchesters and erected a great hall, with spacious private Solar, and kitchens at the other end. The Duke of Bedford had added to this a large and commodious block, in stone, in the early fifteenth century. The Sidneys, although capable of maintaining and caring for such a mansion, had not the means to effect a showy rebuilding, and so, like the Sackvilles at Knole, simply added to and embellished what was already there. Their tenure has endured to the present day, although the name of Sidney has been retained despite a break in the male descent: like the Sackvilles, and at around the same time, the only heir was a daughter, whose grandson John Shelley inherited the house and added the name of Sidney to his own.

Although the buildings of Knole and Penshurst are totally different, there is a similar atmosphere in both, of continuity, of sympathy of current occupants with those of the past, of a long, stable tradition of civilised living, appreciation of beautiful things, of the preservation not only of the material things themselves but also of the spirit in which they were gathered, to be admired and perhaps used with taste, restraint, control: these elusive bases of civilisation. Pulteney's great hall is allowed to stand uncluttered: almost its only furniture is that which Pulteney or one of his near-successors installed, the long tables where people ate, drank, laughed and sang in a way far removed from the elegance of the long table laid with superb Rockingham china and silver-ware in the dining-room, the old Solar. In a way, the great hall is the house's nursery: each addition, through each Sidney generation, is a stage in its adulthood, not in simple physical age but in its progress to civilised living.

The garden is also a place where the spirit of tradition keeps company with present matters of what grows best, and where; fruit-trees and herbs, flowers and lily-ponds and long green walks are only kept from one another by neatly clipped yew hedges, without fuss, without extravagant show, but with the same restraint, that element of restfulness that characterises the rooms and galleries of the house.

Personalities matter: Sir Philip Sidney was born and lived here, who to the Elizabethans was the epitome of Renaissance man, scholar, soldier, poet, courtier, diplomat and, above all, gentleman. Algernon Sidney, the melancholy republican, and his sister the beautiful Dorothy Spencer, Countess of Sunderland, the 'Sacharissa' of the wretched Waller's poems, lived here, walked among these yew hedges, imparted something of their spirit to the accumulative non-substance which is so irreparable, so irreplaceable.

The village of Penshurst, although it bears the Sidney imprint, as at the creeper-covered Leicester Arms (the Sidneys were Earls of Leicester for 100 years whose sign is the same blue wedge, splitting wood, on a gold field which floats on a standard over the great house, has not the look of an estate village, some of which bear a lord's insignia on every cottage. The church is Penshurst's church, with the Sidneys' chapel in it, and the effigy of Sir Stephen de Penchester too to show that the church was there before the Sidneys. So was the house by the lych-gate, whose wholly timbered gable is so old it has gone black.

There is a good footpath from Penshurst which crosses the Eden, where it meanders among the meadows and offers fish to hopeful anglers, climbs up through pastures and woods and comes to Watstock Farm, an old timbered house among modern sheds and barns. Across a lane, another path brings the walker without further trouble to Chiddingstone, also near the Eden. Flanked by its church and an eighteenth-century stone mansion, built on Penshurst lines, which masquerades as a castle, is a row of sixteenth-century houses of such quality that National Trust has bought them to preserve their appearance; in the public bar of the Castle inn at the end of the row might be seen lists of names for the Chiddingstone cricket eleven: they might include the name of Streatfeild (e before i), perhaps twice in one team. In the church, built of local sandstone in the fourteenth century, is a gravestone, made of a slab of iron, of Richard Streatfeild, iron-master, of Chiddingstone, who died in 1601, 'this towne his fame, the poor a portion large of all his worldly stoore'. There are memorials to all other generations of Streatfeilds up to the present day.

The sandstone from which this, and most of the other churches along this range of precipitous hills, are built, outcrops from time to time, often at the roadside on a hill. There is a bulbous outcrop behind the street at Chiddingstone which is known as the 'Chiding stone', alleged as the origin of the village's name (which is probably the usual patriarch's name from *Chid*, his followers from *ing* and the settlement *ton*). The *chiding* supposed to take place was a 'means of persuasion' to better behaviour.

From the lane past the Castle, a footpath, secured between fences, leads across the grounds of Hever Castle, through its fine woods, and reaches a corner of the churchyard. In the church, which has a very tall and slender steeple, is the huge tomb topped by a splendid brass, of 'Sr Thomas Bullen, Knight of the Order of the Garter Erle of Wilscher and Erle of Ormunde wiche decessed the 12 dai of Marche in the iere of our Lorde 1538'. He, owner of Hever Castle, was the grandfather of a queen and the father of another.

Hever Castle, home of Lord Astor, the present Lord Lieutenant of Kent, was carefully and thoughtfully restored by his grandfather between 1903 and 1906. Between Sir Thomas Bullen's death and 1903 the castle had been fitfully occupied, sometimes as a farmhouse, sometimes not at all; unlike Knole and Penshurst, there was no resident family to care for it, and ensure a continuity of possession and occupation.

The moat, gatehouse-keep and curtain wall were constructed in the late thirteenth century by the lord of the manor, William de Hever. In the fifteenth century the manor itself was bought by Sir Geoffrey Bullen, a Norfolk man who had been Lord Mayor of London in 1459. He and his family were social climbers who married into the peerage for three generations, and finally, and disastrously, into royalty. Sir William Bullen, second of the three, built the dwelling-house within the walls, converting what had been a fortified farmhouse into a compact but commodious mansion, retaining the moat and keep for their impressive castellar effect. The painstaking work of the first Lord Astor has, in addition to the building of his 'Tudor village' to accommodate staff and guests, and the laying out of the magnificent gardens, involving the damming of the Eden to make a lake, restored the interior to its Tudor splendour.

The restoration work has been so skilful that it is difficult to distinguish the fifteenth century from the twentieth: the entrance is across a newly made drawbridge which looks ancient, through the vaulted passage beneath the double portcullises of the gatehouse, into the little courtyard where the latticed windows of the Tudor living quarters shine on three sides. The hall leads to an inner hall, rich with carved Italian walnut, and the great dining-hall, hung with tapestries. A long gallery (used for exercise in bad weather) was built by putting in a ceiling to the great hall: it is 100 feet in length, with bay windows and the original Elizabethan panelling in fine-grained oak, evidently added after the demise of the Bullens.

There are some fine things at Hever, notably original Holbeins of Henry VIII and Anne Boleyn and numerous other portraits including a Gheerarts of Elizabeth, and relics and mementoes of Anne and Henry.

The two figures of Anne and Henry VIII dominate Hever, as well they might, for the Bullens' ambitions seem to have created the castle as a scene for them: at the conclusion of the tragedy the scene fades. For a short space this small Kentish castle–manor-house provided the stage to an act of prime importance in deciding the course of English history. The major part, inevitably, was played by the domineering, blustering personality of Henry VIII, a man of some virtues and a great many faults; his most serious fault, for posterity, was his egoism. His first wife Catherine was a model wife, except that the sole survivor of her many pregnancies had been a girl. It was Henry's overriding desire to secure his dynasty by means of a son, and his impatience with Catherine's failure to bear him one (as if it could not have been partly his fault) which led him to tolerate Anne Bullen's (or Boleyn, as she called herself) refusal to be his mistress until she was certain of being his wife. To marry her the king had to divorce Catherine, to divorce her he had to break the tie of the Church in England with the Church Universal. The break, the Reformation, the failure of the Tudor succession, the Stuarts: the snowball began at Hever.

The street at Hever turns sharply round the Henry VIII inn on the corner, and follows the Eden for a couple of miles to Edenbridge. The small town has grown, firstly around the point where one of the Roman *viæ glariatae*, their minor roads built to serve the iron-producing areas of the Weald, crosses the Eden, and secondly, where two railway lines cross one another. The row of timber houses and shops above the bridge, and the old Crown inn, provide evidence of the town's prosperity in the fifteenth century, possibly from the cloth trade or perhaps the growing iron industry, or both. The coming of the railway guaranteed its modern development.

Where the road divides to right and left, south of Edenbridge, the Roman way carries on, straight as a die as usual, into the depths of some very pleasant hilly country, as far as a farm; one can then get easily lost in the woods and hayfields, and just as easily found again with a track or lane from another farm to a lane leading to Cowden. Despite the extremely peaceful rural character of this woody country, it should perhaps be mentioned that while there is no more noise from the ground than occasional sheep-bleats and pigeon-calls, there is a constant procession of airliners overhead.

It is no coincidence that the Romans' iron road passes near to Cowden, because the art of extracting, smelting and forging iron having been rediscovered, a furnace is known to have been established here in the sixteenth century, according to the return of 1573, owned by one Quyntyn. Later in the reign of Elizabeth there was one owned by Michael Weston. There is still a Cinder Lane in the village, and it is said that there are traces of iron slag about. In the church, which has a massive wooden-framed steeple, is another iron grave-slab, similar to that of Richard Streatfeild in Chiddingstone. The village street, on a ridge, forms a close-knit group of church, tile-hung and weatherboarded cottages, all irregularly roofed, shops, post office and inn, and a slightly Continental air given by the trees outside the shops.

Tonbridge, of course, is not at the head of the Medway: but at Penshurst the river is joined by the Eden, and three miles farther up, near Fordcombe, by the Kent Water, and before acting as the county boundary for some distance it not only flows through parts of Sussex but actually rises in that county. For the most important part of its course, nevertheless, it is undoubtedly a Kentish river, and Tonbridge the best starting-point.

Modern Tonbridge has extended mightily, south of the river about the railway station, and north of it around the three major roads which converge on the town. Although, obviously, much smaller in its earlier days, it has always had an importance, firstly because of its stronghold on the river, then later for its capacity to handle river traffic, and for the industries which began to grow up about the two forges and two iron furnaces which are known to have existed in 1573.

Fragments of the castle are still there to testify to the early importance: the earthworks of the Norman motte and bailey are easy

21 *High Street, Tenterden*

22 *Brenchley*

to make out, the motte being particularly high, steep and formidable, although now covered in trees. The gatehouse, the only sizeable construction in masonry left, was added in about 1300, a highly sophisticated defence-work with drawbridge, two portcullises, double doors and three rows of machicolations, some part of which could be operated from each of the three storeys above the gateway. In case that failed, the defences at the inner end of the passage were reversed to cover attack from the bailey. Its early history was stormy, since it was held by the bellicose Bishop Odo of Bayeux, the Conqueror's half-brother, whom the king invested with the earldom of Kent and more than 200 manors scattered throughout the county.

Trade from the navigable river in conjunction with both the wool trade and the iron industry gave Tonbridge affluence in the fifteenth and sixteenth centuries, and it is from the later period that the school, founded in 1553 by Sir Andrew Judd (like Sennocke, a local man who made his wealth in London) and the fine timbered houses in the town date, like the Chequers Inn and the house near it, now Cobleys.

Beginning the progress downriver it is best to leave the right bank by crossing the railway at Tudeley, a small and now insignificant village which nevertheless produced iron throughout the reign of Edward III, the first known works in Kent, although in decline, like everything else, after the first outbreak of the Black Death. At Tudeley Hale, a kind of sub-hamlet half a mile along the way with its own inn, the flat water-meadows begin, lined with willows, and then there is a bridge across the Medway, which is perhaps about 60 feet wide here. Golden Green, on the left bank, is a crossroads village with shop and inn and a little green corrugated-iron chapel with a belfry and a railway-station clock. From here and in fact for miles around can be seen a tall tower, in grey stone, rising from the trees about Hadlow: it is the centrepiece of a madly extravagant nineteenth-century Gothic eccentricity called Hadlow Castle. Much of it has been demolished, but enough remains, of the tower in five stages with a high topmost turret, of subsidiary towers, turrets, minarets, a high brick perimeter wall with corner turrets and arched gateways, of a suitably lunatic gatehouse with two lodges, one

23 *The Pantiles, Tunbridge Wells*

newly whitened and the other covered in ivy, for appreciation of a kind of splendid indulgence which is never seen today.

Normal Hadlow has some good and sensible cottages in the lane by the church, and is now distinguished by the several departments of Hadlow College, the junction of the two former Farm and Horticultural Institutes. We are now back in the hop and orchard country, although the brewers' ability to extract more flavour from each hop flower means that less hops are grown and large numbers of oasts, redundant, are being converted for use as private houses. At Kent House Farm, between Hadlow and East Peckham, this is happening to a large six-kiln oast: it is at least better than demolishing these well-loved Kentish features.

Addlestead, on the edge of East Peckham, has a row of Wealden-style tile-hung cottages and one timbered and thatched: East Peckham itself is not so attractive, except by association with Sir Roger Twysden, who is buried in the church, and his house Roydon Hall, a brick Elizabethan mansion some two miles to the north, which is where the church is, too. Sir Roger was an independent-minded man at a time (the mid-seventeenth century) when it was dangerous to differ from the general run of opinion in the House of Commons: in consequence his estate was despoiled, fines exacted, and there was no end to the 'things caryed out of my house in East Peckham by the Troopers'.

At Branbridges, where the river spreads itself in streams and marshes, there is, beginning at Messrs Arnold and Nathan's yard, a footpath along the river-bank which can be followed all the way to Yalding. The river, if it is a week-end in summer, is lined with anglers and full of boating parties, and has the general appearance, lined with trees on both banks and often rather muddy in colour, of the River Bure in Norfolk, in its upper reaches, except that it is narrower and the boats mercifully smaller. At Yalding bridge, which was one of those maintained at the expense of the County from early times, there is a weir, and if the occasion is similar and the weather hot enough, the water is full of splashing children and a nearby field full of cars. The Teise joins the Medway just upstream from the bridge.

Yalding itself is on the Beult, which brings yet more strength to the major stream, and is crossed by a long stone bridge built in the fifteenth century. The village has a fine street of houses and cottages, from the war memorial down to the church, by the bridge; some are timbered, some weatherboarded, one thatched, some spaciously, stylishly Georgian in brick : none is really outstanding, but all contribute to the harmony. The church tower has a staircase turret with a little Tudor onion spire, just to complete the picture. Close behind the street are several working oasts, for this is deep in hopland, and the right bank of the Medway is lined with hop gardens, cherry orchards and bean rows all the way to Wateringbury. From the lane can be seen, on the far bank above river and railway, the church-and-court group of Nettlestead, the court manor-house in grey stone, gabled and tiled, the nearby church small and squat.

Wateringbury, which on summer Sundays supports another Bank Holiday scene by the bridge, the river lined with anglers, idlers, sunbathers and children and alive with small craft, rises in a street from bridge and railway to the A26 road. A path from this street avoids some of the crush by following a slight stream to the Old Water Mill, its little dammed millpool behind, which is now the Mill Pottery, and reaches the main road by the church. In the church there is an elaborate Jacobean monument to Oliver and Suzanna Style, erected by their son Sir Thomas in 1628. Oliver, who died in 1622 wears in effigy the red robes of the Sheriff of London and is supported by an angel on one side and a Skeletal Death on the other : he lived at Wateringbury Place. Over the main door, inside the church, there hangs the Dumb Borsholder of Chart. This is not so gruesome as it sounds, because it is a dark wooden staff with a chain attached and a spike on one end; it is said to be pre-Norman, and the only one in existence. It comes from a very early policing system whereby ten or twelve householders in a parish group (or borough) would be answerable for their behaviour, through a headman called a Borsholder (from *borhes ealdor* : borough's head). By custom, the official staff or truncheon of the Manor of Chart in Wateringbury was the permanent Borsholder, and therefore a Dumb Borsholder, and the headman was merely its deputy. The last deputy was one Thomas Clampard, a blacksmith, who died in 1748 and is buried in the churchyard.

On the other side of the road from the church is an odd enclave of new houses, in brick, rather squat, all rectangles and long narrow windows, and secretive, like Arab houses with their in-facing court-yard plan.

The river valley at Teston is at its loveliest, but the main road has tended to spoil the village, as in so many cases. A late eighteenth-century rector of Teston was James Ramsay, who having been a naval chaplain in the West Indies and seen conditions there, was determined to do all he could to bring slavery to an end. He wrote a treatise on the subject in 1784 and became an important ally of Wilberforce.

Another medieval bridge crosses the river and the lane climbs to West Farleigh, then along the ridge of the right bank, with West Farleigh church and court a little below and a view of the high-steepled church of Barming on the left bank. Below Barming church is the site of a Roman building, one of many which, as in the Darent valley, give evidence of the prosperity of this fertile vale in the days of the late Empire.

East Farleigh has the third of the vaulted, medieval Medway bridges, with Teston and Yalding (more properly Twyford); it crosses the river a little below the church, which is said to be of tenth-century foundation and has one wall which might be of that date. Near the war memorial is a plain wooden cross and the words: 'In memory of 43 strangers who died of cholera, Sepr. 1849, R.I.P.' The time of year suggests that the outbreak which carried off so many strangers at once was at hop-picking time: no one knew or kept count of the pickers who came down from London. The manor of Gallants in the parish, represented by Gallants Farm and an ele-gant Regency house with a wrought-iron verandah on three sides called Gallants Court, was one of the properties of the Culpepper family in the days when they spread their tentacles all over the county: the reason, perhaps, for this will appear when we visit Goudhurst.

A mile or so after leaving East Farleigh, industrial Maidstone be-gins with the paper mills at Tovil, long established, dwarfed by the mighty works at New Hythe but still functioning: the tavern at the top of the hill proudly proclaims the title, Royal Paper Mill. Entering

Maidstone from this direction, College Road leads quickly to the magnificent group of fourteenth-century buildings by the riverside, subject of generations of paintings, sketches and photographs showing their eminently picturesque reflections in the shining water. From this end, the first set of the ragstone buildings belongs to the college for secular canons established by Archbishop Courtenay in the late fourteenth century to serve his great parish church of All Saints (the next in the range) and probably several of the surrounding parishes. There are in College Avenue the remains of a gateway, another gatehouse or tower used by the Maidstone Sea Cadets, and a large hall with towers which houses the Kent Music Centre, attached to a third crenellated gatehouse. This leads to the church and a tree-shaded walk by the river below the college. The church is wide and high, with a timbered roof: the walls of the chancel were elaborately painted, and the advanced-Gothic reredos erected in 1910. 'At least,' the Vicar comments, 'it saves us from being overpowered by the East Window.' In the north aisle are memorials and all the colours of the old Queen's Own Royal West Kent Regiment, merged with the Buffs in 1961 and now, thus diluted, the 2nd Battalion, the Queen's Regiment. Its depot was the Barracks in Maidstone.

The third group of these medieval buildings by the river is the Archbishop's palace which predates the others: as we have seen, Archbishop Islip finished it in the 1350s with stone taken from his former manor-house at Wrotham. Much of the upper storey was rebuilt, doubtless to a more conveniently modern plan, by Archbishop Morton in the reign of Henry VIII. Near by is a range of stables and a huge barn, and some well-kept gardens where the River Len meets the Medway.

Maidstone's principal streets have some solid Georgian buildings like the Town Hall, and some earlier pargeted houses, rare in Kent, tucked out of the way. There is also, of course, a great deal of modern building, some of which is regrettable. In St Faith Street is Chillington House, a brick Elizabethan house with modern additions in roughly the same style, which houses the County Town's Museum and Art Gallery.

Close by East Station, by the tall Sessions House, the Barracks now occupied by the Royal Engineers, and the prison, the road winds uphill to Penenden Heath. It is mostly built over now, but this hill on the northern side of Maidstone was from the very earliest times of the 'Kentings' their place of assembly, where they gathered for concerted action, or for some great and important legal case. Such a case was that between Archbishop Lanfranc and Bishop Odo the earl, when after three days Lanfranc won back the manors that Odo had presumptuously seized. Such concerted action was that when the Men of Kent rose under Sir Thomas Wyatt, in 1554, to challenge Queen Mary's choice of a husband. The rebels mustered on Penenden Heath, marched to Rochester, gathered more, then marched to London. It was, for a day or two, a serious threat to the Tudor throne, more serious than the other rebellions which tried them during their century of rule because it was near enough to London, the country's nerve-centre, to take effect, which the others, begun from farther afield, were not: as Professor Bindoff observes, 'it may be that we have here one of the clues to our boasted immunity from revolution'. Did not Parliament hold London throughout the Civil War, and was not that fact of prime importance to their conquest of the King's faction? Was not that the reason, when the Men of Kent rose on behalf of the King in 1648 and 'swept away' (according to Gardiner) 'the parliamentary authorities from its northern and eastern seaboard' for the prompt expedition of Fairfax, with 8000 men, who beat the Royalists at Maidstone and was able to withdraw his army after a campaign of only three weeks?

Down from the Heath, across the new by-pass motorway and up the lower slopes of the North Downs, at Boxley there is another reminder of the family Wyatt: in the church is a memorial 'To the memory of Sr Henry Wiat of Alington Castle Knight Banneret descended of that antient family who was imprisoned and tortured in the Tower in the reign of King Richard the third kept in the Dungeon where fed and preserved by a Cat'. To be in politics was to live dangerously: no cat preserved Sir Thomas the rebel from execution.

Park House, south of the churchyard and shrouded by its trees, was once the home of the poet Tennyson's brother-in-law, and Tennyson stayed there in 1842; the parkland is supposed to have inspired the prologue to his poem 'The Princess'. The Pilgrims Way runs along the foot of the Downs, as ever, immediately north of Boxley House, which is now a country club, and across a mighty unbroken succession of cornfields west of the village (the footpath from Forge Cottage is a dead end when the corn is high) there are the surviving buildings of Boxley Abbey.

There are no other Cistercian abbeys in Kent, and in fact so well-cultivated a corner of England was a most unlikely place for the Cistercians to found one, since their principle was to go into the wilderness, away from the world's vanities; but William of Ypres, a son of the Count of Flanders, and Earl of Kent under King Stephen, was a man of such evil reputation that one despaired for his soul: the Cistercians—and the hand of St Bernard looks suspiciously likely in this—promised him absolution of all his sins if he would give them his manor of Boxley for a monastery. The abbey was founded in 1146.

Boxley Abbey is now notorious for having seriously damaged the monastic cause by a long-established fraudulent trick. Its Rood of Grace, a cross with an image which was believed to be gifted with miraculous movement and speech, was found by Thomas Cromwell's agent sent to deface the monastery in 1538, to have 'certain engines and old wire, with old rotten sticks in the back, which caused the eyes to move and stir in the head thereof, like unto a lively thing, and also the nether lip likewise to move as though it should speak'.

Not much is left of the abbey, but a long tiled stone barn, bits of the perimeter wall, and at the hamlet of Abbey Gate, a cottage, part of which is a chapel.

At Sandling, a village caught up in the coils of Maidstone's motorway system, a long-since defunct mill broods over its pool, now a duckpond; over the road from the thatched Running Horse a steep path with steps leads down to the Medwayside near the tree-screened towers and walls of Allington Castle, on the far bank. The cat-succoured Sir Henry, who found favour with Henry VII, bought the castle in 1492; his son the elder Sir Thomas was the eminent (although unpublished in his lifetime) poet; the younger Sir Thomas, the poet's son, was the rebel leader who ended on the block. There were no more Wyatts, and in its later days the castle fell to ruins until restored in the early twentieth century; it now belongs to the Order of Carmelites who run it as a Christian Retreat.

Past the weir and the well-known riverside Malta inn, the new motorway crosses the river by a concrete bridge, and a road along the right bank passes the Elizabethan Cobtree Manor, on a hill out of sight behind trees, on its way to Aylesford. The road is lined with factories and warehouses, and there is a new bridge at Aylesford to supplement the old (which Walter Jerrold thought would probably be necessary, to suit the 'modern traffic' of 1908) and gaps in the rows of old gabled houses in the streets have been filled in a commendably fitting style.

Somewhere near Aylesford was probably fought the third great battle of Hengist and Horsa against the Britons of Vortigern. Nennius, writing in the ninth century, says that it was at Ford, 'in their language called Episford, though in ours Sethirgabail. There Horsus fell, and Catigirn, the son of Vortigern.' The Celtic name given the place is interesting, since it implies that a settlement already existed here: it appears to have done so for a very long time, judging from evidence found in a gravel-pit near by, in what had been a Belgic cremation burial; there were urns, a jug, a pan, two brooches and the famous Aylesford Bucket, a wooden pail with bronze mounts, bronze decoration of animals and scrolls in what is thought to be Greek and Gaulish influence, and handle attachments ornamented with bronze human heads. All the trade-routes from the Continent came through Cantium, and the Old Way under the Downs ran near by.

The church sits on top of Aylesford; in it Sir Thomas Culpepper and his wife, 'by blood and descente descended of many worthy ancestors' recline on their tomb-top; on the floor by them, a small stone lies on Thomas Finch, son of Anthony Finch of 'Coptree', and in the north-east corner is a large and rather vulgar monument to the Banks family, who once owned the Carmelite Friary at Aylesford. The Carmelites abandoned the Holy Land in 1237, one jump ahead of the Moslems. On arrival in England they split into two groups, and one was given land in a manor at Aylesford, where the friars built themselves wooden huts and a chapel. In 1247 they reorganised and built a more permanent structure, and 200 years later rebuilt again. At its dissolution in 1538, Sir Thomas Wyatt, who received it, pulled down church, chapter house and friars' house for their lead roofing, and late in the century the remainder was converted to a private house. About 1675 the Banks family remodelled it again, with new windows, and in 1930 the main block was burnt down. In 1949 the Carmelites returned and restored it to its original use.

On the slopes between Aylesford and the North Downs is the eastern part of the Neolithic necropolis of the middle Medway, described in connection with Coldrum. There have been many more sarsen groups in the past than can be found today, but several, in the way of agricultural operations, were blown up with gunpowder in the last century. The White Horse Stone, connected legendarily with the fallen Horsa (with whom it doubtless had no connection whatever), is hard to find now because yet another new motorway, up Bluebell Hill, has thrown the map into confusion, and fields of high-standing corn make footpath-finding a matter of perspiration and frustration. The Countless Stones, alias Lower Kits Coty, are easier, and best of all is Kits Coty itself, at the end of a long upward path in the trees. The long barrow which once extended westward from the burial chamber has now disappeared, but the huge sarsens remaining have their capstone, a veritable monster of a monolith, in place.

Excavations for chalk in the country north of Aylesford and west of the megalithic monuments uncovered a surprising number of Roman foundations, including one on the riverside at Burham when a factory was being extended in 1895. It was at first thought to be a Mithraic temple: it was underground, with possibly a barrel vault, and there were niches in the walls which might have been for statues of Mithras and his attendants. But there were no actual traces of the cult at all, and there were remains of a timber-fronted wharf on the river, so it seems more likely that the vault was a cellar of a type well known in northern Gaul, for storing wine, oil and perhaps corn for export.

The river between Aylesford and Rochester is inclined to meander between muddy banks, lined with cement works and the remains of old ones, and is less attractive than, say, the reaches around Teston and the Farleighs. Burham Court and church are left stranded on the riverside, their village having moved higher up the hill to a long drab street and a large Victorian Gothic church. Huge old chalk pits, many used by the local council as rubbish tips, are all around. Wouldham, which with a little effort might be a bright riverside village, pays no attention to the river at all and looks run-down: one of its two taverns is closed and unfilled bomb-sites from the war show how short a duration is prosperity from a cement works. The thirteenth-century church, at the end of the village, has a memorial to Morley Monox, dated 1602, in Latin, Italian, French and Spanish, all of which he could apparently speak, but *Non quam diu sed quam bene.*

Halling and Cuxton, sheltering under the edge of the white-scarred Downs, across the river, full of new houses and old chimneys, do not invite closer inspection. A mile past Wouldham is a manor-house of uncertain antiquity (probably much restored and augmented) called Starkey Castle. Downriver a short way from here the M2 crosses the Medway by its handsome concrete bridge, and the lane ducks under it and enters at once the dull streets of Borstal. Its name comes from *beorh stigel,* a way up a hill; the grass-grown shapes on top of the hill are the ramparts of Fort Borstal, which was built as part of the Chatham defences in the late nineteenth century.

The conurbation of Rochester, Chatham and Gillingham, with Strood on the other side, stretches across the Medway mouth to the mud-flats of the estuary. There is not a great deal to be said about Strood: it once had a hospital which the monks of Rochester resented because it was endowed with some of their funds, in fact at one point it had three hospitals, for pilgrims and travellers, and Lambarde says that some of its inhabitants were born with tails for ever after, for being rude to Thomas Becket.

East of Gillingham is a small village called Grange, which in the Cinque Ports' hey-day became a limb of Hastings. None of its present houses is old enough to have existed at that time (although there are some flint and stone walls at Grench Manor which might be) but the tavern is called Hastings Arms to keep the link in mind. The most pleasant part of Gillingham is the Strand, a waterside green with a view of boats, the river with Hoo Salt Marsh and the old fort on it, Kingsnorth Power Station and the nearby gasworks. The hilly back-streets are full of Victorian terraced houses, with views of the ships of the Royal Navy in the dockyards below; the shop-filled High Street adjoins the edge of Chatham and a huge open space where the old fort, Brompton Lines, had its being; horses graze the grass round the tall and dignified Royal Marines memorial. The old ramparts of the Great Lines have given place to service married quarters, but their names, King's Bastion, Sally Port, remain.

By the gate of Kitchener Barracks and near the Naval barrack gate is a fine view of the riverside in Chatham Reach, but Chatham has very little to detain the visitor. Rochester, on the other hand, has a great deal.

The Celtic name of the pre-Roman Belgic *oppidum* on the site now occupied by Rochester was *Durobrivae*, which the Romans adopted. It means 'bridges of the stronghold' which indicates that they had some kind of armed encampment there, and that a bridge or bridges existed. The invading Roman army under Aulus Plautius in A.D. 43, after landing unopposed, evidently found that these bridges had been destroyed and that the Britons had taken up a position on the opposite bank. The Roman cavalry swam the river, while the infantry marched down the bank until they found a place which could be forded: they then took the Britons in the flank. The Britons nevertheless put up a stout resistance, because the battle went on for two days. The Romans as usual won through by sheer dogged persistence, coupled with tactical skill (Vespasian, who 25 years later became emperor, here commanded the Legion II Augusta and won a success with a surprise attack) and were able to pursue the Britons to the Thames.

The Romans constructed a new bridge and later built the town walls. The bridge was the predecessor of the medieval bridge: its characteristic piers were found in the river. Parts of the walls also have been found, some underlying the medieval curtain wall, and some incorporated into the castle walls. The Antonine Itinerary tells us that *Durobrivae* was 25 miles from *Durovernum* (Canterbury), which is quite accurate.

Rochester was the first place in England, after Canterbury, to have an episcopal cathedral and diocese: King Ethelbert built a church for Justus, one of St Augustine's monks, the first bishop, in 604. Nothing now remains of it above ground, but the foundations are under the west end of the present cathedral. The bridge still existed, and surrounding parishes (such as Dowde, as we have seen) were required to maintain it; it was not replaced until 1388, when Sir Robert Knolles, a great commander of the Hundred Years War, and Sir John de Cobham, the builder of Cooling Castle, built a new bridge and provided lands to maintain it. This one lasted until 1856, when it was replaced by the present iron bridge. The balustrade from the old bridge was used for the Esplanade, and that and the old Chapel, incorporated into a Bridge Chamber in 1879, can still be seen.

The Castle was begun by Bishop Gundulph in 1087 and was held against the rebellious William Rufus in 1088. The keep, that immense and enduring monument to the Normans' engineering and architectural abilities, was added in about 1130: it still towers above the whole town and provides a wonderful vantage point for surveying the Medway approaches. It has four storeys, with a tower at each corner. The walls, 12 feet thick at the base, rise 113 feet in the air, and the turrets add another 12 feet to that. The entrance was at second-storey level, and the great hall was at the third storey: the fireplaces and chimney can be seen.

The tower at the south-east corner is round, and the others are square: it had to be rebuilt after King John's siege in 1215. John had secured the sympathy of the Pope, the formidable Innocent III, who condemned Magna Carta and so threw Archbishop Langton and the mediating bishops into despair, because it gave the hotheads among the barons an excuse for armed revolt. The king was at Dover waiting for mercenaries from Flanders; the rebels seized Rochester, whose castle was held by a previously trusted servant of John, Reginald of Cornhill: he opened the gates for them. This infuriated John, whose sometimes violent behaviour was often conditioned by treachery among those who should have been loyal to him. Rochester barred his way to London (the key, as we have seen, to control of the kingdom), so without delay he marched and besieged it. The castle was manned by 95 knights and 45 men-at-arms under William d'Albini, an able commander, but John worked with fierce energy. 'Living memory,' wrote the annalist of Barnwell, 'does not recall a siege so fiercely pressed or so staunchly resisted.' The keep resisted battery from John's siege-engines, so he had a tunnel mined under the south-east tower, filled it with combustible materials and fired it: its shoring timbers burned away, the ground caved in, the tower collapsed. After a siege of only seven weeks—sieges often took as many months—the garrison surrendered.

Bishop Gundulph also built the cathedral and reorganised the priory attached to it. His work is evident in the lovely Romanesque west front, and in the high rounded arches of the nave, which have a characteristic dog-tooth pattern. Outside, the ruins of the monastery buildings surround a quiet garden close.

A great cathedral such as this has many corners; one can find, for example, a brass plate to Charles Dickens' memory, a memorial to Richard Watts, who bequeathed money for an almshouse, or a broken slab which was part of the shrine of St William of Perth, Rochester's answer to St Thomas of Canterbury.

At the dissolution of the monasteries, the cathedral school, like that at Canterbury, was refounded as the King's School, and today it uses some of the old monastic buildings and has spread in various houses in other parts of the town. One of them is opposite a big red-brick Elizabethan house with Flemish gables (and very much eroded in the north wing) where Charles II is supposed to have stayed on his way home to regain his throne in 1660, on account of which it is called Restoration House.

The High Street is full of intriguing buildings, from the cathedral gateway, Chertsey's Gate, to Eastgate House, another late sixteenth-century town-house which accommodates the City Museum and, in its garden, the painted Swiss chalet in which Dickens wrote his last words at Gadshill. There is the bulky Georgian Bull, which became the Royal Victoria and Bull when that monarch stayed there; the Guildhall of 1687 with a gilded ship weather-vane; the Corn Exchange with a large projecting clock, built by Sir Cloudesley Shovell in 1706; and there are several excellent timbered town-houses, now shops and restaurants, which have managed to survive generations of would-be 'developers' and all the dangers of city life.

On either side of Eastgate House, on a site obvious from its name, demolition has uncovered stretches of the medieval city walls. There is much to see in old Rochester.

CHAPTER SEVEN

The Heart of Kent

The ridge of ragstone hills, or the Lower Greensand Ridge, the western part of which formed the subject of an earlier chapter, continues on the eastern side of the Medway, in the same position between the North Downs and the Weald, almost as far as Ashford. In the vale to their north two rivers flow, in opposite directions, the Len to Maidstone, and the Great Stour to Ashford. Geographically, this region is in the middle of the county, and if anyone cares to stand on the hill at, say, Egerton, and look north, south, east and west, he will see nothing which is not Kentish. My chapter heading, therefore, seemed to me appropriate enough.

A railway running through the vale and a junction at either end serve the walker well; I began my journeys from the Ashford end, so that is how I shall describe them. On the Tenterden road, A28, is one of the entrance gates to the park of Godinton, and a little westward of this is a footpath which skirts the parkland, crosses the Great Stour and follows it upstream among grassy meadows with trees all around: the road is forgotten, the river bubbles cleanly between mossy banks and the riverside world of *The Wind in the Willows* comes irresistibly to mind.

There are glimpses of the rosy pink gables and chimneys of Godinton, up on the hillside, among the massed trees: the people who built and lived in it belong to Great Chart and the next chapter. The footpath comes to the farm of Worten, where a lane recrosses the river; on the edge of Godinton Park is Swinford Old Manor, one of those houses which have been growing gradually for some five centuries. Up at Hothfield, whose Common has been preserved as a Nature Reserve, the new houses greatly outnumber the old, some of which were erected as schoolhouses by the Earl of Thanet in 1834.

Below Hothfield the Great Stour cuts through the ridge from the vale between it and the Downs, and across on the far bank the estates of Rooting Manor and, in the distance, Surrenden Dering show among the trees. At Rooting Street, a hamlet of a few cottages, the first examples occur of the Dering window. This is a round-arched window, usually in pairs or threes, and at present outlined in white, and has been inserted into every house and cottage formerly owned by the Derings: of the family, and their influence, there will be more shortly.

Little Chart lies low, on the northern side of the ridge where the Great Stour flirts with the lower slopes. Opposite the inn is a new, simply designed, brick church; it was opened in 1955 to replace the old church whose remains still stand by Chart Court, the old manor, nearly a mile away upstream: in 1944 it was smashed to pieces by a flying-bomb. The new church is heart-warming: in its cream-washed interior, much use is made of the lancet window and high pointed arch, and several treasures have been rescued from the ruins, including the reclining figure in fifteenth-century armour of Sir Robert Darell, who had been a squire to Henry VII. The Darells of Calehill had a chapel of their own in the old church, a notable concession since they remained true to Rome after the Reformation: their modern representatives, whether Roman or not, gave help in the building of the new church.

On the hillside behind the church lies the land of Surrenden Dering, encircled by a high brick wall. The same family, the Derings, held it since before the Norman Conquest, a continuity which, considering the normal run of natural accidents and the uncertainty of fortune which breaks one family and exalts another, over and over again in history, is quite exceptional. The come-down of many, like the Wyatts of Allington, has been political involvement: with two exceptions, the Derings, worthy country squires, knights of the shire and content to remain so, have steered clear, and that may have been their secret. One of the exceptions hardly counts, since he was a younger son, the puritan whom, in his early twenties, Archbishop Parker called 'the greatest learned man in England'; convinced that the clergy needed drastic overhauling he courageously preached at Court, before Queen Elizabeth, in 1570, on Psalm 78,

24 Tenterden

25 Cranbrook

KENTISH WEATHERBOARDING

26 Stocks Mill, Wittersham

27 Goudhurst

28   *St Augustine's Church, Brookland*

29   *St Nicholas's Church, New Romney*

verses 70–72, indicating that these 'hawkers and hunters, dicers and carders, morrowmass priests' had neither integrity of heart nor skilfulness of hands, and wound up directly to the unamused Queen: 'and yet you in the mean-while that all these whoredoms are committed, you at whose hands God will require it, you sit still and are careless, let men do as they list'. He was suspended, reinstated, punished again for further exposures and reinstated again. He died in 1575, aged 36. The other exception was a middle-of-the-way Dering in an age when extremes were normal and moderation unsafe: the mid-seventeenth century. This Sir Edward Dering represented Kent in the Long Parliament, tried, and failed, to steer a middle way between Archbishop Laud and the presbyterians, served a term in the Tower, fought for the King and nearly lost his estates. The legend goes that he escaped capture by the Roundheads through a round-arched window in his house, and commemorated it on his return by changing all the windows on his estate to the same pattern. But he died in 1644, and the windows were inserted by a descendant, another Sir Edward, who lived through all but 11 years of the nineteenth century.

There are no more Derings now, and even the old house, which for some years was a boys' school, was burnt down in 1952; the remaining parts are split into flats.

Pluckley has a brickworks, down by the railway, and all but the modern houses in its steep street, even the 'Black Horse' which was built in about 1470, have Dering windows, in brick, in pairs or threes, with round arches.

The road to Egerton runs along the ridge-top, with views left of the wide Weald, and right of the vale and the Downs. A farmhouse called Pevington is credited in *Domesday Monachorum* with a Saxon church: it is the kind of place whose foundations would probably show that its settlement preceded the church. An encircled mound called on the map Moat could easily have been a patriarch's stronghold.

Egerton is high and windy on the ridge, and has a church tower which can be seen for miles in both directions; its old stone and timber cottages have been augmented in fairly recent years and it has a brand-new primary school, but the names on the local election list pinned to the Post Office are the names which were current 20 years ago. Down past stone Court Lodge a lane goes to pretty Stonebridge Green, and another finds its twisting way among the trees and corn, sheep and cut hay to Boughton Malherbe. Little else on this hilltop exists to share the southward prospect but the church-and-manor-house group, and the farm cottages. The manor was the property of the family of Wotton, who could trace their descent from the original Malherbes, the Norman family who added their name to Bocton or Boughton. One of them was the Sir Henry Wotton who coined the evergreen ambassador's joke (and was reprimanded for it by James I): he was, he said, 'sent to lie abroad for the good of his country'.

Down the slope is Grafty Green, a much more populous hamlet, and lower down still some lanes wind about the fields and orchards to the scattered outposts and farms of Ulcombe, where Joseph Hatch, the famous bell-founder, lived (at a farm near the parish boundary with Broomfield, it is thought). Hatch made his bells during the seventeenth century, to show that something good must have come out of it: they ring in a great many Kent churches today. There are brasses in Ulcombe's church, one of which, to Ralph St Leger and his wife Anne, who died in 1470, is said to be one of the best in Kent, for the period.

There is a footpath from the church to Morry Farm, westward, but maddeningly it refuses to continue, as it should, to East Sutton Park, so one has to go up to Chartway Street and down again. The house of East Sutton, once the home of the pro-monarchical political writer Sir Robert Filmer, is now HM Borstal Institution for girls. It stands near the small church, and on the western side of the park, by the road to Sutton Valence, is a comic hexagonal lodge which has a new battlemented wing, in the same spirit.

Sutton Valence, justly famed for its situation commanding the green-carpeted Wealden acres, owes the second part of its name to a Frenchman. King John's widow Isabel returned to Poitou and married the man from whom John originally took her, Hugh le Brun, Lord of Lusignan. Her sons, half-brothers of Henry III, came to England when that monarch lost Poitou to the French: one of them was William of Valence, called after the Cistercian Abbey near Lusignan where he was born. He married the heiress of the earls of Pembroke and their son Aymer de Valence inherited title and lands, one manor of which was this of Sutton. He built a small castle, which has almost entirely disappeared (Walter Jerrold said there were 'trifling remains' in 1908, and the Ordnance map no longer even marks them); a moderate and sensible man, he was for a while a restraining influence on the ambitious Bartholomew de Badlesmere. Although the king's (Edward II's) friend Piers Gaveston, who invented naughty names for half the barons of England, called him Joseph the Jew, because he was tall and pallid, and insulted him in various other ways, Aymer tried as long as he could to mediate between the rebel earls and the king, and when that failed, supported the king. He died suddenly in France in 1324, and although he had married three times he left no heir: Sutton Valence is therefore one man's addition to Kentish topography, since Aymer's father never owned it in his own right.

Another returning Kentishman from London's wealth, William Lambe, founded the school, a fine ragstone building facing south, in 1575. Many other houses are of ragstone, since it is the material on which they stand, but several also are timber-framed, like Valence House. The church was demolished in 1823 and replaced by the present building, in commendably restrained Gothic.

At Chart Sutton or Chart Corner—and Chart, incidentally, in Kent is simply a piece of common rough ground and rather like a hoath, a minnis or a lees (a forstal is a small one)—there is a bus-route to Maidstone; let us take an imaginary flight to Otham, two miles northward and accessible from Bearsted station.

These ragstone hills are here known as the Quarry Hills, for obvious reasons, and it is partly on account of the quarrying for stone, over an immensely long period, that they have taken on such a sharply corrugated appearance. Otham village (its church is half a mile westward) is all along a street on the side of a precipitous ravine; Stoneacre, down in the hole, although a very fine example and now National Trust property, is only one of a remarkable number of timbered houses, in excellent condition, from the fifteenth century to the seventeenth. Quarrying, evidently, was a profitable business.

There is a curious stream in these hills, which rises at Langley, disappears into a hole in the ground at a farm called Brishing Court and reappears to run through a number of small pools in a magic valley described in a typically intriguing way by Donald Maxwell, in *The Enchanted Road*. At the far end it is joined by a clear spring of water at Salts Place, fills a series of pools for long-forgotten mills, runs, with the lane, under the A229 and then waters the backs and fronts of the houses in Loose. It has often been said that Loose takes its name from this stream, because it loses itself, but unfortunately it appears to be based on a synonym for a pigsty. It is nevertheless a quite enchanting village: a path runs along a causeway between two streams, one of which dives under the front paths of the houses and is joined by bubbling springs on all sides. At the end of the path the streams unite and gush down the race of another old mill; a street climbs to a terraced road and the Wool House, a long two-storeyed timbered hall. The church, by the stream, is in the middle of the village, which is full of houses of all ages and almost equal interest, since many of the new ones are fittingly attractive.

The A229, which swoops across this valley, is of another world; at a crossroads at the top of the hill a road goes off to Coxheath, which once was a useful no-man's-land on which the Army could camp and now supports a hospital, a large modern housing estate and the Bird in Hand; the A229 traffic thunders on over the brow of the hill through Linton, on its south-facing slope. At the back of Linton churchyard is a sundial, and on its plinth is inscribed: 'We the parishioners of Linton give this sundial in affectionate remembrance of our beloved Squire, Fiennes Stanley Wykeham Baron Cornwallis who lived among them for 50 years. In honour chivalrous, in duty valorous, in every thing noble, to the heart's core clean.' This paragon lived at Linton Place, and there is a footpath, beginning at the churchyard, which can be followed, in sections, across four large estates and for two miles, on the edge of the ridge: the first is Linton Place. A big square Georgian house, plastered and painted white, it stands at the end of a long drive and faces the Weald. Horace Walpole, who visited his friend Sir Horace Mann, the owner, wrote: 'the house is fine and stands like the citadel of Kent. The whole county is its garden.'

The footpath passes through the Linton lands—wooded parkland alternating with orchards, currant-bushes and cornfields—and then those of Loddington Farm, and comes to Boughton Place. This is another of the Kentish Boughtons: there are four altogether, Boughton under Blean, Malherbe, Aluph and this one, Monchelsea. Before anyone, fresh from Professor Ekwall's Dictionary of Place-names, starts wondering what a shingle bank has to do with the ragstone hills, it is as well to point out that Monchelsea began life as Monchensie, the name of the Norman lord of the manor. The village, called Boughton Green, lies over the crest of the hill towards Loose: the church and manor-house, which is a charming small stone Elizabethan house, have by far the better situation; the church, much restored, has a churchyard which is a garden, full of roses and wisteria, terraced to a wall which overlooks the greater 'garden', like Linton.

The fourth of the estates crossed by the footpath is Wierton, and there is a way through orchards to Chart Sutton, but we have been that way: up and over the ridge there is a path to Langley which is interesting, if at times not easy. The Langley stream, that which loses itself farther down, flows in its first mile through a shallow valley, where it has been damned to make a lake. A path skirts the lake, which is very overgrown with reeds but provides a good lurking-place for coots and moorhens, through extensive hop gardens. Langley Park House, Georgian in red brick, and its farm are at the end of the lake, and thereafter the path crosses grassy fields—hard going before it has been cut for hay—to Langley, whose church spire can be seen for the last half mile. There is a good hall-house on the corner of the road to Langley Heath, and another, with a later wing added at an angle, in the long street of Leeds. The main part of Leeds is in a little valley made by a tributary to the Len (since these are the northern slopes of the ridge): near the inn there is Manor House, a hall-house with the lower right-hand corner in stone with a pair of trefoil windows, which makes it look as though it might have been a part of the Priory. The latter, which is now being excavated, was on the hill above this house; it was founded in 1119 by Robert de Crevecœur as a priory of Augustinian canons, who would serve the church and other parishes in the vicinity. The church, of St

Nicholas, on the other bank of the valley, has an immense twelfth-century tower, and a fine rood screen of the fifteenth century, 50 feet across; in the north chapel there is an old carved-oak pew for the family from Leeds Castle. The canons continued to perform their duties for this church and the others in their care until the Dissolution, and in 1540 there were still a prior and 14 canons for whom pensions had to be found.

A footpath from the church goes to an ancient stone house called Battel Hall, and another leads into the park, from which one can enjoy a rare sight: as at Ightham Mote, we are back in the fairy-tale world of legend and romance, Camelot, Sir Galahad, Sir Gawain and the Green Knight, for here are rolling green meadows, stately forest trees, a shining lake with white geese and swans, and a castle on islands in it, turreted and battlemented, in creamy stone.

The castle—Leeds Castle—is inhabited, and the park is private (although there is a golf course in it) but from the footpath one can look at it, and that is plenty. The lake was formed by damming the Len, and the islands support barbican, bailey and keep: bridges and drawbridges span the gaps. The work was done first by Normans—possibly Robert de Crevecœur—but the earliest existing walls above ground (there are cellars from the earlier times) date from about 1280, when the castle belonged to the king. Henry VIII added bits here and there, and reconstruction in the last century supplied the present living quarters.

As we have seen, Edward II granted it to Bartholomew de Badlesmere, who moved to take the part of Thomas, Earl of Lancaster, in opposition to the king. An incident sparked off his rebellion. While Bartholomew the castellan of Leeds was away, Queen Isabelle (who was known as 'the she-wolf of France') and her retinue arrived at the castle for lodging. Lady Badlesmere refused to receive her, saying that she would entertain no one without her lord and master's consent. The queen tried to force an entry, and six of her men were killed; furious, the 'she-wolf' demanded to be avenged, and the king complied: it is interesting to note that the response to his summons to the Kentish towns for levies of horse and foot was unexpectedly favourable—the king may have been unpopular among baronial circles, but the commons supported him. This large force (including

Aymer de Valence, Earl of Pembroke) besieged Leeds Castle, and on 31 October 1321 it surrendered. The siege is said to have caused the ruin of the place, but it must have been repaired and restored in order, since Froissart writes that in 1395 'We rode as far as Leeds Castle, to which the King came with all his retinue and where I found my lord Edmund, Duke of York.' He had a richly-bound book of love-poetry to give the king (Richard II) but did not do so at Leeds, 'for Sir Thomas Percy said the time was not yet ripe'.

There is a station at Hollingbourne, not far away, and we shall return to it at the end of the last part of these travels in the Kentish heart-land. Ashford is the starting-point, and the main road, A251, to Faversham the way out: turning left by the gateway to Eastwell Park, a lane follows the park wall under the lee of the heavily wooded Downs of Challock, to Westwell. A quiet, out-of-the-way village, its few cottages, inn and renovated mill-house, whose immobile wheel allows a clear stream to splash through unimpeded, cluster about a small thirteenth-century church; its choir-stalls, for 'singing men' drawn from the parish, were made in the time of Edward III. There is a pathetic little memorial in the Sacristy to the infant son of the Rev. Richard Barham, the author of the *Ingoldsby Legends*, who was curate here from 1814 to 1817.

A long lane through farmland, on the Downland slopes below the escarpment, passes Pett Place on its way to Charing. A fine mansion in red brick, with Flemish-type gables, it is said to have as part of its garage the remains of a pre-Conquest chapel, which is mentioned in *Domesday Monachorum*. The house was a seat of the Honeywoods, a family almost as prolific as the Culpeppers.

Charing has a long street sloping down from the hills to the A20, the Ashford to Maidstone road: it is full of old houses kept in good condition, but its oldest, another palace of the archbishops of Canterbury, is used as farm buildings. It was one of the earliest of archiepiscopal manors, but the present remains were constructed mainly in the fourteenth century by Archbishop John Stratford: he built the gatehouse and much of the hall; it was also used by Archbishops Morton and Warham, and in the days when Henry VIII was yet a devout Catholic it provided lodging for him, for Queen Catherine and part of the enormous retinue which gathered to accompany him to meet King Francis I on the Field of Cloth of Gold; but before embarking, Henry had an anxious few weeks because he wanted to meet the Emperor Charles V first (and the latter wanted to prevent Henry from meeting Francis at all) and the Emperor was held up by adverse winds in the harbour of Corunna, in Spain. At the last moment the wind changed and Henry entertained him in Canterbury for three days; immediately the Emperor departed, Henry gathered his train of over 5000 people, organised by the capable Wolsey, and left for France.

It requires some effort to imagine the crowds, the jostling, the colour, richness and glitter, the lords and ladies, king and queen, among the present straw, cows and heifers, and farmyard litter.

The church, hard by the old palace, having been burnt to the ground accidentally in 1590, was rebuilt in a high and fine style with a well-proportioned tower. In the north transept there are the curious works of a seventeenth-century clock.

Between the railway and the A20, and the Great Stour, there is a low sandy ridge, quantities of which are constantly being carried away by sand-and-gravel firms from great pits in it. A network of lanes connects the scattered hamlets on it (Charing Heath, Lenham Heath, Sandway, as if confirmation were needed of its character) with the vale to the north and the ragstone ridge to the south. Sandway is actually on a farther part of it, beyond where the Great Stour breaks through from the north and trickles under the road by Chapel Farm. From Sandway the road recrosses the railway and leads to Lenham. On the left of this way into Lenham is a fine timbered house with a jetty all along the front, oriel and bay windows, called Honeywood. It was built by a member of that family, Anthony Honeywood, in 1621, a year after the death of another member who added substantially to the population of Kent: in the church, on the left-hand side of the altar, is a memorial tablet to one Robert Thompson, and added to it is a tribute to his grandmother Mary Honeywood, who when she died, aged 92, had 367 descendants living. She had 16 children, 114 grandchildren, 228 great-grandchildren and 9 great-great-grandchildren. Whether or not, as Richard Church asserts, Lenham is 'a spongy village ... the inhabitants are riddled with rheumatism', the Honeywoods seem to have been impervious to all ills.

The Square at Lenham is lined with timbered and brick houses of all ages and great charm, a row of lime trees, two inns and the lych-gate to the church. The old market-house stands, encased in brick and used as shops.

To get to Harrietsham without recourse to the howling A20 it is necessary to cross it and go up the lane to the Pilgrims Way and along it to the rear of a factory and Marley Court, a farm. This gently sloping shoulder of the North Downs is full of springs : to the east of Lenham the Great Stour and several of its tributary streams rise, to the west of it the Len rises; at Harrietsham a brook from a pond near the church feeds the Len. The church at Harrietsham, close by the road from Stede Hill, stands above the village; it has two towers, the main square one of the fourteenth century, and a small one on the north side, said to be Norman. The village is too near the A20 for comfort, but has nevertheless been much increased by new estates of houses; its street has some attractive cottages, notably the row from the Bank House inn which curves away from the road, high on their embankment.

Long leafy lanes guide the walker away from the A20, back up the slopes to Hollingbourne, whose street runs up from the church to the Pilgrims Way and then climbs up into the Downs. In it are an excellent range of timbered and brick-built houses and cottages from the fifteenth century to the eighteenth; the group by the church takes some beating : some cottages by the churchyard gate, a farm down a lane, a large stately white house on the corner, another standing up on a green bank behind a pool. And then, up the street towards the foot of the hill, on the left, a tall brick Tudor house with high chimneys; it was another branch of the Culpeppers who built it and lived in it, the branch which supplied the Thomas Culpepper who lost his life for daring to cuckold the awesome Henry VIII. Henry's fifth wife, Katherine Howard, whom he married in the forlorn hope that she would bear him another son, was not chaste at the wedding : nor was she after it, flirting with courtiers, her former lover Dereham and a gentleman of the Privy Chamber, Culpepper. The chamber might have been privy, but the adultery was blatant :

even so, Henry would not at first believe it. First he raged, then he wept for his ill-luck in marrying such 'ill-conditioned wives'. The story is sour and sad, and Hollingbourne is neither, so let us conclude by recalling Walter Jerrold's story of Nicholas Wood of Hollingbourne who according to Fuller (*Worthies*) suffered from the rare disease Boulimia or Caninus Apetitus, 'insomuch that he would devour at one meal what was provided for twenty men, eat a whole hog at a sitting, and at another time thirty dozen of pigeons . . .'.

CHAPTER EIGHT

The Kentish Weald

The tract of land lying between the ragstone ridge in the north and the Wealden hills in the south is for the most part level: it has hills, especially in its southern region. Marden and Staplehurst are on hills, and so is Frittenden. But its chief characteristics are flatness, immense quantities of trees, and streams. The Beult, rising near Shadoxhurst, flows through most of it, with countless tributaries and hundreds of little ponds and pools, several in one field sometimes; the Teise rises near Tunbridge Wells, flows northward from Lamberhurst and meets the Medway very near where the Beult debouches. In all this region there are few roads, although there is a complex multiplicity of lanes, and only one railway, which runs in a dead straight line from Ashford to Tonbridge. It is one of the most fertile areas in Kent, particularly at its western end, where fruit and hops are predominant. This is that blue-green carpet that lies before the villages of the ragstone ridge, Linton, Sutton Valence, Egerton, a land in which the number of surviving timber-frame houses testifies to the wealth of the late-medieval Kentish yeoman, whose estate was limited by the ancient Jutish law of gavelkind: when an owner died intestate, instead of the land passing to the eldest son, it was split up among all his sons in equal lots. But the yeoman had security of tenure, the fertility of his land ensured his prosperity and he was able to spend enough to build enduringly and well.

Ashford, again, is a good place from which to begin; the A28 road to Tenterden, with a loop south, perhaps, for a glimpse of the manor-house of Singleton, a hall-house converted or modernised in about 1600 with chimneys, a second floor and two-storey porch. Singleton has a moat and has been secure for centuries: but behind it now the sprawling expansion of South Ashford threatens to engulf it, and near by a new road is being cut.

At Great Chart is a street of tile-hung cottages, some of ragstone, many with porches in the Flemish-gable style, built to harmonise with the lord of the manor's Godinton, a mile northwards. The street rises to a hill, on top of which is the church and old manor-house. In front of the church at the roadside is a tiny stone and timber hall called The Pest House, built in the fifteenth century and used now as library, museum and meeting-place. The church had a predecessor in some form, as had so many Kentish churches, which existed in 764; the present building dates from the fourteenth and fifteenth centuries. Several good brasses in it lie over the tombs of Tokes, lords of the manor: there is John Toke, in his fifteenth-century armour, another John and his wife of the next century who endowed the ragstone almshouses in the street, and Nicholas, who died in 1680 at the age of 93 after having married five times and built the great house at Godinton, which was the Tokes' home until the present century; the last Toke died in 1944.

A track through the Manor Farm behind the church (the old house, in stone, is probably older than the church) is muddy at the best of times, but gets one clear of the village and up to a slight hill on which stands the wreck of Goldwell Farm. Another brass in the church commemorates William and Alice Goldwell, whose family married into the Tokes and disappeared: this last relic of their name is now deserted and derelict. The track from it comes to a lane which passes Yardhurst, another timber-framed hall-house, with bricked ends, sheltering behind a high hedge.

Woods are numerous at this end of the Weald, the indigenous oak preponderant, and the farms still give the impression that they are assarts in the forest. The name Weald comes from a word for forest (as in the German *wald*); the whole area called Andredsweald stretched for 100 miles from this eastern edge, through Sussex to Hampshire, filling the bowl between North and South Downs. The Romans cut roads through it to serve the iron-works already well-established, but to the Kentings and the South Saxons it was well-nigh impenetrable. Bit by bit they cleared glades, used the woods for pasturing their pigs—the dens, as in Bethersden, Wissenden,

Brissenden, Plurenden, from *daenne*, a swine-pasture—and built houses and churches on the little hills—the hursts, Staplehurst, Goudhurst, Hawkhurst. These names are all comparatively recent, in Kentish history, because the process only began from about the eighth century onwards.

Bethersden—*Beaduric's-daenne*—has given its name to a grey stone which was quarried in the vicinity; since it could be polished it was called Bethersden marble, and was much in demand for church monuments. The street has some pretty tiled and weather-boarded cottages, and in the lane that turns off by the school is a farmhouse called Lovelace which incorporates a surviving fragment of the Royalist poet's mansion, which he was obliged to sell when he was imprisoned for the second time by the Parliamentarians.

The lane by which Lovelace's old home stood follows, more or less, the infant Beult through oak and beech woods, past an odd-looking brick mansion called Romden Castle, which has a massive tower and began life as a fortified manor-house of the late fifteenth or early sixteenth century. Several converted oasts herald the approaches to Smarden, where the Beult, a slow and muddy stream here, winds its leisurely way through the oak-lined fields. The street of Smarden is justly celebrated for the many medieval timbered houses which line it on both sides, ending with a group, a passage under one of which provides a lych-gate to the church.

From Smarden Bell, which takes its name as a crossroads hamlet from the Bell inn, the lane follows the railway all the way to Headcorn, where the River Sherway joins the Beult from the general direction of Boughton Malherbe. There are good timbered houses, of the sixteenth century, in Headcorn, too, particularly Chequers and Shakespeare House, next door to one another on the south side of the street: these village street houses cannot have been those of yeoman farmers, but many were built by merchants in the cloth trade, on which much Wealden prosperity was founded.

The Beult and the railway have to be crossed again for the long winding lane to the hilltop village of Frittenden, whose sharp-pointed steeple rising from the woods guides one from afar. At the crossroads in the village are two houses which look as if they had once been taverns, and one that still is, with the engaging name of Bell and Jorrocks.

Through a mile or two of woodland a lane from Frittenden reaches the A229 road near Knox Bridge. The bridge is over a stream which once powered a mill on another road, and near the bridge once filled the moat of a small mound which was a stronghold. To what period it belongs is uncertain: C. Roach-Smith, the anti-quarian, writing in 1880, thought it was a 'British moated *oppidum*' of our 'pre-Roman ancestors', but in view of the fact that the Weald was a vast forest in those days, this seems to be debatable. On the other hand, it is in line with one of the Romans' roads which served the iron industry, so perhaps might have been connected with that. Archaeological evidence seems deficient in any case. It is known as Castle Bank, and is one of several clumps of trees visible from the bridge.

Staplehurst, which crowds both sides of the Roman road, now A229, for a mile and a half, is about the biggest village in all this region. Many of its houses followed the arrival of the railway, which runs at right-angles to the road: some were probably already built when on 9 June 1865 the boat-train from Dover to London, carrying among its passengers none other than Charles Dickens, went off the rails near the station. He was not hurt, it seems, but greatly shocked.

There is therefore a great diversity of houses along the street, from the Bell which has a venerable stone wall, and the row of cottages near the church, to the modern shops and houses down the hill. Iden Manor, on the way to Knox Bridge, is now the Convent of the Good Shepherd.

The country west of the road verges on the Wealden hills, and therefore undulates quite sharply. Woods are plentiful, and it is evident from the remarkable number of converted oasts that hop-growing here has given place to the wheat and barley which cover the rolling dales. Going north from the Detention Centre at Blantyre House a lane dipping through the woods passes the end of a garden wall and a little two-storey gatehouse. A fine sixteenth-century timbered manor-house, Hushheath Manor, stands behind a beautiful garden with much topiary. It has close-set upright timbers and the addition of two Jacobean gables; its position, except that it is north-facing, could hardly be bettered, on a hillside, backed by tall trees, with meadow and pasture-land stretching out below, lush green all around, with grazing sheep and cattle.

On the far side, from Hushheath, of some cool beech and oak-woods, at the road to Marden we are suddenly in orchard country. Passing more good Wealden farmhouses at Great and Little Cheveney, a lane crosses a curious branch of the Teise which runs for some four miles northward and joins the Beult. At Claygate, a cross-roads hamlet near a bridge over the Teise and the once-important manor of Bockingfold, the lane joins a road through Collier Street, which owes its name to the Wealden trade of charcoal-burning. There are far more apple trees than any other kind here now: one after another, the orchards line the lanes, replacing many of the old hop gardens, judging, again, by the number of oasts converted into houses or used as fruit-stores. Laddingford, on the Teise, which even after a dry spell is rather murky, is an unpretentious village with two chapels, an oast that looks like a third chapel and another oast with a rare all-brick kiln. Turning towards the Beult now, at Benover is a good timbered house of the seventeenth century called Normans, with two large gables and a smaller one between them. The lane to Hunton crosses the Beult which here, unlike its muddiness at Smarden, looks appealing: it sparkles, shining in the sun (if there is any sun) as though the alchemist Apollo has turned its customary cocoa into molten gold. Water-lilies flower at its edges and fish move darkly in the faintly translucent water.

At Hunton there is a large defunct mill, on a leet from the Beult, an inn, and some cottages by the school where a lane turns off, going nowhere except to a farm. The lane becomes a track and leads across country to a peaceful backwater where a few cottages enjoy as much solitude as anyone could desire: around them, woods and farmland, orchards and cornfields as far as one can see; on the rag-stone hills to the north, the spire of Linton church stands out from the mounds of trees. The track becomes a footpath to a bridge over the Beult and a lane to Chainhurst which, like Laddingford, is a simple village of farms, a few cottages, a post office, inn and chapel, among the orchards and hop gardens. The cottage gardens, as is the general rule throughout the entire county, from spring to autumn are invariably bright with flowers, which turn even the plainest and meanest of dwellings into fit subjects for a painting.

Marden, also on a small hill and also by the railway, has developed a minor industrial estate on its northern side, with a fertiliser depot, a printing works and sundry engineering firms, which employ numerous Marden people. The church, on the highest point of the hill, all of 100 feet above sea-level, rises another 50 or so with a little weatherboarded cap to its tower. At the end of the street of old houses near the church, one of which has recently been uncovered to show its timbers, is a tiny square hut with a tiled roof and weatherboard sides, which serves as a greengrocer's shop. It was Marden's Court Hall, which 100 years ago housed the stocks; according to Mr Kenneth Gravett the weathering on the beams on one side shows that it was originally open, like a market cross. The market at Marden was controlled by the Portreeve of the Hundred of Milton (Milton Regis) which, as we have seen, also has a Court Hall. Another officer attached to the royal manor of Milton was the bailiff whose duty was to administer the dens, the pastures of the Weald, in the Hundred of Marden. In the reign of King John the royal bailiff was one William of Kensham who, when in 1216 England was threatened by invasion, the rebel barons under the nefarious Robert Fitzwalter having invited Prince Louis of France to oust the king, was given powers to maintain a kind of guerrilla band from all the seven Hundreds of the Weald. He became known as Willikin of the Weald, a kind of Robin Hood character who conducted a campaign of sabotage and banditry against Fitzwalter's and Louis's forces on behalf, first of King John and then of his infant son Henry III, which was eventually effective.

A curious discovery at Marden, considering its position in what was for centuries an immense forest, was a hoard of implements in an earthenware pot from the late Bronze Age. What story lies behind it we shall never know, but the Victoria County History says that the hoard was a secret deposit, whose presence does not imply that the district was much frequented during the period. The objects in the pot were mostly broken : could someone have, perhaps, stolen the pot, and bolted into the forest? Or did the objects belong

30   *Martello Towers at Folkestone*

to a fugitive, in hiding? Was their owner devoured by the wild beasts that ranged the Weald in the Bronze Age?

In the extreme west of Kent the range of sharp little hills south of the River Eden continue eastward to Tunbridge Wells, and then south-eastward to Tenterden. On their southern side a series of streams and rivers, the Kent Water, the Kent Ditch, the Rother, form the boundary with Sussex. The hills are part of the Weald, which is to say that until the days when the early Men of Kent began to infiltrate the wooded depths and pasture their pigs and cattle in them, they were merely a small area of the immense forest which stretched from mid-Kent westward to Hampshire, which the Romans called *Silva Anderida*, and the Kentings and South Saxons, *Andreds-weald*.

Gradually, the forest was cleared by assarts, areas cut out for arable farming, and during the middle ages the iron industry, moribund since the fifth-century invasions, started up again. The furnaces and forges needed fuel, and the woods were all around: in a space of 200 years so much was burnt that the government began to fear that not enough would be left to provide timber for ships of the Navy. Coal was discovered near the iron-fields of the north of England, and one by one, the furnaces and forges in the Weald closed down. The greater number had always been in Sussex: by 1740 only four were left in operation in Kent.

It gives one a slight shock of surprise to study John Speed's map of Kent and realise that between Tonbridge and the Sussex border, in the Hundred of Watlingston, there is nothing much beside a walled park called Hungares and some kind of place called Hares-gate. The surprise diminishes when we also realise that Speed published his map in about 1600, and it was not until 1606 that Dudley, Lord North, drank some water from a spring in the Earl of Abergavenny's estate, and was cured of 'the lingering consumptive order he laboured under'; the spring was chalybeate, impregnated by the iron in the local stone. Lord Abergavenny enclosed the spring, and the fame of the Tonbridge Wells began to spread: before long the greater part of high society, escaping from London's plague-ridden streets in the summer, came to the Wells for the good of their health, drank the water (which, wrote Lord Boyle in 1728, 'has a

31 Roman pharos *and Norman keep at Dover*

brackish taste never palatable') and returned to London for the winter and another round of overloading their long-suffering stomachs.

The water still bubbles up in the wells at the Pump-Room, and the graceful houses, built over the colonnade at one side of the tiled walk known as the Pantiles, bear witness to the hey-day of the Wells in the later seventeenth and early eighteenth centuries. The *malades, imaginaires* or otherwise, would be entertained by musicians in the little gallery on the other side of the walk, under the shady trees, and could go and offer grateful thanks for their strengthened constitutions at the brick church, built in 1678 and dedicated to King Charles the Martyr, quite near the Pump-Room.

The Pantiles today preserve their elegance and distinction: the shops, tea-rooms, taverns and coffee-houses seem to have the edge on others in the large and rather shapeless town which, aided by a junction of railways, grew up around the Pantiles and the Wells. The town became known as Tunbridge Wells, with a 'u', to distinguish it from the old town of Tonbridge, and its popularity through nineteenth and twentieth centuries can be seen from the astonishing number of hotels which it supports, facing Hungershall Park. Recently, a new Pantiles area has been created, at the far end of the old one: a shopping precinct for pedestrians only, with a car-park behind and underneath. It lacks entirely the light architectural touch of the original, but is at least in the same spirit, with coffee-houses among the shops and colonnaded walks; perhaps in time it, too, will be visited for itself alone.

The ironstone or sandstone rears up above ground in many places around Tunbridge Wells; at High Rocks, for example, which was adapted in the Iron Age as a fort and is actually just over the border in Sussex; on Rusthall Common where an odd-shaped protrusion is called the Toad Rock, or at Speldhurst, on either side of the steep lane leading from Rusthall Common up to it. The church and manor-house, on top of the hill, are both built of sandstone, but the old George and Dragon inn, which claims 1212 as its date of building, is a timbered house, with the characteristic high tiled roof of early timber-frame houses in Kent, but showing several centuries' additions, such as the two gables, the massive central chimneys and the brick base-wall.

The houses of Tunbridge Wells now spread all the way, along the Tonbridge road, to Southborough, to its outflung hamlet Modest Corner, among the woods and sandstone hillocks, and to High Brooms, a manufacturing, industrial valley in the midst of the high Kentish woods. Beyond High Brooms and the A21 Hastings road, Kent reasserts itself with the dense forest north of Pembury, through which one can walk by footpaths and breathe woodland air after the chemical smells of High Brooms. Capel, on the far side, is on the verge of the Medway valley, but after crossing a couple of its tributary streams and noticing the alder-lined wayside pools, one begins to climb again, up to the old tile-and-brick Wealden house called Crittenden, which has gardens good enough to be opened under the National Gardens Scheme, with a lily-covered pool and a boat. The ascent to Matfield is harder still; at the top is a complex network of crossroads, the pleasant green, the mainly tiled cottages grouped around it, and the road to Brenchley.

The houses of Brenchley are sited mainly around a triangle of roads on a ridge. At one end of the principal street is the war memorial and, opposite it, a timbered house of the late sixteenth century called Poore House, with a two-storeyed porch. On the left, farther down, is the Old Palace, a long, angled house with a continuous jetty in front, broken by a wagon-entry. The brick base and gables facing the street are modern. At one time it was longer still: a crosswing extended northward, and it was a mansion-house belonging to a branch of the Roberts family of Glassenbury, who will appear again later in this chapter. It now constitutes a row of houses, one of which is the post office. On the other side of the road is a working blacksmith's forge, and at the end of the street is a little green with a large oak in the middle, an antique shop on one side, a timber-framed butcher's shop on another and an avenue of clipped yew trees beyond the lych-gate leading to the church door. The church is on the very edge of the southern side of the ridge, and it is only a quarter-mile to its northern side, where from a neatly laid-out semicircle of grass at the roadside the people of Brenchley may sit on the wooden benches and contemplate the wide panorama before them of the valleys of Medway, Teise and Beult, the ragstone ridge beyond and the high Downs shadowy on the far horizon.

Castle Hill, along this ridge-road, a hamlet with an inn and a shop, takes its name from a small earthwork in a wood a short way to the north; it is of uncertain age, and consists simply of a deep moat with the ballast thrown up on both sides to make two circular ramparts.

On the right of the lane from Castle Hill to Horsmonden a tributary stream to the Teise was dammed in the Weald's 'iron age' to form what is still called Furnace Lake. The remains, in the form of foundations, can still be made out of the hammer-mill, near where the stream slips down the long chute. The lake, encircled by tall trees, is quiet and unspoiled, an oasis for wild-fowl, anglers and, perhaps, meditative philosophers. Horsmonden, up on the next hill, is centred around a celebrated cricket-green and a crossroads, some old and many new houses, three inns, a Methodist church and the tiniest shop imaginable which might have been a toll-cottage, since the road was turnpiked in the mid-eighteenth century. The church of Horsmonden is two miles from the village, by way of an immaculate Wealden farmhouse at Hazel Street and the woods of Rectory Park. The question, which is often asked in cases of this sort, why is the church so far away from the village, should really be put the other way round: why is the village so far away from the church? The church nearly always antedates the oldest house in the village, after all, and as we have often seen, was usually built close by the manor-house. There is usually a good reason for the village gradually to move farther away: in this case, probably the iron-forge and furnace in the vale between the two ridges, and then the turnpike road; in other places, whatever industry (like the cement works at Burham) or transport centre (the Medway at East Peckham) or road (Boughton Street) that made habitation near to it preferable to the long journey from around the church.

The church at Horsmonden is called the Gunfounders' church (one of the inns on the green is called The Gun). By the chancel step is an iron tomb-slab for Martha Browne, wife of John Browne who made guns for King and Commonwealth: in 1619 he had 200 men producing guns for Charles I, and in 20 years of royal service is said to have lost £10,000. The church itself is of sandstone, and was built in the thirteenth century; one of its rectors, the Rev. Sir William Smith-Marriott, Baronet, was so impressed by the works of Sir Walter Scott that he erected a tower in Rectory Park to his memory. It is gone now, demolished because too dilapidated for repair. Quaint relics gather in this church, from the guns of John Browne to the literary predilections of a wealthy rector, and then there is another memorial, to John Read, who died in 1847, after inventing the stomach-pump.

The Teise twists through the Wealden Hills in a great arc before finding its way down to Laddingford and the Medway. Before flowing past Horsmonden church and northward to within a mile of that village its fair green-banked valley is crossed by the A21 Hastings to Tonbridge road at the bridge of Lamberhurst. Despite the road, which is as burdensome as all main roads are, Lamberhurst contrives to remain attractive. In its steep street, descending to the Teise and climbing the other side, there are typical tiled and weatherboarded Wealden houses, and some timbered cottages. Two inns, Chequers and George and Dragon, stand on either side of the river, originally for the purpose of coping with travellers stranded by the impassable road in flood-time.

The furnace of Lamberhurst was one of the last in the Weald to close down: it is said to have produced not only cannon for the Navy but also the iron balustrades for St Paul's Cathedral, at a cost of £11,202: there was gold, it seems, in that there iron, which accounts for the fine houses built by the iron-masters. The furnace was upstream from Lamberhurst, not far from the ruins of Bayham Abbey (which is just in Sussex), and quite near Owl House, a lonely place in the woods which acquired its name from the 'owlers' or smugglers, who in the profitable days of the eighteenth century used it as a den.

A walker may leave Lamberhurst with the greatest of ease, by a path at the rear of the Chequers which crosses the cricket pitch and makes for the quiet farmland down-valley. On the hill to the north the church and Court Lodge, both in stone, appear among the trees; the Teise wriggles away towards Horsmonden, and a footpath permits one to climb over the ridge on the southern side and descend to the lane that serves Scotney Castle, by a tributary of the Teise. From the lane, in summer, the gables and chimneys of the great stone house built in 1837 can be seen above the trees, but of the remains of the old castle, which has one complete fourteenth-century round tower, heavily machicolated, among some fragmentary walls and the ruins of an Elizabethan house, not a stone. The stream fills a lily-covered lake, moating the whole crumbled structure, and surrounding it are gardens to which the public is admitted on certain afternoons in the week, by permission of the owner.

During the sixteenth century the castle was owned by the Darell family, the same as those of Calehill whose rescued effigies add the necessary touch of country tradition to the new church of Little Chart. Since, as was observed in that connection, they remained Roman Catholics after Elizabeth's Act of Settlement in 1559, they were obliged to act circumspectly in matters of religion: the house they built in the castle contained a secret chamber for a priest. In 1598 it succeeded in keeping the Jesuit John Blount from capture by the Queen's men.

Scotney's parkland fills the quiet valley with lush pastures and woods; there are no roads but this service lane. Past the farm of Little Scotney the lane crosses the stream and rounds the corner by a tall brick mansion on a rise. From the front the full Queen Anne style can be appreciated: a central three-storey block, with attics, and two lower wings; in the centre, a pediment with a coat of arms, below it a niche with a statue, and below that the round-arched door; tall, narrow windows, symmetrically placed, some with slightly curved tops, some fully rounded; before it, a field with stately trees and grazing sheep. This is Finchcocks, built by one Edward Bathurst in the early eighteenth century: he inherited the manor from a family called Horden who had bought it from the Finchcocks, who gave it their name, in the early years of Henry VI's reign.

The little lane meets the A262 road to Goudhurst at the point where the railway used to cross it. This was the Hawkhurst Branch line, which operated from Tonbridge to the latter village with one track, one tank engine and two carriages; I travelled on it once, from Goudhurst to Horsmonden (the fare was sixpence) but it was closed years ago and the rails have gone. So has the station of Goudhurst, replaced by a house called Haltwhistle; and the Railway Hotel is now the Goudhurst Hotel. Just past it there is a lane which skirts the hill of Goudhurst (which, crowned by its square-towered church, can be seen for miles around) to the B2079 road, on which, close by a high-arched bridge over the vanished railway, stands Pattenden, a large fifteenth-century hall-house with jetties at both ends as well as in front. The immediate vicinity of Goudhurst is full of interesting houses: another timber house, with a stone front, used for many years as a Youth Hostel, is Twyssenden, in a lane off the same road; the lane begins opposite the park, backed by a forest which stretches to the Sussex border, of Bedgebury. We are here in Culpepper country, because this great Kentish family, springing from Bedgebury, issued branches which seem to have borne fruit in half the parishes in the county. There is no trace of them at Bedgebury now, because their manor-house, built no doubt from the profits of their iron-furnace (in a north-eastern corner of their estate is Furnace Farm) was replaced in the nineteenth century by a mansion in the French manner, and even that is now a school, in whose grounds the Forestry Commission has a Pinetum, a nursery for trees.

Farther along this same road, to the right, is Combwell, where until 1536 there was a priory of Praemonstratensian Canons; these were priests who were intended to serve secular needs, although they lived together as regular monks, and were given their cumbersome name because it was a Latin version of their place of origin, Prémontré in France. The priory was founded by Robert de Turneham (the incumbent of Thurnham Castle) during the reign of Henry II, but by the 1230s, only 50 or 60 years later, there was a controversy about whether they followed the Praemonstratensian or the Augustinian order, which were similar in any case. The Archbishop of Canterbury made a visitation and decided on the latter order. A prior and five canons remained to take Henry VIII's oath of Royal Supremacy in 1534, and the priory was suppressed in 1536.

The long hill which brings the B2079 and the traveller to Goudhurst arrives hard by the duckpond, which has chestnut trees and benches on the adjacent green, and the parish hall and some tile-hung cottages around it. Over the way, by the war memorial, is a branch of the National Westminster Bank which must be one of the smallest in England; from the nearby white-weatherboarded Vine inn the steep village street begins to climb to the church, lined with irregularly situated (at odd angles to the road) cottages, also tile-hung and weatherboarded. At the top is a broader space and a cluster of aged and famous inns adjoining the churchyard. The church is basically of the thirteenth century, but the tower was struck by lightning in 1637 and rebuilt a couple of years later. *Blitzen* of a different sort struck in 1940 when bombs smashed most of the glass, plain and coloured.

The story of the Culpeppers can be traced through their monuments in this stately old church of Goudhurst. First, in the Bedgebury Chapel, there is a brass to John Bedgebury, the last of the earlier resident family of the manor, who married one Anne Roper and died in 1424. Anne then married Walter Culpepper, whose heirs inherited the Bedgebury estate: a brass under a stone canopy shows their son Sir John Culpepper, who died in 1480. Then, outside the chapel are the intricately painted wooden recumbent figures of his son Sir Alexander, and his wife, with a helmet above them and carved stone dated 1537. In the chapel there is a huge four-generation monument to Sir Alexander's son Thomas, his son another Sir Alexander and his wife, and their son Sir Anthony and his 12 sons and four daughters: the tomb was built by these in 1608. With so many sons and daughters to provide for, no wonder Sir Anthony extended the Culpepper tentacles to every manor on the market, every eligible heir and heiress in every corner of Kent.

In the north aisle of the church is a memorial to Edward Bathurst, the builder of Finchcocks: he died in 1772, aged 92.

It is perhaps interesting to note, in passing, the fluidity of society in the sixteenth and seventeenth centuries: at Chiddingstone we met Richard Streatfeild, the iron-master who became a country gentleman; at Goudhurst we have the Culpeppers, country gentlemen who became iron-masters, and still remained gentlemen. Industry and trade had not yet become things with which gentlefolk did not meddle.

Along the road eastwards from Goudhurst is the hamlet Iden Green, consisting of some tiny tile-covered cottages, and by the venerable Peacock inn is a lane southward. In the hollow among the trees on the right of this lane is the moated manor-house of Glassenbury: built in the fifteenth century, the warm sandstone has been augmented through the succeeding centuries by wings and projections in brick and tile, beneath an astonishing variety of roofs. It was built by a family who had already lived on the site for 100 years, who could trace their ancestry back for another 200, and whose descendants still live there. The story can mostly be gathered from the monuments in Cranbrook church: the first known ancestor was William Rookehurst, who fled from Scotland in 1103 and bought land somewhere near Winchet Hill, a couple of miles north of Goudhurst, which he called Rookehurstden. He also called himself Roberts, by which name the family was known in the succeeding centuries, when they moved to Glassenbury, until the present century, when the last of the Roberts name died: but his grandchildren, of another name, are there.

Opposite the entrance gate to Glassenbury is a footpath into Angley Wood, an extensive forest where that deep stillness can be felt, the stillness of thousands of years of absence of man: this is one of the small survivors of Andredsweald. There might be woodmen, or a boy with a gun and a dog, but there are no motorists or picnic parties or, so far, surveyors for prospective building sites.

The path comes out into the streets of Cranbrook, to its long High Street, lined on both sides with remnants of old timbered houses among those of all centuries from the seventeenth to the present one, with good examples from each successive age and style. The large, well-proportioned, light and airy church is off the sharp angle at the end of the Street: its south-east chapel is full of memorials and relics of the Roberts family of Glassenbury. One memorial, in stone, shows a huge family tree, from the fifteenth to the eighteenth centuries; another, in pinkish alabaster on the east wall, recounts the story of William Rookehurst: it is dated 1599, and records that the family had already been at Glassenbury for 223 years.

In another corner of the church is an ugly marble obelisk to the Bakers, who bought Sissinghurst Castle and rebuilt it. One, Sir Richard, built the tower: his son, Sir John, who was known as Bloody Baker because of his zeal in punishing Protestant 'heretics' for his mistress Queen Mary, gave it its name. Subsequent descendants of Sir John are listed on the immovable reverse side of the column, permanently out of sight.

Cranbrook School, founded in 1573, still flourishes in the centre of things, and has extended to houses in all directions; Cranbrook Mill, a big old windmill with a plaque to Henry Dobell, 1814, still works as a windmill: the sails go round (when required), the corn of local farmers is ground, the whole place smells delightfully of corn and flour.

Beyond the town and down a side-lane to the east is the Old Cloth Hall, a sixteenth-century timbered house where the weavers wove the fortunes of the Cranbrook clothiers: the cloth trade, the weaving and export of cloth as a finished product, took over from the export of raw wool as the staple industry of the Weald, and many of Cranbrook's fine houses were built from the proceeds; many more of Cranbrook's families owed their livelihoods for generations to it. A path from Coursehorn, now a preparatory school, leads across the fields to Golford, a crossroads where there is a one-storey cottage called Ye old Post Office: a gable under the name is painted with a Union Jack and surrounded with electric lamps, piles of old furniture line the walls outside, and although the proprietor is 'licensed to sell tobacco' and practically everything else, this remarkable establishment has, regrettably, an air of long-postponed disintegration.

North of this stubborn survivor from an age perhaps less concerned with cash-registers is Sissinghurst, a long street of Wealden cottages with a defunct brick chapel, a little Victorian stone church and a site on the corner opposite its predecessor Trinity Chapel, built in Henry VI's reign to enable the inhabitants of Milkhouse Street, as the hamlet was then called, to confess their sins during weather too bad to permit them to do so in Cranbrook. The name Sissinghurst was reserved for the castle which lies at the end of a lane off the A262 Ashford road, in a gentle wooded valley. There was, it seems, never a proper castle here, but there are the remains of three manor-houses; the first, moated, was probably something like Hever or Ightham, a medieval fortified manor-house: two arms of the moat remain and a third, dry and grassed, is part of the garden. There are blocks of stone in the wall at the moat's edge and at the base of the little gazebo which might perhaps have been material from this earliest house. The second building, of the late fifteenth or early sixteenth century, was erected in brick on higher ground west of the original, which was probably by this time ruinous: the low two-storey range across the front of the place now standing is from this second construction. The third, replacing most of the second and including the tall gatehouse-tower, was the great brick mansion of Sir Richard Baker, son of the first Baker, Thomas, to settle at Sissinghurst, and father of the notorious Sir John. Two other fragments of what must have been a splendid palace, the South House and the Priest's House, are left. The whole place was occupied by French prisoners of the Seven Years War in the mid-eighteenth century, and enormous damage done (an inventory is preserved of it), so that it became ruinous and uninhabitable, and most was demolished. The remainder, in a deplorable state, was bought by Sir Harold and Lady Nicolson (Vita Sackville-West) in 1930, and rescued. They repaired the surviving buildings, created a garden out of the wilderness and gave it their own infinitely civilised personality. Today the National Trust cares for the house and gardens, but has made no attempt to interfere with anything that the Nicolsons arranged with their sure touch: the Sackville-West arms fly over the tower, the Nicolson spirit reigns ethereally among the grass walks and the flowers.

A farm-track leads from these Elysian fields to a lane at Bettenham Farm and rejoins the A262 at Three Chimneys, where an inn sign explains, without a word, that these chimneys are really cheminées. The road comes to Biddenden by the churchyard, which is cared for as a garden, and swerves round it to enter the old street with the stone pack-pony trail on the pavements, and the row of timbered houses of the fifteenth and sixteenth centuries, all of which remind us of the importance of the cloth-trade in these years; the Old Cloth Hall, like the one at Cranbrook, was originally the house of the master-clothier, but was lengthened and used as a workplace for the weavers, who required looms and space for their operation; it was built in the sixteenth century, but enlarged in sections eastwards, the last gable having been added in 1672.

A lane through the level land of wood and farms, Washenden Manor, Stede Quarter, Podkin, is by far preferable to the main road as a way to High Halden; houses skirt the A262 as far as the village green, where the ancient and ivy-shrouded Chequers faces the trees which surround the church. Both these buildings call for close attention, inside and out (although the church, like many others in these sacrilegious days, may be locked for protection); the Chequers is said to have been built from ships' timbers in the fifteenth century, and if a patron likes to fancy that the beams above his head were once beneath the feet of King Henry V on his way, with his 'fleet majestical, holding due course to Harfleur', then he may do so, but with little reason, since houses very seldom were built from ships' timbers. The church's chief glory is its timber tower and steeple, which contains a formidable amount of old Wealden oak and is said by the antiquarian Canon Livett to have been constructed in the late thirteenth or early fourteenth century. High Halden is one of the oldest of the 'dens'; in *Domesday Monachorum* it is noted by the name *Hadingwoldungdaenne* and had a church then.

We are now within a couple of miles of Tenterden, at the eastern end of these Wealden Hills; but there is a large tract of country between here and the county boundary, and we shall have to make a looping, sweeping reconnaissance of it before making for 'Tenterden steeple'. It is an area which repays closer inspection.

A mile along the road west of High Halden is a hamlet called Arcadia, a name which should not be taken too literally: from it a lane leads off into some woodland lanes that might be nearer the mark since they are somewhat more peaceful than a main road can be. They skirt a wide forest called Sandpit Wood and reach Clapper Hill, south of Biddenden, from which it is a short way to a crossroads with an inn called Castleton's Oak, named after a legendary parishioner who, at the age of 70, made his own coffin, and then waited another 30 years to fill it. More thick woods line both sides of the road, past Benenden Chest Hospital to Goddard's Green, a row of tiled Wealden cottages facing a neat grassy bank with ornamental trees, and behind them the orderly ranks and spiky skyline of Hemsted Forest, filled with Forestry Commission conifers. Benenden is on a high ridge, its houses distributed along the ridge-road

B2086; there is nothing quite so typically Kentish as the Green, especially at a week-end when a cricket match is in progress. At one end, on the road, there is a row of tile-hung cottages and the white-boarded post office, with a distinguished verandah; the green itself is crisp, close-cut and vivid; trees line both sides, half-way along one of which is the primary school, and at the top the old sandstone church, whose clock chimes the hours for the villagers and for run-chasing batsmen. The church has suffered somewhat, being high on the hill, from lightning, so has less of architectural interest than some, but one might be lucky enough while sauntering round the churchyard to hear the girls from Benenden School (which used to be the Earls of Cranbrook's Hemsted Park) singing inside it. Then church, green and cottages momentarily rise above their material properties.

By a gaunt old windmill on the Beacon Hill a lane winds down to Dingleden, where a timbered fifteenth-century hall-house stands on a hill, presiding over fine gardens and enviable rural tranquillity. A nursery at the end of the hamlet has coloured a hillside bright with roses; near it a lane dives into a tunnel of greenwood in which one might encounter one of the advantages of travelling on foot: a two-foot-long grass snake in the middle of the road. A motorist might not notice it and run it over.

At Iden Green on the far side of the woods there is a way to Hawkhurst which passes through some of the best Wealden scenery and by some fine farmhouses, with picturesque names like Sculls-gate, Little Nineveh and Netters Hall. It reaches the A229 near the former terminus of the Hawkhurst Branch line, now a timber yard (but the old B.R. notice is still there) at Gill's Green, where there is one of Dr Barnardo's homes, Babies' Castle.

A long hill leads up to the middle of tripartite Hawkhurst (Gill's Green, Highgate, the Moor) where the row of shops opposite the Royal Oak inn, built of weatherboard and slate, regularly planned and colonnaded in front, have something of the Pantiles spirit about them. The tall weatherboarded house next to the inn used to be a café called The Smugglers to commemorate the crew of cut-throats called the Hawkhurst Gang who terrorised the entire neighbour-hood in the eighteenth century and were eventually beaten in a pitched battle by the self-organised Goudhurst Militia in 1747. The house is now a Chinese restaurant.

Between Highgate and the Moor is a valley with a stream; the Moor is the oldest part, with a green on one side of the road and the cricket field on the other, white-boarded cottages, an inn, the primary school and the church. A girls' school, Lillesden, occupies Collingwood House opposite the pond by the church, and a road runs past its grounds through a select part of the village and eventually to the A268, which runs along the top of the last ridge of the Wealden Hills in Kent; north of it, the Hexden Channel flows down to Maytham Wharf, and to the south, beyond the Kent Ditch, the hills are in Sussex.

Sandhurst, ranged along this road, is one of those villages which have developed a mile from its church; the latter is on a spur of hill overlooking the Kent Ditch, with a strong sandstone tower and, unusually in Kent, a clerestory. The village has probably been attracted away from it by the road, which was turnpiked in the mid-eighteenth century; many of the cottages seem to belong to this approximate date.

The ridge, and Kent, come to a halt at Newenden, where a hump-backed bridge over the Rother takes the road into Sussex. It is a small village, with a tiny church consisting in a simple sandstone nave, and a clock-tower added as a memorial to George V's coronation; the stone font, carved with figures of wild beasts, is Saxon work and could be from the church which stood here before the Conquest. Most of the houses face the river-levels, in the lane along the base of the ridge leading off from the old White Hart inn, by the cricket field.

For a small and apparently insignificant place, Newenden has excited the passions of antiquarians to a singular degree: Camden said it must have been the *Castra Anderida* of the Romans, because of its position at the end of the ridge between what would then have been the fully tidal channels of Hexden and Rother, and because way out on the levels at the junction of the two streams there is an artificial mound known as Castle Toll. C. Roach Smith in 1880 declared that, while the Toll might be of British origin, it could not be Roman: excavation of it had disclosed no Roman materials, whereas Pevensey has thick Roman walls, to say the least, and since in the fifth-century army list *Notitia Dignitatum* Anderida is mentioned be-tween *Portus Lemanis* (Lympne) and *Portus Adurnis* (probably Portchester), Anderida must be Pevensey.

Newenden could at least boast of its Carmelite Friary at Lossen-ham, near the very end of the ridge, established in 1242 by Sir Thomas Aucher not long after the main Kentish body had settled at Aylesford. The Bishop of Dover, when he accepted their surrender on behalf of the king in 1538, said that the friars were 'honest men' and that their house was poor in building and ready to fall. The name and site are preserved by a farmhouse.

Across the levels of the Hexden Channel the A28 road approaches Rolvenden; from a distance, three of its features can be seen: a black windmill with white sails near Rawlinson Farm (a large and ancient timbered house), the church tower and the steeple, and Great Maytham Hall, an elegant house designed by Sir Edward Lut-yens in a Georgian style. The street of Rolvenden, leading to the church (as so often happens in these Wealden villages) is flanked on both sides with good examples of the prevalent tile-hung and weatherboarded cottages, and the row by the church, the end one timber-gabled, is particularly attractive. The church has a new re-volving door, and in the south-east chapel there is an upper room or pew for the manor-house family, like the one at West Peckham.

Rolvenden Layne, at the other end of Great Maytham's grounds, is principally a large green surrounded by cottages, some of which are single-jetty houses of the fourteenth century, and one of which accommodated Wesley the Evangelist when he preached the Gospel to the populace.

Between Rolvenden and Tenterden is the shallow vale of the Newmill Channel, and the track and station of the Kent and East Sussex Railway. A single-line railway running through a thinly populated rural area and only once—at Tenterden—coming within a mile of a village, might seem to have been an optimistic venture from the start. The line was laid in 1900 to connect Headcorn with Robertsbridge, ostensibly for the benefit of farmers; inevitably, motor transport was soon far quicker, and the line continued to run, until after the 1939–45 war, apparently for the benefit of the late

Will Hay and Mr Rowland Emett. For years railway zealots have tried to revive it, and at Rolvenden station (1¾ miles from Rolvenden) they have assembled a remarkable collection of steam engines and rolling stock. They are now able to operate a part of the line to Bodiam, for tourists and other railway fans.

Most people like Tenterden, because it has a wide street with trees and grass and gracious Georgian houses and is generally reckoned a good place for shops. It also has some older buildings, and from a vantage point by the little five-sided Corner Shop a wholly satisfying few minutes can be spent in contemplating the street scene, beginning with the fifteenth-century Woolpack inn, which has an amazingly lop-sided upper room facing the churchyard, the Town Hall, where geraniums in baskets hang from the pillared portico, and farther down on the left a row of new arcaded shops, well in keeping with the town; over the road there is Tudor House which, since it appears to be a hall-house with the central recess filled in is probably pre-Tudor, the little timbered Spinning Wheel restaurant, and by the cinema which is now a supermarket, a well-known establishment called the Old Cellars. In the corner by the Woolpack (which name serves as a reminder of how the town prospered in the late middle ages) is the churchyard, and the great church of St Mildred. The saint is the abbess of Minster, whose bones worked miracles, and this Wealden church is dedicated to her because the 'den' belonged to the men of Thanet: *Tenet-wara-daenne* became Tenterden. Much of the church is thirteenth century, but the high tower, of Bethersden marble, was built in 1461 by the collective efforts of the local colony of Flemish weavers.

The old saw, that Tenterden steeple (or tower) caused either the decay of Sandwich haven or the inundation of the Goodwin Sands, or both, has exercised a good many minds. Donald Maxwell, for example, went to great lengths to show that the tower made a good landmark for sailors in search of a cargo of cloth, and it was easier for them to dock at Smallhythe, Tenterden's port, than at Sandwich. Others have discovered that some vainglorious bishop spent money on the tower which should have been spent on the sea-wall of Goodwin's estate (this was Earl Godwin, King Harold's father: chronology is about the last thing that matters in the debate). The story

32   *The south door, Barfreston Church*

appears to have been used by Bishop Hugh Latimer in a sermon before Edward VI at Westminster, as an analogy: it was as absurd to
draw the conclusion, he said, that because he preached against
covetousness in Lent, and there was a rebellion in the summer, his
preaching had caused the rebellion, as it was to infer that because a
tower had been built at Tenterden, and after that the haven at Sandwich had become silted up, the tower had caused the haven's decay.

The 'Riddle of Tenterden Tower' is nothing more than a red
herring.

A window in the north-east Lady Chapel is dedicated to the Rev.
Philip Ward, a nineteenth-century vicar who married Horatia Nel-
son: her great-granddaughter, an elderly lady but an undoubted descendant of the little Admiral, still lives in Tenterden.

33 *West gate, Canterbury*

CHAPTER NINE

The Marsh

The mention of Smallhythe, the port of Tenterden ('hythe' is a land-ing-place), in the last chapter, might perplex those who are un-familiar with the changing coastal geography of Kent. The changes have been exceedingly slow, but over a period of some 10,000 years, the area of Romney Marsh has changed from sea to land, back partly to sea, then back to land again. Space here does not permit a full explanation of the vicissitudes, caused by the movement of the earth's crust, but perhaps some should be made of how a village eight miles from the nearest coastline could ever have been a port. For further detail I can recommend the article by C. J. Gilbert, F.G.S., in Vol. XLV of *Archaeologia Cantiana*.

In about 8000 B.C., after the sea had broken through the chalk isthmus connecting England with France, there was an irregular semicircle of high cliffs from Folkestone to Fairlight. The rocks of Oxney and Rye stood out, and the rivers brought down deposits from the remains of the Wealden dome of clay: behind the cliffs lay the forest of Anderida.

Towards the end of the Mesolithic period (*ca.* 3000) the earth's crust sank, the cliffs were cut back, but the upchannel drift kept pace with the depression by spreading deposits of sand and shingle over the bay. By the time Neolithic Man arrived from the Continent the bay had risen above high-tide level and a forest had spread over it. This is why the remains of ancient submerged forests have been discovered under the Marsh surface, in Appledore Dowels, for ex-ample. The bay was dry land, forested.

During this time a shore beach was thrown up on the sea-coast. A further sinking of the earth's surface brought a tidal invasion through the river mouths and low sections of beach, resulting in inundation and the formation of a lagoon behind the shoreline; at high tide the whole bay would be flooded, but at low tide, deposits of sea and river-silt keeping pace with the depression, salt-plants could grow over the whole area. Shingle beaches began to build up, protecting the lagoon behind the eastward end, but the sea continued to scour the cliffs of Rye and Peasmarsh, and Oxney.

The final stage, over the Roman and Saxon periods, the gradual depression continuing, saw the beginning of the shingle bank of Dungeness and the consolidation of the marshland behind the seabeaches. There existed then a wide tidal estuary of the rivers Rother, Brede and Tillingham and the waters round Oxney, extending eastward to Hythe; several islands of shingle to seaward, and behind them a vast acreage of marshy land ripe for reclamation. In 1099 a storm destroyed the island in the farthest east, which is now the Goodwin Sands; in 1250 another swept over Old Winchelsea and partly destroyed it; in 1287 yet another finally demolished it, stopped up the Rother's mouth at Romney and made it flow out at Rye; the town of Romney nearly suffered the same fate as its neighbour Bromhill, but was saved by a slight difference in its height: the west entrance to the church was blocked with shingle, and one still goes down steps to another in the north of the tower.

The Rhee Wall, built between Appledore and Romney, enabled Romney Marsh to be 'inned' or reclaimed. In time it also permitted the land west of the wall to be inned as Walland Marsh; it was completed by the inning of Guldeford Level in 1562, and that was the end of Smallhythe as a port and, virtually, Oxney as an island. The sea was shut out, the rivers brought down their silt and eventually navigation became impossible.

Smallhythe, as Tenterden's port, situated at the head of the waters that encircled Oxney Island, had been important on account of the wool trade, and Tenterden had been incorporated as a member of the Cinque Ports, attached to Rye (one of the two Ancient Towns). It had also been a shipbuilding dockyard. But trade must already have been slackening by 1514, when the best part of the place was burnt down. The most senior of the present buildings were therefore erected after the fire: the brick church, a simple nave, with crow-stepped gables in the Flemish style, the Priest's House next to it, and the Harbour-master's House, which is now known as Ellen Terry's because the great actress spent her last years in it. The latter two are interesting examples of the contemporary development of timber houses, built with two storeys and chimneys, a continuous jetty and close-set upright timbers (studding). Donald Maxwell once pointed out that the church was tiled on the north side and slated on the south, but unfortunately for this delightful story, in 1965 it was re-roofed and tiled all over.

The Reading Sewer is all that remains of the tidal waters of Smallhythe's sea-way (Maxwell, probably rightly, says that they must have been like the present waters around Hayling Island, in Hampshire) and it is soon crossed. The road follows the channel along the windy levels, then climbs to the Isle of Oxney.

The island is likened to a stranded whale for more than the obvious reason that it is no longer surrounded by water (although, pathetically, one must cross some kind of water, even if only a few feet, to reach it): it has, roughly, the shape of a whale, sloping gradually from the low western end to the steep eastern bluff, some four miles' length altogether. Wittersham is its principal parish, and the other is Stone-cum-Ebony. Wittersham is distributed about the road from Tenterden, which dips down the southern side of the island and crosses the Kent Ditch and the Rother (here, separate) on its way to Rye. The central part of the village is the lane from the green, Coronation Garden, and the inn (post office in a curious little cottage) and a converted oast, to the church, which stands on the southern slope. Basically of twelfth-century origin, the church is light and very clean: its early sixteenth-century tower stands up conspicuously and is said once to have had a structure on top in which beacons were flared as part of the coastal defence warning system in Elizabeth's time. There is a memorial in the church to Alfred Lyttleton, 'Athlete, Lawyer, Statesman', who died in 1913: he was one of a group who forlornly hoped to bring some aesthetic ideals into English politics.

Along the ridge-road of Oxney, eastward, there is a white-boarded mill with all its sails, but it does not work. Close to it is an ancient house, with gables all askew, called Stocks, and a small colony of cottages about a crossroads. This is where the road deserts Kent for Sussex. The way along the ridge continues its windy eastward course, however, and the comparative absence of trees permits great sweeping views to right and left, that to northward being particularly striking, on a clear day: the line of the North Downs shows on the horizon, with the gap where the Stour breaks through, the white of the cliffs at Folkestone, the Marsh and the sea, and round to the south-west, the Fairlight Hills.

At the far end of the whale-nose bluff of the island, the lane suddenly dives down the slope northward and runs below a bank whereon stand several fine houses which have the benefit of the full glory of the above-mentioned view, and the full force of the south-westerly gales to go with it. Adjoining the churchyard is what was probably the Priest's House, an excellent hall-house which could be earlier than 1464 if it survived the fire which burnt the church at that date: the latter was rebuilt then so is mainly Perpendicular in style. In the room under the tower, at the west end of the church, are two objects of great interest: one is a glass case containing the bones of an iguanadon found in a quarry at Stone in 1935, and said to be 70 million years old. This figure sounds rather improbable to a layman, but is the one quoted.

The other object in the tower room at Stone church is a rough-cut lump of Kentish ragstone, scarred and cracked all over, with a recessed dish-top and on the lower part the carved figure of a bull. It was dug up in the chancel of the church, probably when a grave was being dug, some time in the eighteenth century, thrown out as being unsuitable for a Christian church, rescued by William Gostling when he was vicar and set up in the vicarage garden, where it stayed until 1926: it has stood here since then. It is said to be an altar of the cult of Mithras, but lacking an inscription or any other firm evidence it is impossible to tell: it may have been sacred to another of the many Romano-British cults. It is possible that it was brought to Stone along the old channel of the River Limen from Lympne and set up by the commander of an outpost or watch-tower, which seems likely on this high cliff, but again there is no evidence. It is probably merely coincidence that the stone is at Stone, and that it bears the figure of an ox in the Isle of Oxney:

when these places were named it might well have been completely unknown and out of sight.

The main part of Stone village is down the hill, sheltered sensibly from the gales; from the crossroads at the Crown inn, looking north-west, one can see a high grassy bank standing a little apart from the whale-back island: this is Chapel Bank, Ebony. In the days of the Kingdom of Kent a church and priory was established on it, colonised from Canterbury. The church is listed in *Domesday Monachorum* and according to A. G. Bradley in his *An Old Gate of England* (which is indispensable for a study of this region) was struck by lightning in Elizabeth I's reign and destroyed. Later, a chapel was built on the site but that, too, has gone, and the only occupants of Ebony now are sheep.

The Reading Sewer is crossed again, to leave the Isle of Oxney, by the Stone Ferry Inn, which has a list of charges painted in perpetuity on the wall, scaled according to the size of the load to be ferried; the ferry has been replaced by a bridge, for the Sewer is only about 20 feet across now.

It is not hard to imagine how the land used to lie when all the present grassy levels were covered with water: Appledore is on the very end of a spit of land reaching out into what must have been a maze of mud-flats and saltings at low tide, and a distinctly unfriendly wind-lashed estuary at high tide. The sense of difference in surroundings on leaving the street by the sharp little dip past the church is maintained by the necessity to cross the Royal Military Canal before entering the altogether strange land of the Marsh. Most of the village is along this street, a mixture of houses from about the sixteenth century to a representative of the Space Age, tile-hung and flat-roofed, with an all-round jetty deeper by far than any medieval timbered house, executed in concrete. The church, which has the royal arms carved in stone over the west door, stands within the traces of an ancient earthwork, said to be that thrown up by the Danish army which encamped here and breathed defiance at King Alfred in 893: the Marsh was then in its state of lagoons and tidal swamps protected by the beach islands around its rim, and the Danes probably sailed up the old course of the Limen, by Hythe.

Appledore Heath is an inland hamlet, from which a road runs

eastward past Horne's Place, a good seventeenth-century farmhouse to which is attached, left untouched from a former dwelling-place, a private chapel built of stone in the late fourteenth century: the family of Horne owned the place for some 350 years until the time of Elizabeth.

Continuing along the edge of the low hills above the Marsh, one comes to a string of villages all the way to Lympne, many of which shall be described shortly. First I must mention the area behind them, a stretch of country which is heavily afforested, crossed by many lanes but measuring some seven miles by three, which is a sizeable acreage. At the western verge of this series of forests, standing on a rise near Kenardington the spire of Woodchurch appears two miles away above a mass of trees: it is a large village but none of its houses (many of which, old and new, are single-storey) can be seen. There are farmsteads and hamlets in this land of woods, but only two other villages, Shadoxhurst, where there is a little church with some original early fourteenth-century glass and a stone cottage with Flemish gables that used to be the schoolhouse, and Orlestone, little more than church and manor-house because its main part has moved down to crossroads and railway station at Ham Street.

The church of Kenardington stands rather forlornly on the edge of the hill above the village, on the remains of another ancient earthwork which the Victoria County History suggests might be that which the Danes stormed and overthrew in 893 before establishing themselves at Appledore. The church has some Norman work, but is much truncated and reduced, having been struck by lightning at about the same time as the old priory church at Ebony. Inside it is painfully simple, a bare nave, tiled floor, two pews and the rest chairs, a table altar; there are no decorations but for texts on either side of the door (Isaiah left, St Mark right); there is no electricity, either, so candles and gas-lamps must be used. Nicholas Ridley would have been delighted with it.

Warehorne, which stands on a promontory overlooking the railway, the Royal Military Canal and the Marsh (this part of the Marsh between Warehorne and Appledore is called the Dowels, and is in parts below sea-level) consists mainly in a pleasant group of cottages and an inn on the other side of the road from the church. The Rev. R. H. Barham, who wrote the *Ingoldsby Legends*, after his curacy at Westwell, was appointed rector of Snargate, down on the Marsh, and curate of Warehorne, at the same time (1817). Sensibly, he lived on the slightly healthier upland of Warehorne.

At a crossroads near Warehorne called the Leacon the B2067 arrives from Woodchurch and follows the Marshward edge of the Clay Hills all the way to Hythe. At Ham Street it is crossed by an Ashford road from the Marsh and by the railway; at Ruckinge it comes nearest to the canal, which I have already mentioned and will now observe that it was constructed in the early years of the nineteenth century, from Hythe to Rye, when invasion was threatened by Napoleon Bonaparte. It was designed with a kink every 400 yards so that cannon could be placed there to enfilade attacks across it: no doubt it would not have deterred an invading army for long, but it would have given time for the marshalling of a defending force in the hills. The same idea appears to have occurred to ministerial minds in 1940, judging by the number of concrete blockhouses or 'pillboxes' which still stand on the landward side. The Canal is lined with elms for miles of its length and is much favoured by anglers, moorhens, ducks and algae.

Ruckinge is a small village with a correspondingly small church, of Norman origin, with two remaining decorated doorways, on the west side of the tower and in the south wall of the nave. Most of it was rebuilt in the fourteenth century after a fire. In the churchyard, a rough plank on three iron supports is the grave of the two Ransley brothers, leaders of a smuggling band, who were hung on Penenden Heath in 1800 for highway robbery; on the other side of the road a row of handsome new houses on a bank is called Ransley Green, to commemorate these villains. On the way to Bilsington, on the left past the Blue Anchor is a field bank with a good collection of farm wains and old ploughs, painted and preserved.

On the highest bank of the hill at Bilsington, by a miracle the Cosway Obelisk still stands, despite being struck by lightning in 1967. It calls to memory a squire of Court Lodge here, Sir William Cosway, who was in no way outstanding but seems to have been a kind landlord who in the bad agricultural days of the 1820s and

1830s helped Bilsington families to emigrate to America. He was killed in a coach accident in 1834, and in case the obelisk does fall down, the cottages near it are also named after him. Church and manor-house stand together on the edge of the hill; the church, and probably several others on the Clay Hills, was served by canons from Bilsington Priory, of Augustinian order, the roofed towers of which, attached to an Edwardian mansion ('a modern country house', says Bradley in 1917), can be seen from the road, looking like a French *château*.

Bonnington is scattered all over the bounds of its parish, and its church, St Rumwold's, is down the hill by the canal, a tiny building with a two-window nave, minute chancel and squat tower, capped by a little Tudor onion spire: Barham had it in mind for his legend of the hard-swearing Sir Alured Denne who,

> ... *always in metaphor rich,*
> *Call'd his priest an 'old son of —' some animal—which*
> *Is not worth the inquiry ...*

A large, partly timbered house called Goldenhurst stands on the edge of the hill under Aldington Knoll, the highest point of the Clay Hills, and a lane runs up through the woods to Aldington Corner, which is the main part of this village. The church stands up high on a hill eastwards, and in the valley in between is Cobb's Hall, a timbered house with close-studding and continuous jetty which must have been brand-new when Elizabeth Barton, the Holy Maid of Kent, lived in it as a servant, in about 1519. She had had visions, uttered prophecies and been publicly cured of a disease, and had thereafter retired to a convent in Canterbury, from which in 1527 she spoke out against Henry VIII's proposed divorce. At first she warned the king on her own behalf to expect damnation, but later she was manipulated by a circle of clergy led by one Dr Bocking, and prophesied that the king would die a villain after marrying Anne Boleyn: the whiff of treason involved other leading opponents of the divorce, like Bishop Fisher and Sir Thomas More, and meant trouble for all. Eventually in 1533 Henry struck: the wretched girl, Bocking and four others were hanged at Tyburn.

Aldington church, with an early sixteenth-century tower built by Archbishop Warham (Aldington was always an archiepiscopal manor), stands on a hill up a lane past old Ruffins Farm, and seems at first to be all mixed up with the farm buildings of the Court Lodge. It is an interesting church, partly for its own sake—a church attached to an archbishops' palace (which has vanished) must be appropriately magnificent: there are fine choir stalls and misericords of fourteenth-century carved oak, and a pulpit with a carved pelican on the front. There is also a blocked-in window in the north wall of the chancel which might testify that part of the fabric is pre-Conquest in origin. The list of rectors shows that Erasmus of Rotterdam, the great theologian and scholar, was given the living in 1511 by Archbishop Warham. Unfortunately he knew no English, his parishioners, neither Latin nor Dutch; in just over a year he resigned in consideration of a pension, and was replaced, according to the list, by one John Thornton, who held the dignity of Bishop of Sirmium, an erstwhile Roman imperial city (on the Sava in Yugoslavia) which had been entirely demolished in the fifth century.

Court-at-Street, on the hilltop road, once had a chapel in the woods downhill towards the Marsh where the Holy Maid was supposed to have prayed and uttered her prophecies. It would be difficult for anyone to concentrate hard enough to produce any kind of spiritual response nowadays, because Lympne Airport having been promoted to Ashford Airport and enlarged to accommodate much larger aircraft than the old Dakotas which used to scatter the sheep on take-off, the droning and screeching from it is truly tremendous. The noise permeates all over the neighbourhood of Lympne, entering the formerly peaceful precincts of the castle and church on the hill. At this eastern end, the Clay Hills are much higher and are thickly tree-clad. The village of Lympne huddles among the trees around the castle walls (pretending to ignore the aircraft) on the very edge of the hill; the castle's east tower was built on the site of a Roman watch-tower in Norman times, but the great hall was rebuilt in 1361, with a crown-post timbered roof. The west tower was added in the fifteenth century. The hall, and adjacent parlour and kitchen, with Tudor and later furniture, is opened to the public, who may climb the towers and admire the view across the Marsh to the sea. St Stephen's church, next to the castle, has been much restored but has a nucleus of a large, square Norman tower.

By the side of the castle wall a footpath descends precipitously down the hill to a range of crumbled blocks of masonry known as Stutfall Castle. Their last useful function was as part of the walls of a fort which the Romans built in the early fourth century, but the material and the site had had a longer history. Soon after the invasion of A.D. 43 the Romans established a naval base here at the mouth of what was either one of the tidal inlets to the lagoon behind the shingle islands of the incipient coastline, or the mouth of a river, perhaps an earlier course of the Rother; in either case the waterway was called Limen and the naval base, *Portus Lemanis*. The fleet called *Classis Britannicus* operated from this port. Among the building material of the fort an altar-stone was found inscribed: 'Aufidius Pantera, admiral of the British Fleet, erected this altar.' He possibly did so in the second century, but when in the late third century its admiral, Carausius, deputed to repel Saxon pirates, used the fleet to establish himself as an autonomous British emperor, clearly its existence had become dangerous. When the province had been restored to Roman rule the fleet was disbanded, and possibly the port dismantled. The fort which was built on the present site was a part of a new defence system under a command called in *Notitia Dignitatum*, *Litus Saxonicum*; the Count of this Saxon Shore commanded nine forts and garrisons in all, and as in this case often building material was used from old installations. The fort called *Lemanis* covered 10–11 acres, roughly rectangularly, and the surviving portions are parts of the east, north and west walls. Their downfall was not due to the besieging prowess of the Saxons (or Jutes) but to the springs which welled up all over this hillside (one still runs) and undermined the whole foundation.

The existence of the Limen as a river is debatable, but it has been shown (from grants of land by kings of Kent) that between 724 and 732, at least, the River Limen ran along the north-west side of Romney Marsh to an exit somewhere south of West Hythe. It is perhaps significant to note that a road south of this course, from Sherlock's Bridge to Botolph's Bridge, is a parish boundary along the whole of its length, and that a farm on the way is called Lower Wall: it could indicate the ancient course of the river.

At the top of a steep hill up from West Hythe is a cross, erected by Lord Beauchamp when he was Lord Warden of the Cinque Ports in 1923: it marks the site of the old Shepway Cross, where all important meetings of the Portsmen were held (out of doors, as was usual in the middle ages: even churches would not hold a great multitude, and no other building was large enough). The Cinque Ports (Hastings, Romney, Hythe, Dover and Sandwich) and the Two Ancient Towns (Winchelsea and Rye), and all their associated limbs or members, were granted all manner of privileges by the king in return for furnishing him with ships and men when he wanted them. It was an ancient custom which evolved into a Confederation, and was granted a charter of confirmation by Henry III in 1260. Most of its usages were much older than this and had hardened into jealously guarded rights. Probably the Cinque Ports' most efficient time was under Edward I in the late thirteenth century: by the mid-fourteenth century some of the ports were being deserted by the sea and their prosperity was ebbing. Their nadir came in the 1370s when the French raiding parties burnt and looted with impunity. The odd, and typically English feature of the Confederation is that although it has served no useful function for 600 years it still exists, and still has a Lord Warden.

At Hythe, to which we shall return later, is the terminus of the Romney, Hythe and Dymchurch Railway, which runs a regular service on a very narrow-gauged track, with nine or so miniature replicas of famous steam engines of the past and covered carriages with sliding doors, glassed windows and comfortable seats. The old nostalgic smells and sounds are reproduced, the trains puff along at a fair speed, and a very entertaining way is provided of travelling from Hythe to Romney.

The station half-way is Dymchurch; in Walter Jerrold's day (1908) it was 'a quiet, scattered village', and 'a delightful place, far from the madding crowd'; anyone who has been there in recent years would agree that these descriptions can no longer be said to fit. Chalets and caravans, *etcetera*, nothwithstanding, Dymchurch has a Norman church, of St Mary, and an ancient Court Hall, which was the headquarters of the Lords, Bailiffs and Jurats of the Level of Romney Marsh who, since like the Cinque Ports the Marsh itself was a liberty, acted as magistrates and weighed up evidence in all cases brought before them. Kipling, Davidson and Russell Thorndike have all ensured that the reading public is aware of Dymchurch, and the multitudes who have spent holidays there are probably aware of the Martello Towers along the Wall: they were another part of the anti-Napoleonic defences, based on the design of a tower at Cape Mortella in the *Golf de St-Florent*, Corsica (which island had been in Britain's possession for a couple of years in the 1790s). Since they are practically indestructible they have lasted well and are part of the Romney Marsh scenery, like the canal.

New Romney is an important station on the railway (the line goes on to Dungeness) and it has been a town of some moment since Saxon times: it has only been 'New' since the fifteenth century to distinguish it from 'Old' Romney, although neither antedates the other, but were merely two churches serving the same, widespread, parish, along with a third, Hope All Saints, the ruins of which can still be seen from the Ivychurch road. New Romney's church, of St Nicholas, is a great Norman church with a massive square tower, built in the eleventh century, not long after the Conquest: the chancel and side-aisles were added later. Each of the Cinque Ports had its own mayor and jurats, who commonly met in the church; a brass plate on a large tomb in the south chapel reads: 'Here lyeth buryed the bodye of Richard Stuppenye Jurate of this towne in the first yeare of King Henry VIII who dyed in the XVIII yeare of the sayde kinges reigne of whose memorye Clement Stuppenye of the same Port his great grandsonne hath caused this tombe to be new erected for the use of the auncient meeting and election of maior and jurats of this Port Towne June the 10th Anno Dn. 1622.' As a port, the town had already been in decline since 1287 when the terrible storm which changed the course of the Rother deprived it of a harbour. The flood-marks from this frightful inundation and tempest can still be seen on the massive round pillars in the church, and the whole ground-level outside has never sunk to its old position, because of the shingle-storm.

The Street of Romney has several Georgian houses, and some

fragments of medieval buildings, some timbered and some stone, like the one in Ashford Road with gargoyles over the arches, and another in West Street opposite the Cinque Ports Arms. The New Inn, behind a Georgian façade, is anything but new, but is not a survivor from the disaster of 1287.

The church tower of Lydd can be seen from Romney, and vice versa; the road between the two towns crosses a flat piece of treeless country which the sheep, skylarks, wheat and potatoes have mostly to themselves. Also visible from both towns and half the Marsh are the bulking shapes of the new power-station at Dungeness: the scenery on the great shingle headland has changed in many ways since the inception of this plant, and the Marsh skyline now includes the lines of electricity pylons which radiate from it.

All Saints, Lydd, sometimes called the Cathedral of the Marshes, is a very ancient foundation. Lydd was built on one of the shingle islands on the rim of the estuarial marshes, and until the fateful storms of the thirteenth century, culminating in the worst in 1287, which so blocked the mouth of the Rother at Romney that it had to find a new way to the sea at Rye, was a flourishing seaport. From earliest times, therefore, it could afford a fine church, and the form of its pre-Conquest building can be seen in the north-west walls of All Saints, with narrow Romanesque arches. Another church was built on the spot in Norman times, and pieces of it were found in the rubble of the chancel after it had been knocked flat by a bomb in 1940. Its rebuilding has been well-accomplished, with three narrow lancets, new coloured glass and a beautifully painted ceiling. Between the chancel and the north-east chapel is the tomb of another Stuppenye which is also the focal point for the election of bailiff and jurats.

Lydd is quieter than Romney (it has military appendages where Romney has seaside holiday camps) and has a good wide street of Georgian houses and a dignified Guildhall.

A chapter about the Marsh usually turns into a catalogue of churches; this is because there are plenty of them and they are mostly worth mentioning, which is more than can be said for the greater part of Marsh domestic architecture. Nor is the preponderance of fine churches an indication, as Cobbett might have inferred, that the Marsh formerly supported a much higher population: it demonstrates that agriculture on the Marsh was and is a profitable business, and whether out of piety or pride (charity would prefer the former) the Marshmen wished to build to the greater glory of God in the best way that they could. Most of these churches deserve a mention because they are worth seeing.

The pedestrian on the Marsh is at no advantage because it is perilous in the extreme to use footpaths unless he has used them since he could walk (there are too many watercourses) and as Kipling has written, the roads lead him in all directions so that he walks three miles to reach a place within two. On the other hand, there is no other way in which one can experience the Marsh atmosphere: the silence which, if analysed, is not silence but full of sheep-bleats, larksong and the humming of insects; the feel of the wind and the consciousness of so much open sky, the complete yawning cloudscape in a mighty circle around one tiny focus, which imparts a kind of luminous lustre to the land; the cabbage smells, and water smells, and earth, and corn, and cattle and sheep. A little scene on the road from Brookland to Snargate sticks in the mind: a corner, with a little brick bridge, orange with lichen, a willow by it and a dyke beneath it, running along the edge of a grassy field full of Romney Marsh sheep; swallows and swifts flitting about the willows, and the odd sound-filled Marsh silence.

On the way out from Lydd to Old Romney the sole surviving gable-end of Midley church can be seen among the meadows, an old 'redundant' church. At Old Romney, in a clump of trees, are a few cottages about an inn, and at the entrance to the church lane, an old brick cottage with an amazingly undulating tiled roof; the church, St Clement's, mainly thirteenth century, has a contemporary font of Purbeck marble and eighteenth-century wooden gallery and box pews, all now in a pretty dove-pink.

Old Romney is on the Rhee Wall, the ancient retaining wall for the first inning of Romney Marsh, and the road runs along it to Brenzett, a cluster of cottages round a couple of crossroads. St Eanswith's church is also mainly thirteenth century; in the north-east chapel is a tomb with the alabaster figures, in cavalier dress, of John

Fagge and his son John, of Rye, who died in 1639 and 1646 respectively, owners of the manor. Sheep graze in the churchyard. West of the Rhee Wall is a complex net of lanes around Brookland, which is in two groups, round the Woolpack inn and round the church, St Augustine's. It is one of the best-known Marsh churches (this is Walland Marsh): the soil beneath was too uncertain to bear too much weight, so instead of building a high stone tower they erected a separate wooden belfry. It is a complicated structure, the belfry, in stages like the candle-snuffer spires of Upchurch and Bexley: Mr Kenneth Gravett says that the lower timbers could well be the original Norman work of the eleventh century, but that the top part was replaced and the whole extended to its octagonal shape in the fifteenth century. Among many other interesting features of this church are the high box pews and the lead font of about 1150, said to be the best of its kind in England, and depicting the signs of the zodiac and their appropriate seasonable occupations in the country. Fairfield church, a couple of miles from Brookland, is one of the Marsh wonders, since unlike the Marsh's redundant stone churches, Fairfield was built as a temporary structure of timber, lath and plaster, in the thirteenth century, to serve a scattered population. Its exterior has been strengthened from time to time with brick, and in 1913 the whole building was carefully reconstructed and encased, to preserve it. It is the only church in the diocese of Canterbury dedicated to St Thomas Becket.

Snargate, Barham's rectory from 1817 for five years, is smaller than Warehorne, his curacy at the same time: the church is large but the village is very small. St Augustine's at Snave is on a mound behind the customary Marsh screen of trees (the mound is also usual) and is one of the plainest and humblest and, for that reason, one of the best. The village is a mere half-dozen cottages. On the road to Ivychurch (all the roads, as I have mentioned, behave with extreme drunkenness because they have to negotiate the highly complicated system of sluices and watercourses, without which the Marsh would swiftly become real marsh again) there is at Chapel Farm a one-storey white cottage which ought to be, but is not, typical of Marsh dwellings: many are new, plain and utilitarian. Great use is made, in numerous cases, of corrugated iron.

34 *The Nave, looking eastward, Canterbury Cathedral*

Ivychurch (whose name has nothing to do with ivy but derives from words meaning church of the island in the waters: that speaks for itself, referring to early Marsh conditions) has an attractive group of new and fairly old cottages and an inn, The Bell, hard by the churchyard. The church, St George's, is one of those whose dimensions speak more of the depth of the residents' pockets than their multiplicity. It was built in the 1360s, when the trade in raw wool was still good, on the site of its predecessor; it has two great arcades of octagonal pillars and a quatrefoil clerestory which in the nave has been blocked in, but is still open in the chancel. To add to the effect of light and spaciousness there is no chancel arch, and at present there are no pews or chairs either: the weakest may still go to the wall, where there is a short length of the original stone bench for that purpose. The embattled porch has two storeys, is vaulted and has benches, because it used to be the village school.

The Marsh, although flat, is by no means treeless, especially about this central part, actual Romney Marsh east of the Rhee Wall. The lane between Ivychurch and Newchurch is one of the most eccentric, weaving and swooping about and sometimes leading one in quite the opposite direction, then back again; it is one of the best, despite this, for walking, for here one can feel to the full the Marsh magic, among the spaced trees, the wide acres, thousands of sheep and the occasional lonely 'looker's' (shepherd) cottage; dykes everywhere, moorhens in them, swallows and swifts, lapwings and rooks and pigeons; the feeling of timelessness.

Newchurch has a church similar to St George's but smaller, and its porch houses an old metal plough. The Marsh parishes are now organised as the Romney Marsh Group of Parishes: there are ten, and are administered by one Rector and two assistants, who have nevertheless so arranged the services so that there is one in most of the ten churches on most Sundays.

At Sherlock's Bridge the road that seems once to have run along the wall of the old river Limen leads off, and another goes south to Eastbridge, where on a mound by a modern brick cottage a fragment of the old church still points a stone finger skywards. Potato and wheatfields line the way to Burmarsh, where the usual group of cottages, inn and church huddle among the trees. A footbridge across a

35 *The churchyard, Fordwich*

dyke takes one to the church, where over the Norman south door a face grins like an African mask; the church is mainly twelfth century, and has a crenellated nave and tower, but windows of later dates. Burmarsh's name comes from *Burgh-wara-marsh*: marshland of the men of the borough, in this case Canterbury. Strips of the Marsh's reclaimed land were owned by many apparently far-flung landlords.

The Marsh at this eastern end narrows: the sea-wall is near on one's right, the Clay Hills and Lympne on the left. From Botolph's Bridge the lane comes alongside the Royal Military Canal, and a footpath on the north side of it leads pleasantly to Hythe.

One of the original Cinque Ports, Hythe lost its importance when it lost its harbour: formed from the old mouth of the Limen, the inlet which made a haven for the hythe or landing-place became gradually filled with shingle, deposited by the channel current and the south-westerly gales. The town has suffered more recent changes of fortune too, for its School of Infantry is closed down, and the fine Georgian barrack buildings which housed it are even threatened with demolition; the brewery, too, which must have provided jobs for generations of Hythe men, is also defunct. The High Street is nevertheless crowded in summer with trippers and tourists, and there is a new industrial estate off the road to Dymchurch.

The parish church of St Leonard is perched high on the town's steep hill, where a long and stepped lane is full of good-looking houses bright with flowers. The church is large and magnificent: it has traces of the original Norman church of the late eleventh century (not really original, since there was an earlier Saxon church), which was extended with transepts in the late twelfth century, and in 1220 the tower, choir and sanctuary were added: the crypt beneath the chancel, whose roof is higher than that of the nave, was intended as an ambulatory, so that processions (as at Wrotham) could stay within consecrated ground. In it are 1200 skulls and 8000 thigh-bones (from about 4000 bodies), all of the thirteenth and fourteenth centuries, which it is thought were probably dug up to make room for victims of the endemic and recurrent Black Death.

A hint of the importance attached to the Cinque Ports' past glories is given by a stone on the wall under the tower, which reads: 'Here lieth the bodi of Thomas Spratt Iuratt and Susan his first wife who whilst he lived was thris (thrice) Mayor and Baylif to Yarmoth and on (one) of those that did cary the canopye over the kinge at his cronation who died the 21 of Ianry 1619.'

CHAPTER TEN

Stour

There has probably always been a certain amount of mild controversy on the question of which of the two head-waters of the Stour is the greater, which the lesser. The western stream, rising at Lenham, is generally called the Great Stour, and the eastern, at Postling, is known as the East Stour, and yet the latter, when joined by the former at Ashford, is already greater. For the purpose of this chapter I have followed the East Stour valley from the hills behind Hythe, around the shoulder of the Downs and northwards through the gap cut by the combined streams, now definitely the Great Stour, to Canterbury. The Stour is a chalk stream from both head-springs, and is clear and fresh, harbouring plants and creatures greatly valued by botanists and naturalists. Not only people with these interests but many who prize the river for itself have been worried recently by the tendency for millions of gallons of water to be pumped out of the river, for public use, and for quantities of noxious matter to be pumped into it, from factories and sewage works: this has been checked but attention is constantly needed to ensure that Kent's only chalk stream retains its character.

Between the Downs and the coast at Hythe is Saltwood, which has been a fairly ordinary village and is now a residential suburb of Hythe, but was once a very important manor, owned by the archbishops of Canterbury. It was important because it was a large manor in a vulnerable position, and Duke William of Normandy, when he had beaten the English army and had himself crowned king, wanted it in safe hands; he could not deprive the archbishop of one of his possessions, so he granted it, as tenant, to Hugh de Montfort, a loyal knight whom he had created Constable of England.

Hugh built a castle, which although rebuilt in the next century and augmented with curtain walls and a gatehouse in the fourteenth century, is the nucleus of the building which stands there today. It is said to have been the meeting-place of the four knights who took too literally an angry comment of Henry II, on their way to Canterbury and the most famous murder of the middle ages. An indication of the importance of the manor of Saltwood is that it included Hythe, whose parish church until 1844 was merely a chapel of Saltwood, greater and more magnificent though it was. The castle was rescued from decay and made habitable in the last century and today is the home of Lord Clark, whose television series on Civilisation has been of such interest to so many people.

The road from Saltwood to Sandling runs beside Sandling Park, on the edge of which stands a fine early timbered house with a crosswing called Slaybrook; north of a turning in the A2o at Postling Wents (a Kentish term for a road: crossroads here and there are called Four Wents or Five Wents) is the village of Postling. Hasted was unusually rude about it ('unpleasant and unfrequented . . . very wet and swampy') and today it is small, without either inn or shop, but its church, of St Mary and St Radigund, is partly pre-Conquest in origin (just: early eleventh century) and has a stone in the north wall of the chancel which reads (in Latin): 'The 19th of the Calends of September, on the day of St Eusebius, Confessor, the Church was dedicated in honour of Blessed Mary, Mother of God.' The year is omitted, but might have been late seventh century: a dedication to 'Mary, Mother of God' is rare in the western Church but not in the eastern, so it is possible that it was made by Theodore of Tarsus, who was Archbishop of Canterbury in 668. Later, in about 1200, the church was given to the Abbot of St Radigund's, near Dover, so the other saint's name was added.

It is near Postling that the East Stour springs from the hillside, close under the escarpment of the Downs, at the roadside between the church and a farmhouse called The Pent, which was once rented by Joseph Conrad for some 20 years from its owner Ford Maddox Hueffer. The infant river flows down to Stone Street and the village named from it, Stanford; it runs then under the road and under the railway near Westenhanger station (which functions as a phantom station, without staff), round the back of Folkestone Racecourse and around the remains of a battered old manor-house, Westenhanger House. This strange place is only reached through the litter-strewn rear parts of the racecourse and would be better seen from the train if longer than two seconds were permitted. There is a legend which says that Rosamund Clifford, Henry II's unfortunate mistress, lived here, and one of the two surviving towers is known as 'Fair Rosamund's Bower'; the towers in question, along with the rest of the remaining fortifications, were not built until the fourteenth century, so this seems unlikely. There might have been a previous fortress or manor-house here, but evidence is scanty. The remains of a house, attached to the castle ruins, belong to the sixteenth century, when a remarkable character called Smith, who made a formidable amount of money in the City, married Alice, the daughter of Sir Andrew Judde, the founder of Tonbridge School, and secured the highly lucrative farm of the customs collected from the ports of London, Sandwich, Chichester and Southampton; from this he acquired the name of Customer Smith, Smyth or Smythe, and a considerable fortune, some of which he exchanged for the manor of Westenhanger, which had been augmented by Sir Edward Poynings with splendid apartments, cloisters and chapel. Most of all this has gone: some is incorporated into a Georgian house, stones from the rest have gone to build barns and sheds, for it became a farmhouse. Ivy-covered and inaccessible, Westenhanger remains oddly romantic.

The country between the East Stour and the North Downs, which generally speaking slopes up from one to the other, mostly well wooded, is difficult to explore without some back-tracking, because there is much of interest in it which should not be missed. From Stanford (it is impossible to go anywhere from Westenhanger except back to the racecourse) a lane runs past an old windmill without sails, through low hills to Horton Priory, where from a footpath along a tributary to the Stour one can glimpse through the trees a large stone mansion built in the last century. The stone from the priory buildings was used for the construction of Deal Castle by order of Henry VIII, so very little remains of them. The priory was a cell of Lewes, in Sussex, which was one of the 'congregation' of the great house of Cluny, in Burgundy: all members accepted the auth-

ority of the Abbot of Cluny in return for the protection of his immensely prestigious name. Since, however, Cluny was not in England, and England was often at war with France, Lewes and Horton
were treated as alien and taken into the king's hands: the prior was
obliged to prove that he was English by paying an annual sum to the
king. Eventually in 1373 Lewes and its cells were declared 'denizen',
and remained so until dissolution in 1536.

Footpath and tributary both come to Sellindge, which is unfortunately on the A20; opposite its church the road to Brabourne leads
off into the stream's valley, past an old wisteria-covered house with
the stream in its garden. The road climbs gradually from an area of
sandpits and rubbish dumps to the chalk slopes of the Downs and
Brabourne, whose street lies along the slope below the Pilgrims
Way. In the street are some good old brick cottages, a stout seventeenth-century farmhouse, and by a very attractive group of houses
at the end, the path to the church: this celebrated building has
some excellent twelfth-century Norman work, including the chancel arch and its carved capitals, and even a window in the north
wall of the chancel with the original Norman glass, a design of
circles, semicircles and squares in colours. The nave and south aisle
are later, and the tower fell down and was repaired in the fifteenth
century. The chancel and south-east chapel are full of memorials
and tombs of the Scott family of Scotts Hall, Smeeth, a building
which has entirely disappeared. They stemmed from the probable
owner of the heart in the little shrine here, John Baliol de Scot, who
founded Balliol College, Oxford, and was the father of the John
Baliol whom Edward I chose out of the 13 claimants for the Scottish
throne when the Maid of Norway died in 1290.

The Pilgrims Way, the ancient pre-Roman trade-route, runs along
the foot of the Downs and can be followed for some three miles,
passing below the Wye and Crundale Downs Nature Reserve and by
the lovely gardens of Fishponds Farm, where at the mouth of a re-
entrant in the chalk a stream provides the series of fish-ponds. A
turning south from the Way goes through Brook, a long street of
the usual mixture of old and new houses, with another outstanding
church and a museum. The latter, housed in a good, probably late
fourteenth-century, timber-framed barn built by Christ Church

Priory, Canterbury, is a collection of farm implements and wagons made by Wye College. Admission is free and one may inspect at will the ploughs, seed-drills, threshing and reaping machines of the earliest design, all well displayed and labelled. The church, close at hand, built all of flint, has a tower, nave and chancel of the eleventh century, and on its interior walls a series of mural paintings, showing the lives of Christ and the Virgin Mary, said to be contemporary (although some texts have been added which are obviously much later since they are in Authorised Version English). They were restored in 1965 by the Pilgrim Trust. Mural paintings like these were quite common in early English churches, helping to explain to the unlettered what they could not read. Many were painted out by reformers with the same kind of simplistic zeal that made Blue-skin Dick Culmer smash the windows of Minster church.

Down the hill towards Ashford, on the sandy ridge, is Hinxhill, where below the small shingle-spired church is the manor-house, a solid Georgian place, cream-painted and slate-roofed, with a big pillared porch. A few cottages complete the village; at Ousely Farm a footpath saves us from going to Ashford yet and leads instead across fields to Quarrington Farm, where an unidentified moat, all tree-grown, probably once surrounded an ancient manor-house. Hatch Park, adjoining, shows to the road a little pool where antlered roe stags might be drinking and grazing: a footpath across the Park, through stands of tall trees, sandy banks, bracken and gorse, and by a reed-fringed mere, gives elusive glimpses of the great mansion, designed by Robert Adam, of Mersham-le-Hatch, home of the family of Knatchbull.

Like other prominent Kentish families, the Knatchbulls of Mersham have given, in return for land, wealth and position, their due portion of service. One, Sir Norton, founded in 1638 the Free Grammar School in Ashford (to which no boy was to be admitted until he could read the Bible in English) and served for many years as M.P. for Romney. Another, Sir Edward, 4th baronet, served (after, admittedly, changing from Tory to Whig) under Sir Robert Walpole in his much-criticised but stabilising ministry of the early eighteenth century; another Sir Edward, 9th baronet, replaced his father as M.P. in 1830 and served under Peel in his great ministry of 1841. When elevated to the Upper House, they gave military service: the war memorial at Smeeth testifies that the 3rd Lord Brabourne was killed in the war of 1914–18, his successor in the war of 1939–45.

The church of Smeeth also has Norman work in the tower and chancel arch. The vanished Scott's Hall is shown on Speed's map of 1600 to be between Smeeth and Sellindge: north of this region there is a Lodge House, south of it there is Park Wood, and Evegate Farm, west of the latter, is built suspiciously of stone: perhaps from the demolished manor?

Mersham village is divided by the railway, and the prettiest part is south of it, where the East Stour runs by a mill and under the road by an older mill-house. The houses of Ashford have spread out nearly as far as Sevington and have engulfed Willesborough, so that the way into the centre of Ashford seems very long.

It is hardly surprising that the junction-point of two streams to make a third, six major roads and five railway lines, should become important as a centre of population. The situation, at the end of the gap in the Downs made by the Stour at the point where it could be forded—*Esshetisford*, the ford of the water—and the traces of the old Roman iron-roads from the Weald, would appeal to the early settlers, for a start. The wool trade, the cloth trade and Sir John Fogge brought prosperity and the great church-tower to Ashford, Sir Norton Knatchbull gave it a school, and the South-Eastern Railway Company made it the hub of its system and a centre of railway engineering in the mid-nineteenth century. Now it is a very big town indeed, with plenty of industries of all descriptions, and its housing estates (built, regrettably, often with the customary modern mediocrity) spread far and are planned to spread farther.

In the middle of all this, there is not a great deal for a visitor to see; there is a busy and well-stocked High Street, and an area between it and the church of narrow back-streets with the remaining sixteenth- to eighteenth-century houses and inns of the old town. Other period houses in the High Street and adjoining roads appear somewhat neglected. The large cruciform church was repaired and its pinnacled tower built in the fifteenth century out of the pocket of Sir John Fogge of Ripton Manor, who was Treasurer of Edward IV's Household, outlawed by Richard III and restored to his lands by

Henry VII; he is buried in the church, and so is that flamboyant Elizabethan merchant, Customer Smythe.

The way out of Ashford, down-valley, is through the uninspiring residential district of Kennington, which from its name (from *Cyning*, king and ton, a homestead or manor) was probably a manor of the Kings of Kent. On the road to Faversham, past all the modern houses and a girls' school, a large, turreted and highly decorated Victorian gatehouse stands on the corner of Eastwell Park. From the road to Westwell a lane leads into the Park, across the head of a long, shining mere grown with lilies and inhabited by moorhens and coots, and entirely surrounded by trees. At one end is a small balconied boathouse, at the other—the lane end—an old high-roofed cottage, deserted and empty, which is said to have within it a hall of the thirteenth century: it is called Lake House. Near by is the ruined church of Eastwell, whose tower still stands, but little else except the little chapel, built out from what was the south aisle, which used to house the memorial to a Lady Winchelsea who died in 1849. Eastwell Park was the home of the Earls of Winchelsea, one of whose ancestors, Sir Thomas Moyle, having the manor-house rebuilt, is said to have discovered one of the bricklayers reading a book in Latin, and on questioning the man, who was elderly, found that he was a natural son of Richard III, who had fled after Bosworth and hidden himself in obscurity for fear of Tudor persecution (justifiably, considering their record of eliminating all Yorkist survivors). Sir Thomas gave him a pension and a house in one of his fields, and there he died, and here, in the ruins of the church, is the plain tomb generally regarded as his, Richard's, the last Plantagenet.

The church is a fairly recent ruin, having been damaged by a bomb and still more by neglect, and Eastwell Park is grazed by cattle and sheep and managed as a farm. The footpath through it (the lane ends at the church) emerges at Boughton Lees, where old cottages and an inn flank two sides and some new 'regency-style' houses the third, of a large triangular green. It is the main part of a far-flung parish called Boughton Aluph—the fourth and last of the Boughtons. Its church is a mile away on a section of the recently opened North Downs Way, a continuous run of footpaths which traverses the length of the Kentish North Downs. A cottage at the end of the church lane, and the Flying Horse at the Lees, both suggest by their round-headed windows, in pairs, that they were once the property of the Derings of Pluckley: the signature is unmistakable.

Between Boughton Aluph on the west and Wye on the east bank, the hills close in on the Stour as it wriggles through the gap. The Downs on both sides are high and bear a deep carpet of green-wood trees: above Boughton, Challock Forest, above Wye, Crundale Downs—and the crown-shape cut in the hillside below the woods by students of the Agricultural College to mark Edward VII's coronation. The road dips to the valley, crosses the railway and then the bridge, whose inscription tells us that it was built in 1638 at the charge of the County, over the smooth-gliding Stour. A mill-race hurls its waters past a long-gone mill-wheel whose weatherboarded premises are now used by a seed merchant. A gap, filled by new houses, evidently separated the river from the little town of Wye, which stands on rising ground. Recently, in October 1972 in fact, the foundations were found in much lower ground near the river, at Harville, of an important Roman settlement; living-quarters, out-buildings and walls, and a bronzesmith's workshop covered about an acre. There was evidence of occupation at three different times in the Roman period, the earliest of which boasted a good hypocaust central-heating system. Having examined it and removed all they could, the archaeologists had to fill it in again and return it to the plough.

Whether or not any of these buildings remained in the days of the early Kentings is unknown: but the name of Wye means a place for idols, or a heathen temple, and some local occupation supplied the burials which have in the past been found in the Downs near by. Christian Wye once had a graceful, finely proportioned church (a good model of which stands at the present west end) with a central steepled tower and transepts, but it suffered two disasters. In the centre of the nave is the gravestone of Gregory Brett, who helped to rebuild the steeple after it was struck by lightning and burnt in 1572. But too long a time elapsed before any adequate repairs were made, the weather did its work, and in 1686 the steeple crashed into the chancel. The present tower is over the old north transept, the chancel is apsidal, in the classic renaissance style and new-painted in dark and light grey, white and gold, on the site of the old tower: the effect is to truncate and spoil the old proportions.

Before these catastrophes struck, the nearby manor-house of Olantigh had supplied an archbishop of Canterbury, John Kempe, and Kempe, in the fifteenth century, had endowed his native town and its 'feir, large' church with a college of priests. Some of the buildings, east of the churchyard, are now incorporated into a different college, that of Agriculture whose various departments are distributed all around the town, to the benefit of husbandry in Kent and many other places in past, present and future years.

Olantigh, by the river, is passed by a long straight road north of Wye: it was rebuilt in the eighteenth century in brick, with a colonnaded portico, by the resident Sawbridges who have a formidable tomb to themselves in the churchyard, in reddish marble. The house now provides a centre for the annual Stour Music Festival.

A footpath from this road, past the old farmhouse Trimworth Manor, goes under the railway to the A28 and over the river to Godmersham church, which stands in the woods beneath the hill of Godmersham Downs: it has early Norman work of the eleventh century in the north wall, as can be seen from the windows in it, and a blocked-up Norman door in the west wall. There is a memorial on the north wall to Edward Knight, the brother of Jane Austen, who changed his name to Knight in order to inherit the house and manor of Godmersham, which lies behind a high brick wall just west of the church. The river here, crossed by a small bridge, is at its loveliest, which is more than can be said for the A28: on the far side of it is the village of Godmersham, most of which seems to have been built, judging by the inscriptions on the brick porches, by Edward Knight in 1833. There is unfortunately no alternative to following the main road for a mile to East Stour Farm, where a footbridge crosses the river and a path heads uncertainly for Mountain Street, an outlying hamlet on the hillside south of Chilham Castle. Monckton Manor and Heron Manor here are basically hall-houses, probably of the fifteenth century. The lane runs along the base of the Castle's walled grounds, where enclosures come into view of types of deer and wild pigs, of the sort that the early Men of Kent must have put to pasture in the 'dens' to root for acorns and beechmast. It is invisible from this hillside because of screening trees, but on the far side of river, road and railway is a Neolithic long barrow known, for unhistorical reasons, as Juliberrie's Grave.

Chilham Castle, whose grounds were laid out by Capability Brown, is a Jacobean mansion of great charm standing on the site of a medieval baronial hall, the castle keep of which, a grim old Norman tower, still remains. It played an important part in the complicated feudal structure which provided a garrison for Dover Castle, and later when its inefficiency had been appreciated and replaced, it was granted, as we have seen, by Edward II to Bartholomew de Badlesmere. After his demise it passed through many hands until it came to Sir Dudley Digges, who married the granddaughter of Sir Thomas Kempe of Olantigh, the current owner. Sir Dudley had the old hall pulled down and the mansion, which is another of those that might have been designed by Inigo Jones, built: Jones visited Italy in 1604, and may have been inspired by the geometrical lay-out of Cardinal Farnese's palace between Viterbo and Rome. Chilham is hexagonal, with the sixth side open.

The square of Chilham, on the end of a ridge with steep streets descending on all sides, is famous for the well-preserved timbered cottages on two of its sides: on the third are the Castle's gatehouse and trees, and on the fourth the churchyard. The church is fourteenth century, with octagonal columns, and is full of memorials and tombs, mostly of successive Castle-owners; one, to two Hardy boys who died young, has them in marble with battledore, shuttlecock and a book; another is the massive, square Digges memorial, with a marble obelisk, four Virtues, one classically posed on each corner, and four plaques, two of which refer to Sir Dudley, 'whose death the wisest men doe reckon amongst public calamities of these times' and his wife Mary. Sir Dudley, who died in 1658, had been ambassador to Russia and Master of the Rolls to James I.

Past Chilham station, down at river-level, a lane climbs the opposite side of the valley to the corner of Mystole House's grounds (once the home of the Fagg family, now divided into flats) and down again to Shalmsford Street, an offshoot of Chartham, then along the side of the railway to Chartham itself. From the triangular green can be seen the houses more frequently glimpsed from the railway:

some ancient, some merely old, some new, one timber-framed and lop-sided, one tall and straight with a bust in a niche in front, a new row, bow-fronted, near the churchyard. The church, in dark flint, has an admirable timber roof with even a timber cross-vault, and some oddly designed 'Kentish tracery' in the chancel windows. There are some good brasses, especially that of Sir Robert de Septvans, who was lord of the manor of Milton; the brass, of 1306, is one of the four earliest in England.

By the river at Chartham are the paper-mill works, latest in a long line, and nearby a dubious footpath leaves the road and is supposed to go to Horton, where a little medieval chapel lurks behind a high wall of trees, and then to Milton, the former manor of the Septvans family; the parish of Milton is restricted mainly to the farmhouse and cottages, but its church, the manor chapel, remains: a simple rectangle of flint ashlar, it was restored, says a date on it, in 1820.

There is little left of the Stourside journey now except the last mile or two to Canterbury, and two places visible and accessible from the road. One is Tonford Manor, between the two railway lines that converge on Canterbury, a farmhouse built from the remains of an ancient moated manor; the other, looming over the same side of the valley, is a wooded eminence which was adapted by one of the Belgic tribes which invaded Cantium in the Iron Age: Bigberry Camp. It was a defended *oppidum*, protected by ditches which follow the contours of the spur of land, and although it was probably created a century or so before Caesar's raids, it seems likely that it was the 'well-fortified post of great natural strength' from which he chased the Britons during his second expedition of 54 B.C. His 'night march of about 12 miles' would have had to be nearer 16, from Deal, but the river and the camp correspond.

CHAPTER ELEVEN

The Eastern Downs

The North Downs between Canterbury and Folkestone, a roughly triangular area east of the Stour gap and west of the A2 and the A260 (Folkestone road), are not higher than elsewhere along the range: in fact they are not as high as the hills above Wrotham, Kemsing or Chevening. But seen from the East Stour valley, or from the sea, with their crest of thick trees like the palisade of an ancient hill-fort, they give an impression of impregnable strength. The extensive woods and unpopulous valleys of this Downland offer some of the least spoilt rural scenery and best walking country in Kent. There are no main roads through it, although Stone Street, the Roman road from Canterbury to *Portus Lemanis*, is still important and well-used; there once was a railway, a single-track line from Canterbury along the Elham valley built in the late 1880s, but it has been long defunct.

The dry valleys and consequently most of the lanes run north to south, so exploration of the area, on paper, takes on a slightly lunatic zig-zag effect. Canterbury is the best place from which to begin, because of its variety of transport: a train to Chartham permits a sidelong climb into the Downs by way of the road past St Augustine's Hospital and the only exception to the north–south rule for direction of valleys. At once, the commotion of road and railway in the Stour valley are left behind: in 2½ miles this little dale is disturbed by no more than two farms, the manor-house Kenfield Hall, and on its southern side the hamlet of Garlinge Green. Behind the latter the mass of Denge Wood stretches over the hills south-westwards; a lane through orchards drops to the first of the long probing finger-valleys running southwards from Petham, where there are some attractive cottages, particularly a timbered one on the corner of the lane to the church. One lane follows the valley bottom to

Ansdore, another, called Broadway, climbs through thick woods on the ridge to Waltham, skirts the edge of Denge Wood by the somnolent hamlet Solestreet, then dips first into a small and, but for a couple of farmsteads and the sixteenth-century mansion Huntstreet, uninhabited valley; in the next, larger vale is Crundale.

A village in a valley not on a route to anywhere else is less likely than some to be crowded in summer, but is also apt to be cut off by heavy snowfalls in winter: this happens now and then to Crundale, and probably always has. The church, on the ridge between the two valleys, those of Huntstreet and Crundale, is small and unpretentious, a mixture of stone, plaster, flint ashlar and brick with a reconstructed chancel window dated 1894, and inside a coat of arms of Queen Anne. The village is protected on all sides by the tree-topped hills and is small and fairly compact; two of the cottages are attached to small and non-operative chapels, and the inn is now a private house. The manor-house, in the hollow just below the church, was built in 1660.

Despite the comparative scarcity of modern population, in ancient times this area appears to have been well settled: a local antiquarian of the eighteenth century, the Rev. Brian Faussett, investigated a number of burial-mounds which he found in the woods on Tremworth Down, west of the village; there were some cinerary urns of the first and second centuries, some third-century burials and early Jutish remains blending with the late Romano-British; in addition to this some more urns were found at Garlinge Green, thought to be Romano-British, and a lead coffin containing a child's skeleton; a large two-handled amphora turned up at Anvil Green, Waltham, in 1902. As a medieval village, Crundale managed to produce two master masons: when Edward I's Queen Eleanor died, her funeral procession was commemorated by the erection of a series of crosses on the route. The Clerk of the King's Works employed one Master Richard of Crundale to construct Charing Cross: he died in 1293 and the work was finished by Roger of Crundale, perhaps a brother. Because of the large amount of Purbeck marble used, Charing Cross was the most expensive of all the crosses, costing over £700, a huge sum for the thirteenth century. The present Charing Cross is a copy of it.

A footpath from the church along the top of the ridge can be warmly recommended because it provides an excellent way of seeing this remote and unspoilt country: the Crundale valley, traversed only by the private road belonging to the manor-house, lies on the right, and the smaller and even lonelier vale, continuing past Hunt-street, on the left. The path passes through some fine beech woods, which seem to thrive on chalk: Caesar's comment, that 'there is timber of every kind, as in Gaul, except beech and fir' is mistaken, since both are indigenous. Perhaps his night march across the Downs to the Stour valley precluded, as would hardly be surprising, any serious study of the vegetation.

The path, after about a mile and a half, comes to a farm-track, to a seventeenth-century inn at Hassell Street which precariously preserves, in these changing times, old values and standards, and also to another footpath: there might be a struggle here with mud and stinging-nettles, but it slips into the end of the Crundale valley at Big Coombe Farm and climbs out again to the hills, which are Wye Downs. From the farm the path has been elevated to the status of a lane, and immediately opposite its junction with the Wye Downs road is a stile in a fence, on the far side of which is the Wye and Crundale Downs Nature Reserve.

A mile and a half of escarpment, covering 250 acres, has been preserved by Nature Conservancy, a government agency, to protect one of the best remaining examples of Kentish Downland, which tends to deteriorate rapidly as a result of modern farming methods. Experiments are carried out in grassland management, to maintain a proper balance of flowers, grass and insects; there are about 100 acres of woodland, predominantly ash, there are singing birds like willow warbler, whitethroat and nightingale in the thorn scrub, there are small animals, the occasional fox and badger and sometimes even fallow deer. There are also countless kinds of insect including several species of butterflies, chalk-based wild flowers including orchids of 17 varieties, and to most of all this the public is allowed access, provided that a few simple rules are observed: one must stay on the paths (nature trails can be arranged through the acres normally circumscribed), disturb neither trees, nor flowers, nor creatures, keep dogs well under control, shut gates, take litter home and refrain from setting fire to anything. These, in fact, are the normal rules of the Country Code and ought to be borne in mind wherever one goes.

There is of course a wide prospect over the East Stour valley and the woods and fields around Brook, Hinxhill and Mersham, the Weald beyond them and the dim shapes of the Wealden Hills in the far distance. One of the Reserve's many paths skirts a deep and narrow re-entrant called the Devil's Kneading-trough, crosses the sheep-pastures where skylarks sing and regains the road that runs along the tops to Hastingleigh. This is a high and unfrequented place which, like Crundale, is often isolated in snowy weather; its name seems to derive from 'woodland belonging to the *Haestingas*', who were a tribe or following of early Germanic settlers who occupied most of East Sussex (their name is commemorated in Hastings) and, evidently, much of the low-lying country between the Sussex hills and these eastern Downs. Hastingleigh may have been so-called to distinguish the border territory of the *Haestingas* from that of the *Canter-wara*, the Men of Kent.

The village is grouped about a crossroads, and the church and manor-house are half a mile away. One of the lanes leading from it descends to the very end of the Petham valley, where a stretch of evident parkland marks the site of Evington Court: this, by all accounts, was a great, gloomy mansion built by the Honeywoods on the site of a much more attractive house. The Honeywoods were a branch of the family encountered at Charing and Lenham and, like the Culpeppers, were once very numerous in East Kent; considering that prolificacy of Mary Honeywood with her 367 living offspring, this is hardly surprising. Generations of them are buried in Elmsted church, high on the next ridge: it has a curious shingled tower-top, with a spire, which overlaps the stone tower like the lid of a font; the structure is basically twelfth century, with many later additions and alterations. Elmsted village, which the church serves, consists only in a few farmsteads and cottages, but there are several outlying hamlets like Whatsole Street and Bodsham Green; as on the Marsh, a country parish covers a very large area. Beyond Whatsole Street Stone Street runs due south along a high ridge, marked by the dark serrated outline of Lyminge Forest. Stowting Common is tucked under the lee of the forest, and a lane from it descends the escarpment into a re-entrant which shelters Stowting from the northern cold. When this lane was being cut out of the chalk in 1844, the workmen came across graves containing 30 or more human skeletons, along with fragments of weapons, pottery and some coins of the late Roman Empire; in 1866, 25 more were uncovered not far away, with relics of a similar period.

Stowting is small, secluded and attractive, with a small church and cottage gardens brighter, it seems, than any with flowers. It is connected by a steep lane and a couple of murderous footpaths with Stone Street, which today performs the same function as it did when the Romans laid it, in connecting Canterbury with Lympne. Three miles from Canterbury the modern road leaves the ancient and serves such villages as Nackington, which has a Norman church, and Lower Hardres, which is a suitable place from which to begin the next southward probe.

The church at Lower Hardres is in early nineteenth-century Gothic, but it replaced an earlier building whose five-shafted thirteenth-century font was tranferred into the new church when it was built in 1830.

The best course for a walker here is to take the right fork past the inn at the end of the Lower Hardres street and pass gently through a mile-long dale, tree-lined on both ridges and supporting just two farmsteads; it ends at Upper Hardres Wood, where a lane climbs a short way to Upper Hardres Court. Domesday Book records that the lands of this manor were held of the Archbishop by one Robert de Hardres, who is supposed to have been a member of the Conqueror's invading force; if so, he may have been one of the family who emerged as Châtelains of Ardres, vassals of the Count of Guines, near Calais, in about 1030. The family were still in possession during the reign of Henry VIII, when in 1544 Thomas Hardres gave the king valuable assistance in his siege of Boulogne. When the town surrendered, the king permitted Thomas to take home and erect in his garden a pair of gates from the city, made of iron. The king, furthermore, is said to have stayed with Thomas at his manor on the way home. The gates were still there in Hasted's time, but were later sold for scrap iron.

The church, in which members of the Hardres family from the eleventh to the eighteenth centuries were buried, suffered a very bad fire in September 1972, which destroyed the wooden gallery and the whole of the nave roof, and worst of all, smashed the three medallions of twelfth- and thirteenth-century glass, which came from Christ Church Priory, Canterbury, and were probably acquired by Thomas Hardres when the priory was dissolved.

Only the manor farm and cottages make up the dwellings at Upper Hardres, but the neighbouring village of Bossingham is within the parish boundary, which runs into the valley of Pett, to the east. To reach this there is a footpath, leading off the lane to Bursted Manor, through Bursted Wood which offers a pleasant walk among the cool beeches. The Pett valley is long, very thinly populated and heavily wooded on both banks; near Lynsore Bottom, where a group of ancient cottages in timber and brick, and a converted oast enjoy a view down the valley uncluttered but for a line of pylons, a baffling maze of lanes runs up and down the eastern bank, and it is quite easy to get lost. This eventuality is not greatly to be dreaded because all the lanes lead somewhere and the scenery in any case, much of it wooded but affording glimpses down into the Pett valley and across to the hills on the other side of the next, Elham valley, is so rich. One of the advantages of travelling on foot is that full benefit can be derived from the benign, undisturbed, timeless atmosphere of lanes like these: such an atmosphere, spoiled only by a noisy intruder, cannot be experienced if, in a car, one is that intruder.

The network of lanes having been negotiated, farther along the Pett valley, under the dark pinewoods of Lyminge Forest, the road leads to a hamlet of farms and cottages with the engaging name of Wheelbarrow Town. From it a lane runs up to Stelling Minnis; a minnis is a common, and here the houses lie scattered about haphazardly between tracts of grass, bracken and gorse as if each cottager still kept pigs and goats on it. The houses have multiplied in modern times, but still in an agreeably untidy fashion, and the village spreads itself over several square miles.

Lyminge Forest, which lies on the ridge between the Pett and Elham valleys, belongs to the Forestry Commission, which means pine trees, but means also miles of well-cleared paths for walkers and riders and a total absence of motor traffic, which is forbidden access to it. Crossed by three or four roads from one valley to the other, it covers a very great area, stretching along the ridge for six or seven miles.

A ten-minute bus-ride from Canterbury to Bridge is probably the best way to begin an exploration of the Elham valley. The lane by Bridge church goes through Bourne Park, where the Nailbourne, when it flows at all, does so from a lake; it is a mysterious and unpredictable stream, called sometimes the Woe waters, since after a long completely dry spell of years it will suddenly flood and catch everyone by surprise, and furthermore in times past was usually taken to be an omen predicting plague, famine or war. The name nailbourne, meaning an occasional stream like the West Country winterbournes, comes from the Old English *eylebourn*, a spring or well stream.

Bourne Place, standing in an imposing position on the east-facing side of the valley, is a classically designed house of the Queen Anne period, owned for about 100 years by the Beckingham family. Until recently it has been a Benedictine monastery. Bishopsbourne, on the far side of Bourne Park, was called in Domesday Book Burnes, but was held of the Archbishop, hence Bishop's Burne. A white-painted house called 'Oswalds' close by the churchyard was rented from 1919 to 1924 (after his stay at Pent Farm, Postling) by Joseph Conrad: in the latter year, he died there. The rector of Bishopsbourne from 1595 to 1600, when he too died, was Richard Hooker, a quiet and unassuming man, but a brilliant academic: the Church of England, established by Queen Elizabeth's Act of Settlement in 1559, was susceptible to criticism from Calvinist and Catholic alike because it lacked a theological and philosophical basis. Hooker supplied one, for the first time: his *Laws of Ecclesiastical Polity* was so well-written and cogently argued that it filled the gap. He completed it in his last years here at Bishopsbourne: a bust in the church commemorates him, over a slab which is supposed to be his gravestone; there are also some interesting early fourteenth-century wall-paintings above the arches of the nave.

A path beyond the small village street leads through Charlton Park, where another large house, once the residence of the Prince

Regent, who stayed there in 1798, and currently painted a kind of custard-yellow, stands in a similarly good position on the hillside. The path, following the dry bed of the Nailbourne, emerges at Kingston, which stands on the western side of the valley: the Dover road traffic can be seen on the crest of Barham Downs, opposite. The church is at the top of the village, where a brand-new rectory replaces the lofty Victorian pile once considered suitable. The rescue of its font is described on a tablet on the wall of the tower-room, where it stands:

'This Font, as old, as we may believe, as the Church of Kingston in this neighbourhood, but cast out of that church on account of its age, and for many years, shameful to relate, used to hold pigs' food, was at length rescued from profanation and placed here as it were under the protection of St Augustine, as an act of respect by Bryan Faussett, A.D. 1775.'

In an angle of the wall is set a stone head (presumably meant as St Augustine): the head, the font and the inscription were found in a summerhouse at Heppington House, Faussett's home, reconsecrated and replaced in the church in 1931. Font and church both date from the early thirteenth century. Faussett, in addition to his activities on Tremworth Hill, opened no less than 308 graves on Kingston Down near by, finding that their contents, judging by the extremely valuable objects placed in them with the skeletons, were of dates ranging from the first to the seventh centuries. In one of them he found a brooch which is one of the best examples of its kind and serves to illustrate the advanced culture of the invading Jutes.

The high, bald Barham Downs, where the Watling Street runs from Canterbury to Dover, are also dotted with *tumuli*, burial mounds, and the fragmentary remains of some defensive earthwork. As usual, these have been linked with Caesar, but in fact the Downs have been utilised for military camps whenever emergencies have arisen, from Caesar's opponents, the *Catuvellauni*, to King John, from Simon de Montfort to the Spanish Armada scare, from the Civil War Royalists to the Napoleonic Wars and from the Kaiser's war to Hitler's. The boots and shovels of so many generations of soldiers have rendered the identification of the earthworks impossible. The

Downs here were once crowned with a windmill, a well-known landmark, but it recently burned down, past repair.

Barham, along the valley road from Kingston, rises from the dry bed of the Nailbourne to the top of the hill. It is as well to climb this hill, admiring the old cottages, some of which are end-on to the road, to the green-spired church at the top, because the valley road through Derringstone has tended to attract a great many builders of modern houses which are rather uninteresting. There is a good lane through Walderchain Wood, on Breach Down, where in the nineteenth century the antiquarian Lord Conyngham opened over 100 more burials and found in them the bones and effects of Jutish men and women of the sixth and seventh centuries.

Below a beechwood the lane drops to the valley through which the road forks off from Watling Street on its way to Folkestone. In the parkland on the left can be seen the fine rose-red Caroline mansion called Broome Park, once the home of generations of Oxendens (many of whom are buried in Barham church) and for a while the home of Lord Kitchener. It is now an hotel. The busy road runs past, through the village of Denton, where a group of ancient cottages face the inn across a green. Beyond it, a lane leads off left to the church and manor-house: Denton Court is a turreted and spired Victorian mansion which no doubt occupies the site of sundry predecessors; the little church, screened by tall trees, is an excellent example of a simple early thirteenth-century village church, with a narrow chancel arch and lancet windows, and a curious and apparently inexplicable stone cross, with indecipherable lettering, set in the wall near the pulpit.

Back across the Folkestone road, a lane climbs the hillside and a farm-track on its left runs behind Tappington Hall, and then follows another otherwise trackless valley for over a mile.

Tappington, in which Richard Harris Barham installed several generations of nobly-born Ingoldsbys to suit his fertile imagination, actually was in the possession of his own family (he was born in Burgate, in Canterbury: his father is buried in Upper Hardres church). It is an aged, timbered, gabled farmhouse whose mossy tiled roof undulates like an old cloak, and it is easy enough to imagine in its connection the 'wailing voices, sounds of woe', which 'that fatal night round Tappington go, its long-drawn roofs and its gable ends . . .'.

There is only one other house in the little valley behind Tappington, tree-screened from the world: another farmhouse called Gatteridge. The farm-track thereafter becomes a footpath and follows the lonely vale until it reaches Rakesole Farm and a road; a sharp right turn along this brings one over the hill and down again to the Nailbourne valley: from the hill there is a good view of the village of Elham, compact still even with its modern extensions. It has a wide street with good timbered houses, some jettied, of the sixteenth and seventeenth centuries, a little square lined with Georgian houses of that stylish grace which never has been rivalled, and a large church; to a Norman nave and chancel were added in succeeding centuries, aisles, cinquefoil lights, a tower and chancel arch, and a chapel and clerestory. Each addition improved the general appearance and proportions and supply now a useful lesson in ecclesiastical architecture. There is also a yew-trunk chest of the thirteenth century.

There are still traces of the vanished railway all along the Nailbourne valley: bridges across the roads, embankments, lines of trees along the track, and in Elham active coal-yards behind the phantom station.

Lyminge, the last village of the valley (Ethelburga's spring, one of those by which the Nailbourne makes its allegedly prophetic appearance rises from a field below the church) is not as architecturally satisfying as Elham, but it has a longer known history. Since Roman tiles are present in the walls of the present church (and were no doubt employed in its predecessor) it is reasonable to suppose that there was a Romano-British farmstead here, although its foundations have never been found. The best indication of very early Jutish occupation of the site (a cemetery on the Elham road confirms it) lies in the name: Lyminge, as indicated in the first chapter of this book, is derived from Limen -*geh* (the last word similar to the German *gau*), district on the Limen. The latter, as we have seen, was the river or inlet which flowed past the Romans' port and fort *Portus Lemanis*, which means that, since it is about five miles from Lyminge, the district must have been quite extensive and Lyminge itself probably the chief village in it. This would explain its pre-eminence in 633, when King Edwin of Northumbria was killed in battle against the heathen Mercians: he had married Ethelburga, daughter of the King Ethelbert of Kent who had been St Augustine's most important convert. Ethelburga, with Bishop Paulinus (one of Augustine's monks) returned to Kent where her brother, now King Eadbald, granted her land at 'Limninge': she founded here a double monastery, for men and women, and took the veil herself. She died in 647, was canonised, and her remains were enshrined. Her monastery was probably destroyed by the marauding Danes in 840 since nothing more is heard of it, but in 960 the land came into the possession of Archbishop Dunstan of Canterbury, and a new church was built over the ruins of the old one. These ruins have been uncovered and can be seen partly under the present church, on the south side. The off-setting of the building may have been done in order to incorporate the tomb of St Ethelburga, formerly in the centre of the old church, into the wall of the new one. The chancel, showing the Roman tiles, is the surviving part of this second church, built about 965. Archbishop Lanfranc, a century later, translated St Ethelburga's relics to Canterbury, but a plaque on the outside south wall shows where they had rested.

Several paths and lanes lead back into the hills from Lyminge to Acrise, which stands on the ridge above the far end of the Tappington vale: at least, the church and manor-house do, the village is half a mile away. The manor-house is a stately seventeenth-century mansion, with tall windows in semicircular bays (it was 'modernised' in the early nineteenth century) and smooth green lawns; the little church, close at hand, is an uncomplicated Norman structure which is evidently in better repair than in 1502, when Rector John wrote to the officials of the Archdeacon's Court:

'It', *The rofe of the body of our church is at reparacon, it rayns therein.*

'Our *stepull is at reparacon & bot yf it be* (not) *holpe ryzt* (right) *sone, it wyll fall down for it raynit in and rots the timber.*

'It', *our churchyard is hopyn* (open) *yt all manner of beasts may come in.*

Paddlesworth, reached from Acrise by greenwood-shaded lanes, is the highest village (at 612 feet) in East Kent: it is comprised of a few cottages, an inn called The Cat and Custard Pot and a little Norman church unusually dedicated to St Oswald (a Northumbrian relative of St Ethelburga).

The last of the undulating Downland stops short at a dramatically sharp cliff-drop, and suddenly there is the whole coastal plain and the sea. If it is clear, the cliffs of France appear smudgily on the far left, and far right the humps of Dungeness power-stations show up below the dim Fairlight hills. Immediately below, in the plain, are the rows of huts in the army camp in St Martin's Plain, and all round are streets of houses and factories. This is the area which, if the current plans are eventually effected, will be transformed by the opening of the Channel Tunnel. A cross-channel tunnel has been discussed for so long and rejected as impracticable or undesirable so frequently that, even now, Kentish people will probably believe it only when they see it. Yet, with Britain participating in a Europe more close-knit than at any time since the fall of the western Roman Empire, it seems that, this time, it may be both practicable and desirable. But how will it affect Kent? Hostility to it, naturally, is strong: will more waves of huge unmanageable lorries emerge from it, will the terminal require so many yards and warehouses and offices that yet another large area of fertile Kent will disappear for ever? Or will it be restricted to a railway, with a new, fast line built through the Kentish fields, channelling many of these fears away to London and the industrial north? Some of these decisions have probably already been taken, but speculation among Kentishmen will continue until the tunnel is completed and operating.

The Down-top road runs along to Castle Hill, which is exactly what it has been: it is sometimes (inevitably) called Caesar's Camp, but is an Iron Age earthwork, and therefore existed when Caesar came. It was adapted by the Normans as a motte-and-bailey castle centuries later, perhaps during the late eleventh century, or even as late as King Stephen's reign.

Sandgate itself, due south of this hill, is not remarkably interesting: it has the battered remains of one of Henry VIII's coastal-defence castles, which has fought a losing battle against the sea, and close by the piers of the old Sandgate lift is Spade House, where H. G. Wells lived and worked. The road from here to Folkestone, along the Lees, has an attraction for anyone who likes to be near the evocative sea smells.

Folkestone's chief glories may be principally in the past, but it is still a very popular holiday resort: it has elegant clifftop hotels, a funicular lift to take their patrons to the beaches, a harbour, with fishing-boats and cross-channel ships, a southern aspect and protection from the cold north winds. This last factor may have attracted settlers in other ages, since some Neolithic remains have been found, a Roman villa, probably of the late first century A.D. with subsequent additions, was unearthed on the western shore of East Wear Bay, and a nunnery was founded on the clifftop above the harbour, at about the same time as that at Lyminge, by Eanswyth, daughter of King Eadbald. Like Ethelburga's abbey, it was destroyed by the Danes in the ninth century, replaced by a later Benedictine priory, and then by a parish church (still St Eanswyth's) in the early thirteenth century.

Folkestone is still growing, and like the rest of the area, speculating on the possible benefits or drawbacks of the Channel Tunnel: these are always inconstant, since what is a benefit for one may be a drawback for another. For example, the twentieth century's contribution to Folkestone's architectural treasury is, among other delights, a tall tower building on the clifftop west of the church: doubtless it is of inestimable benefit to its owners and to those who wish to study the coast of France from its top, and possibly also to mariners, but one could not envisage its unqualified approval by, say, Inigo Jones.

The only remaining Downland left to describe is that from Canterbury to the sea between Deal and Dover: the coastline is perhaps the best-known in England, because its chalky cliffs greet every homecoming traveller from the Continent across the narrow Straits. Although it was a small part of what the Romans called the Saxon Shore (the nine forts in their defence system extended from Norfolk to Hampshire) because it was the shore most susceptible to attacks from Saxon pirates, it became later the symbolic key to the kingdom when the Saxons themselves were in possession: the mighty Norman castle at Dover, Henry VIII's forts at Deal, the armed camp that the whole clifftop became in the two twentieth-century wars emphasise the importance of this most vulnerable corner of the island, separated from hostile nations only by these 22 miles of sea. Herein lie some of the fears for the consequences of constructing the cross-channel tunnel.

The triangle of land formed by the A2, the Folkestone road and the sea can be inspected from a route beginning at Kearsney station, in the narrow valley of the Dour below Temple Ewell. A hard climb up Minnis Lane, through the suburban village of River, scales the Downs to a level plain of sheep-grazed grassland and cornfields, a long straight lane across which leads to the remains of St Radegund's Abbey. These are considerable, and worth a visit because they are mainly the same as those erected in the 1190s by Canon Hugh and his monks sent from Prémontré to colonise the new abbey. The gatehouse, which was really the tower, in dark flint with an odd triangular pattern on the buttresses, and the chapter-house, refectory and cellarer's buildings have been allowed to stand and in parts incorporated, with adjustments in the sixteenth century, into a farmhouse and barns: the architecture is plain and simple, with the earliest type of pointed arch.

The 'pleasant footpath ... from the Abbey to Copt Hill' which Walter Jerrold mentions is (in season) obliterated by fields of barley and wheat, and therefore needs some astute navigation. But the grassy track on the far side of the cornfields is worth reaching because it leads into a narrow valley in which the farmhouse of Poulton (once a big enough settlement to rate a church, listed in *Domesday Monachorum*), served only by a long unmade track, gives the impression of extreme remoteness; down the valley eastwards the bulk of Dover Castle shows above the hills, but westward only the old house on Copt Hill can be seen, and while the footpath out of it to Hougham is negotiable, it is by no means easy going.

West Hougham is a quiet hilltop village with several Georgian and brick-and-timber houses, and a Methodist church; a twisting lane from it comes to the Dover to Folkestone clifftop road, the houses of Capel-le-ferne and the fearsome heights of the Warren, overlooking East Wear Bay. Most of Capel-le-ferne owes its origin to unambitious builders of the 1930s: the parish church is a mile away farther inland, by a farm marking the vanished manor-house. It is a small flint church, with unusual tracery in the windows, and huge reddish quoin stones, one of which, on the south-east corner of the chancel, has a little sacramental cross carved near the edge.

The high windy uplands here limit visibility as if in a heavy sea—one is always between billows—and it comes as a surprise when the road dives suddenly into a valley (past a footpath to Mount Ararat); the valley carries the B2060 from Kearsney to Folkestone, a long lateral rift in the chalk, and here it passes through Alkham, clustered round the crossroads. The church is interesting: it was rebuilt by the monks of St Radegund's in the early thirteenth century, and again later in the same century when the north aisle was pulled down and a chapel built instead which has fine mural arcading; in it is the tomb of the first named rector, Herbert, with the earliest epitaph (he may have died in 1199) in East Kent, written of course in Latin.

It is, of necessity, a long and tortuous route out of Alkham's valley, over the hill, down into another, quite uninhabited and used by the Army for training purposes, and out of that through the woods to Swingfield Street, a place of small, humble cottages, an equally tiny inn and a simple church. Round a couple more corners, by St John's Farm, there is a chapel of the Knights of St John, at least as big as Swingfield church, also of flint and just as simple: it is in course of repair by the Department of the Environment, not before time.

A long lane to Wootton between high hedges and beside woods finds a quiet little green with some old houses offset by four fairly new and certainly not unattractive cottages, and the little church of St Martin, also of flint and built in the thirteenth century: in it is the family vault and several memorials of the Bridges (or Brydges), lords of the now vanished Wootton Court. One of this family, James Brydges, determined to remain in governmental office, changed from Tory to Whig when Queen Anne died and bought his way to the Dukedom of Chandos. 'By 1715,' says Professor J. H. Plumb, 'he was on the same easy familiar terms with Walpole and Townshend as he had been with Bolingbroke and Oxford in 1714.' An early nineteenth-century Brydges, who was supposed to be a Rector of Wootton, tried to recapture by law what his ancestor had achieved by studied bribery, but 'the protracted litigation of his claim to the ancient Barony of Chandos, which wasted so many years of his existence, were at length too much for a delicate constitution, and he sank into the grave'. Later in the century, as if to make up for the Reverend Edward, the family produced a Poet Laureate, Robert Bridges.

East of Wootton progress for the walker becomes problematical because a footpath from Geddinge Farm fails before it has begun in a sea of barley, and there is no other way to Lydden but by the side of the fearful A2, encountered after the way into Lydden race-track. This is an experience which can on no account be recommended, but gives an insight to what the inhabitants of such places as Bridge, Boughton and Lydden must endure every day: the traffic, which for many years has been non-stop, is nowadays augmented by monstrous Continental lorries of great weight, noise and potential danger to life, limb and the nervous system. A row of little crooked-roofed cottages at Lydden look as if they have been shaken that way by the traffic; the church, of thirteenth-century flint, has Norman work which shows in the blocked-up windows in the tower. An escape-route can be found up a lane round the corner of the hill back to the billowy Downland country, and down to Ewell Minnis, where the B2060 runs along its valley below a handsome beechwood which overhangs the hillside. This road arrives back in Kearsney, where a walled garden, formerly the grounds of a mansion called Kearsney Abbey, encloses lawns and ponds from the waters of the Dour, well laid-out and open to the public.

The rest of the area, on the north-eastern side of the A2, can be examined in slices, beginning near Canterbury and ending at Dover; Bridge is a good starting-point again because from it the lane follows the dry Nailbourne to Patrixbourne, past Bifrons Park. In the 1860s, no doubt to the great delight of the antiquarian Lord Conyngham who lived there, more than 100 graves were found and opened on the Bifrons estate: they disclosed plentiful evidence of the style of jewellery used by the early Jutish settlers, which was like other finds in parts of the Continent inhabited by the Franks of the middle

Rhine, and unlike anything found in graves of the northern Anglo-Saxons.

Lord Conyngham, and two other marquises of his family who lived at Bifrons, are buried and commemorated in the famous church of St Mary, Patrixbourne, whose doorway reproduces, in miniature, the twelfth-century masterpieces of, for example, St Trophîme in Arles, St-Gilles and Oloron-Ste-Marie. Within a semicircular design, concentric carved figures, of animals, birds, men and their heads, flowers and leaves, converge on a central Christ in Majesty. In the east wall of the chancel is a circular rose window above three small round-headed lancets, with a carved head above them. For a small parish church, this ornamentation is unusually rich.

Some Patrixbourne cottages, in Victorian mock-Tudor, owe their existence to the same Lord Conyngham who conducted the grave-digging operations in the district; they have now adjusted far enough to fit in with the older, Flemish-gabled brick houses. It is a short way to Bekesbourne, whose church is curiously placed on a rise behind an orchard, without visible access to the road. The cottages are mainly grouped by the railway station and bridge; along the Littlebourne road is the mansion Howletts, whose present owner has established a zoo in its grounds. A notice at the gate says, 'Beware: gorillas, rhinos, tigers, wolves, elephants', and perhaps to illustrate the force of this a cage near the road is full of apes which crash about and make unearthly noises. A slightly bizarre feature of Bekesbourne is that in the middle ages it became linked, as a Limb, with the Cinque Port of Hastings, of all places, apparently for land-owning reasons.

On the right of the road past Howletts is a track to Garrington Farm, and half-way along this is a wood in which is a spring of water, and behind the wood the flint and stone fragments, much ivy-grown but recognisably rectangular, of Well Chapel; in 1194 it was the subject of a dispute between Richard de Garwynton and the Abbot of St Augustine's, which ended in the Abbot's grant to Richard and his heirs of the right to have divine office said three times a week in the chapel by the priest of Littlebourne.

At Littlebourne the Nailbourne, now properly flowing because of the copious supplies from the Garrington Well, becomes the Lesser

Stour, which reserves Littlebourne for the next chapter. The way to Wingham, along the A257, lies through Bramling, where there is a large and pleasantly baroque brick mansion, now an hotel.

In a field on the right of the road before Wingham is a trace, in the form of an embankment, of another of Kent's vanished railways, the East Kent Light Railway, which had a shorter life than any since it was only opened in 1916 and has been dead, except for the coal-mine stretch to Eythorne, for many years.

Wingham had a college, of six canons and a master or provost, established by Archbishop Pecham in 1286 and lasting until the first year of young Edward VI's reign, 1547. The fact that some of the canons' houses have survived would not be so remarkable if, as at Cobham, they had been built of stone: but they were timber-framed, and although they have been much altered, enlarged and strengthened, the houses now called the Old Canonry, the Dog inn, the Old Forge House and the Red Lion inn, reading from right to left are basically those built in 1286. The church was rebuilt at the same time, in flint: decorated windows were added in the next century, and the green copper-plated spire in the fifteenth. The manor belonged to the archbishop, and part of the hall survives in Wingham Court, across the road. One extraordinary feature of the church is that when the nave was rebuilt in the sixteenth century, for the supporting columns chestnut was used instead of stone. There is in the south-east chapel a great obelisk memorial, built in 1682, with a black ox-head on each corner, to the Oxenden family of Deane House, who inhabited the Wingham district from 1440 to 1920.

Trees are scarcer in these northern slopes: church spires show on the skyline, and the cooling towers of Ebbsfleet power-station. At Staple are several thatched cottages, a form of roofing uncommon in the rest of Kent: one at the nearby hamlet of Barnsole is timber-framed and brick-filled and therefore probably of the seventeenth century; the influence of the immigrant Flemings, escaping from the religious wars which tore Europe apart in the seventeenth century, can be seen in many of the brick houses, like Selson Farm.

The early importance of Eastry as the chief village of the Eastor-geh was marked by a palace there of the kings of Kent, but all trace of it seems to have disappeared, and the only things to distinguish the village now are the stylish Georgian and Regency houses in the street (which, since it is also the A256, is rather hectic), a black-boarded windmill without sails and a pretty street leading to the church.

Attempts to reach the church and manor-house of Knowlton from the lane that runs from Eastry alongside the track of the old railway may be difficult, because the footpath tends to lead into the railway-cutting instead of across the fields; it is nevertheless possible to find a longer way round by road and then go to Chillenden, where the Griffin's Head inn is an early hall-house of the fourteenth century, much amended, and the tiny flint church, with a little spire, might remind us of the famous Prior Chillenden under whom Henry Yevele rebuilt the nave of Canterbury Cathedral.

A little white mill, with sails, on a hilltop, marks the way to Goodnestone, which shelters behind the tall trees of Goodnestone House. Nearly all the houses in the village are fitted with what I have previously called Dering windows, round-headed brick frames, in pairs and threes: another example of estate building and prob-ably copied from Pluckley. The church is in flint ashlar, of the thirteenth century. Footpaths from the churchyard are, again, apt to become confounded by broad acres of corn belonging to the owner of Goodnestone House (which is in the classical style, with a pillared porch), so another way round must be found to Adisham: Ratling Court, on the way, is worth noticing, a venerable manor-house with thatched farm-buildings. The cottages of Adisham are in a street below the large flint cruciform church, with long lancet windows: close by is the Court, in brick with Flemish gables. None of these buildings is far from the railway station, on the Canterbury line.

Another useful station on the same line is Snowdown, which may be a little off-putting because it serves one of the Kentish coal-mines, three of which are still being worked. In Nightingale Lane one finds the incongruity of normal Kentish woods and fields to one side of the road, and towering black slag-heaps and pit-head derricks and wheels on the other. A few paces farther, through some woods, and the coal-mine is forgotten; from Frogham the lane goes down to Barfreston (or Barfreystone), a pretty, compact village with the finest example of a complete church in the Romanesque style of the twelfth-century renaissance in Kent: it is smaller than Patrix-bourne, but although carefully restored from time to time has never been subject to additions or subtractions from its form of nave and chancel, with no tower. It is carved inside and out with the animal, floral and dog-tooth designs of the period, has a rose window over the three lancets in the east wall, and grimacing human heads all round the outside chancel wall; Barfreston can never have been a large or important place, and this little church speaks volumes for the spirit which moved its builders. Modern cynics can only under-stand the care lavished on great cathedrals in terms of 'conspicuous consumption': here the consumption is far from conspicuous, but the care in the ornamentation of an obscure little parish church is proportionately the same.

Eythorne, a mile from Barfreston, has the nucleus of its old village around the church, but is supplemented by large housing estates and shops for the miners at nearby Tilmanstone Colliery. Tilmanstone itself is 2½ miles away, a pretty and so far unspoilt village with the usual flint church. Around the corner of Betteshanger House's grounds (the house is now a school) is the road to Northbourne, on which at a crossroads is the famous signpost which says

HAM   1½
SANDWICH 4

Betteshanger Colliery, the last of the three, is nearer Northbourne than Betteshanger; Northbourne exists around its Court and church, and the latter is basically twelfth-century, but later than Bar-freston: in flint, and cruciform, it has a chevron-patterned but pointed chancel arch and round-headed windows in the nave. There was accommodation for a priest in the tower (his little window shows above the chancel arch); in the south transept is a huge seven-teenth-century monument in alabaster to Sir Edwin and Lady Sandys: as Treasurer of the Virginia Company he devised a consti-tution for Virginia, whose Assembly first met in 1619, which served as a model for the other American colonies.

Northbourne Court, a large brick mansion built in 1750, is

screened from the colliery by its tree-lined valley, out of which the road climbs the hill to Great Mongeham, then plunges into the housing estates of Upper Deal.

Julius Caesar, in both of his exploratory expeditions to Britain, is reckoned to have landed at Deal, because after reaching a place from which 'javelins could be hurled from the cliffs right on to the narrow beach' he anchored, waited for the wind and tide, 'and after proceeding for about seven miles ran his ships aground on an evenly sloping beach'. But Caesar's evenly sloping beach was not the beach which lines Deal's modern waterfront: the storms which battered his ships as they lay aground on the beach were instalments in a long geological story. The eastward drift of the tides and storms, which eroded chalk and clay cliffs, broke them up into nodules and moved them as shingle, gradually building up beaches and, in time, filling in estuaries and havens from Winchelsea to Sandwich, threw up a line of beach in front of the shoreline at Deal. It created what was called a 'sea-valley' in between, from the cliffs at Walmer along the coast to Sandwich Bay. In the sixteenth century Henry VIII's engineers were able to build castles on the beach, and gradually houses began to fill in the valley and keep the castles company on the new coastline. Caesar's landing-place was about a mile inshore of the new beach.

But its present beach, like its old one, is still one on which boats can be grounded, and to a certain extent Deal had preserved its fishing tradition and maritime character. Its church reflects this: significantly, although the present building dates from the late seventeenth century, it stands on the rising ground landwards of the 'sea-valley'; the parish church of St Leonard has a medieval chancel with piscina and sedilia. Its agreeably light and airy nave has a wooden organ-loft and gallery built, as a plaque proclaims, by the Pilots of Deal. There are memorials to several naval families, and a new model of one of the ships lost in a great storm in 1703 in which, as reported by one Colonel Culpepper when petitioning Queen Anne for a light on the Goodwins, 'fower ships of war of the Royall Navey of England and other ships perished and 1,800 men were drowned'.

The railway runs through the 'sea-valley', and Deal's old weather-

boarded and brick houses of the seventeenth and eighteenth centuries, grand hotels, small hotels and castle stand on the beach. The
castle is the best-preserved of all the five coastal-defence bastions
which Henry VIII had built in the 1540s, when he was waging war
yet again against France; Sandown has completely disappeared,
Sandgate is half in the sea, Camber is a crumbled ruin and Walmer
has been converted to a residence, but Deal is very much in its original condition. It is built on a concentric plan, with huge bastions
mounted with cannon, a basement magazine and first-floor living-
quarters with messes, fireplaces and ovens. In the gatehouse the
Department of the Environment has installed a museum of local
finds, of Neolithic, Bronze and Iron Age and Anglo-Saxon flints, pots
and tools, and in the living-quarters is a good explanatory exhibition
of plans, pictures and maps of all the Henrician defences.

There is a detailed plan near the pier at Deal showing the Goodwin Sands and pointing out the ships wrecked on it (their masts can
be seen at low tide). Like the Tenterden steeple legend, the origins of
the Goodwins have induced considerable ink-spilling in the past and
much theorising. They were, according to a favourite theory, a
highly fertile island called Lomea which, since their immunity from
inundation by the sea depended on the maintenance of sea-walls,
and the archbishop responsible preferred to spend the income for
this on other things (Tenterden blamed again) a great storm in 1099
was permitted to overwhelm the lands and wash away the soil:
Lomea, Earl Godwin's land, became the Goodwin Sands. Evidence
certainly points to the building up, at a similar time to the coastal
rim of the Marsh, of a beach of shingle like those on which Winchelsea, Broomhill, Lydd and Dymchurch were founded; early
writers refer to an *Infera Insula* (low island, hence Lomea) lying
south-east of Thanet, and the *Anglo-Saxon Chronicle*, against the
date 1099, observes that 'in this year also, at Martinmas, the incom-
ing tide rushed up so strongly and did so much damage that no one
remembered anything like it before', but it does not mention the
destruction of Lomea. Failure to record it does not preclude it, but it
makes less likely the probability that it was either inhabited or fertile. Doubtless it belonged, for what it was worth, to Earl Godwin,
who was Earl of Kent, but no one need pay much attention to rum-

ours about extravagant and negligent archbishops.

Walmer, due south of Deal, is now joined to it as a kind of suburb, and the most pleasant way to it is by walking along the beach-path. The castle, surrounded by gardens and trees, was long ago rendered habitable and comfortable as official residence of the Lord Warden of the Cinque Ports, a sinecure post usually given to elder statesmen: past holders and occasional occupants of the castle have included William Pitt, the first Duke of Wellington, Lord Curzon and Sir Winston Churchill; like Deal the castle is concentric and of stone, with deep-splayed gun-ports to seaward. The moat is all garden and lawn.

Beyond Walmer the cliffs begin to rise, and at Kingsdown the street of pretty cottages is on quite a sharp hill. At the top the scenery is again undulating Downland, and along a high ridge the A258 to Dover runs past Ringwould, a small village with a flint church of the thirteenth century distinguished by a brick and flint tower built in 1628 and capped with a lead cupola, a little onion turret roof. In a wood on the left of the road, on a high bank among the trees stand four walls and a gable, the ruins of St Nicholas, Oxney Court. Two little round-headed windows pierce the north wall; a few headstones remain, with memorials of the La Coste family of Oxney Court (on the edge of the wood), dated late nineteenth and early twentieth century: either the church has fallen into ruin since then, or these people were buried in the ruins.

A long road leads from the A258 across the dipping Downland to St Margaret-at-Cliffe, a hilltop village built mainly of flint and brick and including a surprising number of taverns. Its church is a fine mid-twelfth-century building, with vast columns and arches and patterns more geometric than animal. The inner door-case of the porch (north side, entered from the road) is particularly notable. A precipitous winding road brings one with a sense of finality (it leads nowhere else and is hard to get back up again) to the beach of St Margaret's Bay, a sheltered cove in the chalk cliffs with a sense of privacy, some good hotels poised among the cliffs and, for comfort, a small flint-built inn, for years the Green Man but now the Coast-guard.

Public transport in the form of a bus from St Margaret-at-Cliffe to

Dover enables a reluctant departure from this pleasant haven, and the last stage of the present exploration may begin at the station of Shepherdswell, also known as Sibertswold, where the village has grown, around the railway, away from its old nucleus up Church Hill on the green; the Victorian–Gothic church stands among eighteenth-century, and earlier, gravestones, so replaces an earlier building. A shallow valley separates it from Coldred, where a much wider green gives an impression of space between the white-boarded, brick and flint cottages: down the lane is Coldred Court, where on the roadside by the solid brick seventeenth-century farmhouse is a little square black-boarded grain-store, on mushroom-shaped stilts. The churchyard is just beyond it, with a small flint church of simple nave and chancel standing in the middle of an ancient fortress, a ditch with ballast thrown inwards to make a rampart, probably of Romano-British origin.

Immediately outside the ramparts is a crossroads and the corner of Waldershare Park, the estate of the Earl of Guilford. The lane runs along its border to Eythorne, with the curiously Kentish blend of woods, cornfields and pit-head machinery on the skyline, then along its northern edge to the A256 road to Sandwich. In a dip below this is an exercise in architecture, Malmains Farm: a square-fronted eighteenth-century farmhouse is attached as a crosswing to an early timber-framed house, to the farther end of which is joined a brick Flemish gable of, possibly, the seventeenth century. The main road can be crossed at once and a lane taken to Ashley, a homely village with small cottages, an inn and a Baptist chapel. Beyond this, East Studdal is a long strip of uninspiring modern houses leading to Sutton, a pretty village where a thatched cottage faces one with the locally prevalent Flemish influence, below a small medieval church, of flint, with picturesque nineteenth-century embellishments. Up on the high and windy Sutton Downs, mostly cornfields with rows of trees running at right angles to the contour-lines as windbreaks, skylarks and gulls share the only interruption of silence.

A track from this high road runs down into a secluded valley where Langdon Abbey Farm contains the few flint walls remaining of the Abbey of West Langdon, which was founded by one William de Auberville and colonised from the Praemonstratensian Abbey of Leiston in Suffolk, in 1189. It is often mentioned in Praemonstratensian records, seeming on the whole to have been well-conducted: as late as 1482 it had an 'excellent abbot', in 1488 the house was free from debt and well-provisioned, in 1494 was still prosperous and in 1500 had a debt of £60 but was still well provided; the report of Thomas Cromwell's commissioner in 1535, therefore, that he found the abbot with 'gentlewomen' and the house in 'utter decay and will shortly tumble down' should perhaps be viewed with suspicion. The abbey was obliged to surrender, and its lands went to help the king out of his financial difficulties.

East Langdon and Guston share the characteristics of the above-mentioned villages: they are attractive and unspoilt without being remarkable or architecturally distinguished. From the latter the road to Dover passes the buildings and playing fields of the Duke of York's Royal Military School; on the hill before the castle it passes an infantry barracks, reminders of the continuing tradition of the King's (or Queen's) garrison of Dover, from King John's Constable, Hubert de Burgh, to the orderly officer of the day in the army of Queen Elizabeth II.

There is far more of military, nautical, ecclesiastical and recent history of Dover than can be squeezed into the space available here; the town, a settlement even in Neolithic times, an Iron Age village and fortress turned into the Roman town of *Dubris*, one of their channel ports important enough to be lit by two *phari* or light-houses, one now nearly vanished on the Western Heights, the other still standing if abbreviated, attached to the Saxon church within the castle; the later Roman fort of the Saxon Shore, which has recently come to light in the course of some road construction, and then the long Anglo-Saxon (or Jutish) period, its accent post-597 far more on ecclesiastical than military considerations. There was a priory, founded first by King Eadbald of Kent in the seventh century, which lasted in one form or another in continuity until 1535: Richard Layton (he who had reported dubiously on West Langdon) told Cromwell that the prior and monks were immoral and as bad as any. The prior, John Lambert, wrote to Cromwell himself, pointing out that he had spent much to repair and improve the priory and asked Cromwell to consider deeds rather than words which might not be true. But the priory must be surrendered. Those who took the surrender confirmed the truth: the house was well repaired, the prior had reduced the debt, and the honest people of Dover were sorry to see the monks go.

The Hospital of St Mary, called Domus Dei or Maison Dieu, founded in 1203 by Hubert de Burgh to accommodate pilgrims and other travellers in and out of the port, lasted until 1544. A hall and tower were added to the original buildings in the late thirteenth century, and still stand, much restored and attached to the Victorian Town Hall: they are worth a visit.

The port, throughout the middle ages, continued to play a vital part as England's nearest link with the Continent and as a trading and naval base. Dover was one of the Cinque Ports, providing the king with ships and men in return for corporate privileges and liberties. Like the other ports it fought a continual battle with the sea, which persisted in filling the harbour with shingle, but could not win: by 1572, out of 135 ships in the whole of England of 100 tons or more, only one belonged to Dover. More efforts were made to improve the harbour, because it was still the nearest to France, and at last in 1924 the great encircling moles were built to make a safe anchorage for the fleet of cross-channel ferry-boats which are constantly steaming out and in, performing the same function as ever despite airlines, hovercraft and the projected tunnel.

The castle dominates Dover: it is really very fortunate that the nearest port to France should be overlooked by such a naturally defensible position, but it was Henry II who perceived that it should be crowned by the strongest and most modern of castles. A castle of some sort, perhaps mainly of wood, had existed before the Conquest, and it seems likely that it was replaced by one of stone later, but the prodigious expenditure of Henry II (over £7000 in all) created a defence-work which remained usable for 800 years. The massive central keep and the inner curtain wall are his work, begun in about 1168 and finished in the 1180s. His son John and grandson Henry III added more. John's Constable, Hubert de Burgh, defended the castle against a determined attack by the rebel barons and Prince Louis of France, and managed to hold out until John's death and the accession of his infant son brought about Louis's withdrawal. Between 1217 and 1256 another £7500 was spent in strengthening and increasing the fortifications, and the results are still visible. They would be more complete and better-looking, had it not been for work carried out in the 1790s, in the early phases of the Napoleonic Wars, when parts of the walls were demolished and other parts bolstered by earthen ramparts: tower-tops were levelled to make gun-platforms and the medieval underground passages extended. For students of medieval military architecture this transformation was tragic, but it serves to show that the 'key of England', as Matthew Paris had called it in Henry III's time, was still worth polishing and oiling, so to speak. Batteries of guns were added in various corners of the castle and cliffs later in the nineteenth century, and the complex redoubt built on Western Heights. Some of them were brought up to date in 1939–45 with anti-aircraft guns: the last garrison left the castle in 1958.

The castle today is immaculately preserved and opened to the public by the Department of the Environment, and anyone who goes to visit it may learn far more than I have space to tell them here: they may see the Roman *pharos* and the (much restored) Saxon church of St Mary-in-Castro on, the castle's bailey, the 24-foot cannon, presented by the Emperor Charles V to Henry VIII and known as Queen Elizabeth's Pocket Pistol, and the model, in one of the rooms of the castle keep, of part of the Battle of Waterloo, beautifully made by Captain Siborne early in the last century. Visitors may also climb up the wide stone stairs past the two fine Norman chapels, the great halls with their armour and fireplaces carved with graffiti by French prisoners-of-war, to the heights of the keep, even to one of the four corner turrets, and see below them the whole complex embattled hilltop, the town squeezed in between the hills in the narrow Dour valley, the wide harbour within its protective moles, the sea and the misty outline of the French coast. It is one of the best places in which to reflect on the importance to England of the port of Dover and the clifftop bastions built to defend it.

CHAPTER TWELVE

Canterbury to the Sea

Trying to describe Canterbury in a part of a chapter is rather like a ten-minute summary of a Shakespeare play: the structure is crudely comprehensible but the poetry is lost. Some might say that the poetry of Canterbury is lost in any case because of certain modern additions to it, but probably that is debatable.

The first known town of Canterbury was a huddle of huts on either side of the crossing of the Stour called by the Iron Age Britons *Durovernon*. During the 400 years of imperial rule, as a focal meeting-point of roads from Lympne, Dover, Richborough, Reculver, the Weald and London, it acquired a street-plan on the usual grid-system, a wall, baths, a theatre and several fine houses (like the one with a mosaic pavement, preserved for public inspection beneath Butchery Lane); it was called *Durovernum Cantiacorum*. As Roman civic discipline declined, early Germanic mercenaries lived in the town: the sites of their squalid hutments have been found. When in the mid-fifth century they ousted the Romano-British inhabitants, houses were built in the old streets and places, and the whole plan changed. The town was never deserted. By 597 King Ethelbert had his palace there: he gave it to St Augustine for a church, the basis of Christ Church Priory and cathedral church of the archbishops of Canterbury, primates of England. From St Augustine's time to the Reformation Canterbury was primarily ecclesiastical and monastic: when its two great houses were dissolved part of its function, to serve them, disappeared and it began a long decline, despite its continued position as primatial see of the Anglican Communion (but the archbishop was so often at Lambeth Palace) to the status of simple country market town. Only comparatively recently has it revived, with new commercial interests and industries: this is the two-edged sword which has sliced several layers off the architectural poetry, but I shall return to that later.

The accident of Becket's murder in his own cathedral made medieval Canterbury, and the wealth poured out by pilgrims and pious benefactors contributed hugely to its material survivors into modern times. There is a surprisingly large number of them, but there are also plenty of houses remaining from its later days, when the power of the church had waned. A brief itinerary of the city will probably resemble a kaleidoscope, but is at least one way of sketching the chief lines in what ought to be a detailed portrait. Outside the city walls, at the end of the London road is St Dunstan's, a church with a slender tower and, in its south-east chapel the vault of the Roper family, in which is a casket containing the head of Sir Thomas More, which his daughter Margaret Roper managed to rescue from London Bridge. Farther down the street is Roper Gate, the sole relic of their mansion, in Tudor brick; nearer the city there are famous old houses like the House of Agnes, borrowed by Dickens for one of his characters, and the Falstaff inn, built in 1403, end-on to the street. The Westgate is the only one of the city's fortified gates left: it was part of the refortifying work carried out by Archbishop Simon of Sudbury in about 1380, when castles and walls all over the south-east of England were built to repel the French, who had already effected some disastrous raids in the 1370s. There is now a museum of arms and armour in the Westgate, under which traffic still passes into the city (but round it, out). St Peter's Street, named from the little St Peter's church on the left, is lined on both sides with an interesting array of timbered houses, many of which have had brick fronts inserted to disguise their age: several are much older than they look. At the end, by the bridge over a stream of the Stour (another flows before the Westgate as a moat) is a many-gabled house called the Weavers, an equivalent of the Biddenden and Cranbrook cloth-halls. On the other side of the bridge and actually over the stream is the Eastbridge Hospital, founded by Archbishop Becket for the relief of poor pilgrims and later dedicated to him: miraculously, it still exists, as an almshouse with residents in the brick seventeenth-century building attached to the old hall, chapel and undercroft, administered by the Church.

In Stour Street, round the corner of the Post Office, an archway under a house leads to a garden where a stream of the Stour flows beneath a little flint building which in 1268 was built to accommodate the Franciscan (grey) friars, some of whom had lived in the city since 1224. They had previously been lodged in the nearby Poor Priests' Hospital, in Stour Street, a stone house of the twelfth century which was established as the hospital for poor and indigent priests in about 1200; it houses a clinic and a museum for the Buffs, the former Royal East Kent Regiment who were merged with the Royal West Kents in 1961. It is a full and interesting collection, of regimental relics and medals, but could do with more space. At the end of Stour Street, near the rapidly disappearing remains of the gasworks, is St Mildred's church, one of the oldest in the city, whose Anglo-Saxon origin can be deduced from the enormous stones used as quoins. At the end of Gas Street, up from the church, is the crumbled stump of the Norman castle, built soon after the Conquest in about 1080: it is in such a bad state now because the upper storey was pulled down in the early nineteenth century for sale as building materials.

From the castle, curving round eastward, is the best part of Sudbury's flint walls, with semicircular towers at intervals, and behind them are some very pleasant gardens named after a puzzling artificial mound called Dane John: innumerable suggestions have been made to account for it, but it is either a pre-Roman or Romano-British burial mound. The line of the Roman city wall changes direction to avoid it. Its appearance was considerably altered by 'landscaping' in the eighteenth century.

The east end of the city, from the Dane John Gardens to Burgate and from Butchery Lane to St George's Gate, was heavily bombed in 1942, and for years after the war only the propped-up halves of buildings and temporary huts could be seen in all the area. The work of clearance and rebuilding permitted excavation, in places for the first time ever, and more of Canterbury's Roman and medieval past came to light than would have been possible without Hitler's help. Most of it had to be reburied, but the mosaic floors under Butchery Lane were kept in situ, in a cellar eight feet below the street surface. The other corollary of the destruction of so many of Canterbury's old buildings was that new ones had to take their place: in part, this was well done, and in Burgate and the south side of St George's Street the arcaded shops seem already to belong to the general tone of the city. Other additions were not so happy: rectangular blocks of glass and steel, and a towering concrete car-park may be fully representative of twentieth-century architecture and not artificial mock-ups of some bygone age, but they say little for this century's abilities, spirit or taste.

In a short time the new buildings will probably be accepted as a fitting accompaniment to the ancient glories; perhaps the underlying reason for their radically, brutally unaesthetic design is that they are built for commercial purposes in as economic a way as possible, and until money is spent on what is commonly regarded as frivolous and extravagant embellishment of buildings whose prime function is not geared to the production of wealth, we in modern times will probably never realise our potential for creative design, and our most ambitious schemes will never rival the achievements of our medieval ancestors, despite their absurdly limited facilities, compared with ours, for large-scale construction.

Destruction of Canterbury's architectural treasures was not, of course, limited to Hitler. St Augustine's Abbey, in its hey-day, must have been as magnificent in its way as the great cathedral of its rival, Christ Church. 'Augustine,' says the Venerable Bede, our authority for these momentous historical happenings (he wrote in about 730), 'also erected a monastery to the east of the town, in which by his exhortation and direction King Ethelbert ordered a church to be erected of becoming splendour, dedicated to the blessed apostles Peter and Paul, and endowed it with a variety of gifts; in which church the body of Augustine and also those of all bishops and kings of Canterbury might be laid.' This took place in 598. Kings and bishops, abbots and saints, all were buried in the great church until 758 when the custom was broken.

The church was enlarged by St Dunstan in 978, and Abbot Wulfric in 1049 began to build a rotunda to connect the abbey church of St Peter and St Paul with the middle of the three, St Mary's. The third, St Pancras, is probably the oldest, and current excavations may be able to establish its date of building. The first Norman abbot, Scotland (a monk of Mont-St-Michel), reorganised the whole structure and rebuilt it, and the result stood with only minor alterations until 1538 when the abbey was surrendered to the king's commissioners by its last abbot, John Foche, and 30 monks. The remains, carefully excavated, turfed and gravelled, are almost impossible to understand without a plan and guide, because the whole complex was demolished shortly after dissolution, except for some walls of the nave which were incorporated into a house that the king had built for himself, and a tower. After the house became derelict half the tower fell in 1722 and the other half 100 years later. In 1844 the site was purchased for a missionary college, and in the next year work began on buildings for it, designed by William Butterfield. Part of the remaining abbey buildings were used, including the turreted gatehouse, built by Abbot Fyndon in 1300–9; excavations began on the main part of the site in 1901 and have proceeded intermittently ever since.

The church then, of St Augustine's Abbey, was swiftly destroyed; that of the other Canterbury monastery, Christ Church (whose earlier name was Holy Trinity), survived because it was also the cathedral church of the archbishops of Canterbury, who had also until the dissolution been abbots of the monastery. Even some of the abbey (or, rather, priory, because the prior was effectually in command) buildings were allowed to remain, such as the cloisters, and parts of the cathedral school which was refounded as the King's School. Except for some further demolition, some of which has now been made good, by the agents of Adolf Hitler, most of what was left after the dissolution still stands.

A little street, Mercery Lane, leads from the High Street to Christ Church Gate: the street has long-jettied, three-storey buildings on either side which have stood for 500 years or more. That on the left shows the stone ground-floor of the old Chequers hotel, which has stood for long enough to have accommodated pilgrims to the shrine of St Thomas in Chaucer's time. At the end of the lane is the place where the Buttermarket used to stand, and facing it is the well-restored late-Perpendicular Gateway, which nearly succumbed to another would-be despoiler, Colonel Edwin Sandys. He, grandson of a notable archbishop of York and son of the Virginian administrator of Northbourne, fired 40 discharges of cannon at the gate to destroy the figure of Christ in the central niche, then smashed his way through the cathedral, breaking and spoiling all he could, allegedly in the name of purification.

The entrance through the gateway comes to the south-west porch of the cathedral: the building which confronts one is so tall, so immense that there is difficulty in comprehending it at all. It has come to us through all these dangers and distresses of the near and distant past: its fabric has been burnt three times, in 1011 by the invading Danes, in 1067 and in 1174 by accident. Parts of each rebuilding are left: the lovely Romanesque arches of the twelfth-century work of William of Sens and his successor William the Englishman; the awesome nave, replacing Lanfranc's work of the eleventh century, designed by Henry Yevele and built under Prior Chillenden in the 1390s. The work was undertaken from funds raised by public subscription, and finished in 1411, the year Chillenden died.

No verbal description can convey adequately the feelings evoked in almost anyone who enters the cathedral and gazes up at the towering forest of arches in the nave, to the steps before the screen. This is the work of men, hundreds of years before us: of course, we know little of what architects, overseers, masons and labourers thought about it, and they may have regarded the building operations as just another job for which they would be paid; but the pay came not from the profits of some industrial complex, nor from grudgingly paid taxes, but from the results of Archbishop Sudbury's appeal of 1378, and no doubt from subsequent appeals by his successors, for contributions from the Christian public. Whatever spirit animated the builders, and those of the earlier reconstructions, the result speaks not of 'conspicuous consumption', nor of a suitable building for the cathedral church of the primate of the Church in England (and later of the Church of England), but of a place made and dedicated by humble men to the best of their ability to the greater glory of God.

No matter how many times a visitor may walk around the cathedral, into its crypt or along its dark exterior passages, there is always something new to notice, and to admire: there is plenty to see, far more than can be even mentioned here, rich stained glass, tombs of archbishops, priors, kings and princes, the spot where Archbishop Becket was murdered, the little ceremony of the Warriors' Chapel, the half-incredulity in looking up into the great tower, Bell Harry; the best a writer can do is say, go and see.

Harbledown, which Chaucer called 'Bob-up-and-down' because that is what travellers through it do, is the last village on the Watling Street before Canterbury. On the edge of the Forest of Blean, it was probably a wood-cutters' village at first; Archbishop Lanfranc, the brilliant monk of Bec who became the first Norman primate under the Conqueror, founded a hospital there for the relief of lepers, in 1084. By the mid-twelfth century leprosy was on the wane and the hospital gradually became almshouses, for the care of the aged; coupled with Eastbridge Hospital, it remains so today. The present buildings, modernised, replaced the current houses in the nineteenth century, but the church has some of the original eleventh-century fabric in its nave and a substantial part of the twelfth-century additions: the north aisle, the arcade and the tower. On the hillside below the Hospital but above a fine thatched wooden barn belonging to Hospital Farm is a well decorated with the Prince of Wales's three feathers and called the Black Prince's Well: there is a tradition (unsubstantiated as far as I know) that the Prince called for some of its medicinal waters during his last illness. The waters are far from medicinal today because of oil seepage from the road, which, as the A2, taking the full force of traffic, can still be crossed if one waits for long enough and is reasonably agile. On its opposite bank from the Hospital is the parish church of St Michael and All Angels, built in the twelfth and enlarged in the fifteenth century.

The Downland hills on the left bank of the Stour behind Canterbury are now crowned with the new, imposing and interesting buildings of the University of Kent at Canterbury, a small collegiate university with a particularly impressive library, both architecturally and academically. One of its colleges, Darwin, is on the site where Bartholomew de Badlesmere is said to have been hanged, and the name of its neighbouring village, Tyler Hill, was recently made fully explicit by the discovery in a field of the foundations of one of the tile-kilns. Below the hill but still above the river-level is the village of Hackington, often better known by the name of its church,

St Stephen's, which has always been more or less a suburb of Canterbury (its houses are now adjoining); facing the green is a row of brick Elizabethan almshouses, contemporary with and adjacent to the Beverley inn, home of the Canterbury game of Bat and Trap. The church, at the end of the green, was the centre of a major twelfth-century ecclesiastical row, because Archbishop Baldwin, having quarrelled with the monks of Christ Church Priory, proposed to establish a collegiate church at Hackington with prebendary stalls for the king and all bishops, which would have surpassed the Priory in prestige, as Baldwin intended, and circumvented the monks' right to elect the archbishop, who was also their abbot (there was always a dispute at each election, the monks' candidate against the bishops'); the monks appealed to the new king, Richard I, who ordered a compromise. Baldwin withdrew, and retrieved his reputation by going on Crusade and dying at Acre in 1190. The church remains, but has always been merely a parish church.

Beyond the latest extension to Hackington, a housing estate at Hales Place, the hillside remains rural as far as Sturry. Here the Roman roads from Reculver and Thanet (by a ferry) met, and shortly after the 1939–45 war, in the course of some excavations for gravel the jetties were found of the port which served *Durovernum*: the river was much wider and the tide came up to a point near where the railway runs below the road. Sturry's name is one of the earliest Jutish names, from *Stour-geh*, district on the Stour. The southern parish boundary is the Roman road to Thanet, the northern, the edge of the Forest of Blean: originally it probably included Chislet and Hoath as far as Reculver. Its manor belonged for a while to St Mildred's monastery at Minster, then to St Augustine's Abbey: it was to Sturry Court that John Foche, the last abbot, came with his pension in retirement. The house which now serves as part of Junior King's School is part of a mansion built after 1578 by Customer Smyth (Smythe or Smith) when on his way up to his Westenhanger status. Near it and at right-angles to the church is an immense timber-and-brick barn, of the late seventeenth century, one of the longest in Kent. The church is of Norman origin, built like many others on the site of a Saxon chapel, and greatly altered and increased in size in the thirteenth and fourteenth centuries.

The parish of Westbere fills in the gap between the A28, the Roman road and the present course of the river; the village itself hangs on the hillside, shrouded in woods, a quiet place apart from the main road's clamour, with several interesting houses and cottages, including one dated 1356 but much bricked-up on all sides, and the timbered inn, the Yew Tree; the church is a simple small nave and chancel, with no tower.

On the Sturry side of the A28 is the Reculver road, along which one comes to Hoath: a little farther on, towards Reculver, is a farm called Ford Manor, which conceals the fragmentary remains of a manor-house built by Archbishop Morton in the 1480s. It was used by subsequent archbishops, particularly Cranmer, who went there from Lambeth in 1537 to avoid an outbreak of plague; it was eventually demolished by order of the Commonwealth in 1658. It stands in a little fold in the hills, the valley of a small stream whose ford gave a name to it.

A lane across the wide open cornfield country leads through a farm-and-cottage group called Chislet Forstal, where there is a 'Tudor House' which is almost certainly pre-Tudor but was augmented with chimneys, oriel window and porch in the sixteenth century, to Chislet: a single street of houses, with a Victorian primary school and an inn, it has a church with a curiously truncated spire, squared off less than half-way up. Chislet is on the northern side of the Sarre Penn, a tributary to the Wantsum which makes a long valley in the hills behind the Stour bank, rising in the Forest of Blean. On its southern side is the fourth Kentish coal-mine, called Chislet but served by the mining village of Hersden, and now closed down; at the very end of the ridge is Upstreet and Wall End, both self-explanatory names when one considers the behaviour of the old Roman street and the beginning of the Sarre Wall across the levels to Thanet.

Across the river from Sturry is Fordwich: Sturry was the Romans' port for *Durovernum*, but Fordwich was the medieval port for Canterbury, the highest navigable point on the river. In Domesday Book it appears as one of the only eight boroughs in Kent, with most of its land in the possession of the abbot of St Augustine's Abbey. By the end of the thirteenth century it had acquired a mayor, jurats and freemen, and the rights, privileges and liberties granted to a Limb of a Cinque Port, in this case Sandwich. It served as a port for unloading victuals for both the great monastic establishments of Canterbury, who waged a constant war of attrition over rights of wharfage: stone from Caen was unloaded for the rebuilding of the Cathedral, the abbot of St Augustine's bailiff was in perpetual odium for infringing the rights of the freemen, ships were sent to fulfil the king's demands from Sandwich, cases were tried in the little Court Hall, thieves were drowned in the 'Thefeswell', mayors were elected every year by the freemen in the church. Much of this air of importance still hangs over the little town (which has never been more populous than a small village): there is a street of good-looking 'town' houses, with the George and Dragon inn (which once had the farm for collecting tolls on the bridge) at one end, and the old Court Hall at the other; the latter has a stone base containing a gaol and a jettied upper room of timber and brick, with a tiled and hipped roof. On its river-fronting end is a black-boarded shed and the Town Crane, a piece of machinery which was still in use in the nineteenth-century last days of Fordwich as a port (there are photographs of barges being unloaded). The old corporation, inspected and found wanting in 1835, lingered on until 1886 when it was wound up: but traditions are tenacious, and Fordwich still has a mayor-deputy who is still elected every year, with a ceremony in the Court Hall and a service, in which the mayors of Canterbury and Sandwich participate, in the church. Now, with local government being reorganised, even Canterbury and Sandwich will be deprived of mayors so perhaps all such spirits of the past will have to be laid.

St Mary the Virgin, Fordwich, is a small, mainly thirteenth-century church with a tall shingled steeple and box pews: the mayor's pew, with the iron stands for the mace, is of course in the front on the left. There is an old stone sarcophagus with a fish-scale pattern in the north aisle, and a solid wooden penitents' stool; above the chancel arch is a rarity, a tympanum with the arms of William III and the ten commandments, a celebration of the 'Glorious Revolution' of 1688.

On the hills above Fordwich there are woods and orchards all

235

the way to Littlebourne, giving way to farmland downriver towards Stodmarsh. In the little vale of a stream there is a hall-house, El-bridge, which as a farmhouse has been in the possession of the same family, the Holdstocks, for hundreds of years.

Littlebourne, on the Nailbourne where it becomes the Lesser Stour, has two groups of houses, around the church which has a high thirteenth-century chancel, with lancet windows, and a great wooden thatched barn between it and the Court Lodge, and along the A257, the Sandwich road; a lane follows the shallow stream at right-angles to the main road, past a converted mill of white weatherboard to a larger one of similar design, still in use, at Wickhambreux. The small triangular green of Wickhambreux, set about with chestnut trees, flanked with cottages, the church, stately Georgian houses, an inn and some timbered houses, is justly famous and in summer often attracts a surprising number of coach parties.

Ickham is only half a mile away and easily accessible, a wide street of brick and weatherboarded houses on one side and the church and Court Lodge, with farm, on the other: Stodmarsh is oddly isolated, approached by an almost gratuitously tortuous net-work of lanes, on the edge of the lower river-marshes of the Stour. It is a compact and attractive village, with a tiny thirteenth-century church, one of whose lancet windows has all its original glass.

The rivers are wider, the marshy levels broader here, and bridges rarer; there is only one bridge, replacing the Grove Ferry, between Fordwich and Plucks Gutter, seven miles farther down: there is only one on the Lesser Stour between Wickhambreux and its junc-tion with the Great Stour at Plucks Gutter. Across this on the last north-eastern undulations of the North Downs are Preston and Stourmouth, whose name demonstrates amply enough where it once stood: near the meeting of the Stour with the Wantsum Channel. West Stourmouth is on a road to nowhere and therefore is fortunate in its tranquillity: it is an old settlement of farms and cottages, and at its very end is a little church, All Saints. The road through Preston and East Stourmouth almost rivals a Romney Marsh road in its eccentricity on its way to Plucks Gutter, the Wantsum levels and Thanet: east of it and north of the Sandwich road is a stretch of country which, like West Stourmouth, possesses that enviable property, peace, from absence of through motor traffic. It is a country of wide, slightly convex fields of potatoes, corn and orchards, scattered farmsteads and small hamlets. Elmstone has a tiny flint church and both it and Walmstone, hardly more than a farm now, are listed in *Domesday Monachorum* as having had Saxon churches. Ware, on the edge of a sudden dip made by a stream to the Wantsum, has a nineteenth-century chapel, now in use as a barn. This sparsely inhabited but intensively cultivated, and almost unknown country, while short on definite attractions, has a rare allure for those who, on foot, prefer to be out of earshot of traffic-rumble.

The latter is encountered in full force again at Ash, on the Sandwich road: a street of good brick seventeenth- and eighteenth-century houses, with a high-standing spired church; the western end of it, with circular pillars of different thicknesses, is of the late twelfth century, the chancel, transepts and chapel, of the thirteenth. There are a number of tombs with effigies of their occupants, and some brasses to a branch of the Septvans family, previously encountered at Chartham.

New Street, Ash, leads down from the ridge along which the road runs, to Woodnesborough. Although evidently derived from Woden's burgh, it has been suggested that the name, in addition to being the Teutonic god's, was also a man's name, judging by the frequency with which it occurs. The little church, on a hill with a tower capped by a wooden balustrade, a square wooden belfry and an onion spire, has a new rood cross, of wrought-iron by a local man and a brass centrepiece worked by a nun of Minster.

Across two of the main roads converging on Sandwich and in a world of its own, like Stourmouth, is Worth, a street of brick cottages with a Flemish flavour by a duckpond, which is said to be the remains of the creek which once connected it with the sea, and a twelfth-century church. Due south of the church there was discovered the remains of a Roman temple, which at one time was thought to have been a signal-station or watch-tower for the benefit of shipping on its way to the port of *Rutupiae* or Richborough.

A good footpath with an asphalt surface goes all the way across dykes, sluices and cornfields from Worth to Sandwich, arriving hard by the railway station. Sandwich was one of the original Cinque Ports, with duties in return for privileges marked out as early as Domesday Book (1085) and throughout the middle ages until the Wantsum Channel and the Stour Estuary between them silted up and made navigation extremely difficult, was one of the most important of Channel ports. It had walls for defence at the time of Domesday, it acquired four hospitals for the care of poor travellers and pilgrims (one of which, St Bartholomew's, was founded with proceeds from booty captured in Hubert de Burgh's great naval victory over the rebels supporting Prince Louis of France, on St Bartholomew's Day, 1217); another St Bartholomew's Day, in 1572, was the occasion, obliquely, for the town's rescue from decline as its status as a port vanished with the silting up of the haven: the massacre of protestant Huguenots on the eve of that day (24 August) moved others of their persuasion to emigrate in haste, and large numbers settled in the nearest port, Sandwich, and began to practise their arts of weaving serge cloth, growing market-garden produce and making silk. Colonies of them in Canterbury and all corners of East Kent, as can be seen from the surviving characteristic gables in the houses they built, were further swelled during the seventeenth century by persecution on the Continent, and many names in modern Kent (such as Kemp and, in some cases, Jenkins) owe their origin to them.

Sandwich has streets of maze-like complexity, lined with houses from all centuries from the fourteenth to the twentieth: most are of brick, several of timber, and some of flint and stone. The earthen ramparts which encircle the town, erected in the 1380s to keep out the French (who had already been, disastrously, on a raid in 1377), included in their fortifications the Fishergate, on the quayside, and possibly also the Barbican, much restored, where tolls are collected from the endless stream of motorists crossing the bridge. The parish church, St Clement's, has Norman work in the base of its tower and a brick top, with an ogival onion spire; the flint and stone in the nave walls are strengthened with courses of tile, perhaps taken from nearby Richborough. The Town Hall or Guildhall was rebuilt early in this century but inside is much material, such as the wooden panelling in the Court Room, taken from its medieval predecessor. It is being extended at the rear, in a style consistent with the earlier building and well in keeping with the town. The game of golf, which is played on the miles of level sand-dunes which were originally responsible for the town's decline, since they prevented ships from finding an easy way into the haven, has gone a long way towards restoring it; now there are industries established across the bridge at Great Stonar, a modern place on the site of a vanished medieval town which used to exist on the shingle spit south of Ebbsfleet, with the same name. The traffic through the narrow streets of Sandwich, from the four converging main roads from Canterbury, Thanet, Deal and Dover, is incessant and very troublesome.

A lane from the Canterbury road, near an old windmill, follows the railway and the river northward from Sandwich towards a low tongue of land stretching out into the levels: on the very end of this are the very substantial remains of the principal port of Roman Britannia, *Rutupiae* (which became *Raette-burgh* and subsequently Richborough). The invading army of the Emperor Claudius, under the command of Aulus Plautius, taking note of the storms which damaged Caesar's ships when he beached them at Deal, made for this sheltered haven in the Wantsum Channel: 'it is probable', says J. P. Bushe-Fox, in his pamphlet, 'that the whole force' (four legions plus auxiliaries) 'landed here, because defensive ditches of the period have been found enclosing a large area'. The base was consolidated as a supply depot, and became the principal communications port with Gaul and Rome: during the reign of the Emperor Domitian, in about A.D. 85, probably to mark the completion of the conquest of Britain by his general Agricola (the subject of a biography by his son-in-law, Tacitus), a mighty and awe-inspiring triumphal arch was erected on the site of some of the former wooden buildings of the port, cased in marble and decked with bronze statues. The massive foundations of this monument suggest, by their thickness, that it must have been of colossal size: a cruciform platform, 30 feet thick, is made of layers of flints embedded in mortar. Thinking that it concealed a chamber in its centre, a drilling was made some years ago, finding none: the mortar is so hard that the drill often penetrated the flints rather than the mortar. One imagines that the monument must have been of a size which could be seen, as the towers of the power-station at Ebbsfleet are seen today, for many miles inland and out to sea.

In the third century the raids on the south coast by Saxon pirates began, and new earthen fortifications were dug; when Carausius was put in charge of the British Fleet (*Classis Britannicus*) and, in a time of imperial confusion, usurped an autonomous command over the whole province, he began to erect a series of fortifications on the south-eastern coast: the walls here at Richborough are of this date (287–93) and are among the most complete of those surviving. They are two-and-a-half-sided: the whole eastern and half the southern walls have collapsed and vanished from erosion by the tidal seas, but the remainder, using parts of the great monument which must have been demolished for the purpose, still stand 25 feet high in places. This fort of Carausius was in the fourth century incorporated into the Saxon Shore Fort system, along with Reculver, Dover and Lympne, and at one point was garrisoned, according to the army list *Notitia Dignitatum*, by the Legion II Augusta, which had spent most of its career after the invasion of A.D. 43 stationed at Caerleon. When in the fifth century the troops were withdrawn from Britain in order to defend parts of the empire nearer to Rome, *Rutupiae* began to decline, disappearing from recorded history. The foundations of a Saxon chapel on the farthest eastern part before the eroded slope down to the railway and river, show that there was an awareness of the importance of these mighty walls: St Augustine was said to have set foot ashore here on his way to the mainland and King Ethelbert's city of Canterbury, and that foot was supposed to have left a print on a stone which was preserved in the chapel, and shown to generations of pilgrims.

Christianity came to Kent in Roman times, as we know from the chapel at Lullingstone villa and from a number of finds, such as the silver spoons at Canterbury marked with the *chi-rho* monogram; the faith also preceded St Augustine, because King Ethelbert had married a Frankish princess who was already Christian and brought her own chaplain, Liudhard, with her. They had built (or perhaps rebuilt an existing structure) a church on the hill behind Canterbury, dedicated to St Martin. Parts of it can still be seen, Roman tile and brick coursed with flint and stone, in the present choir of the church of St Martin, which makes it the oldest in continuous use in England.

At Richborough one can stand in the marked foundations of the chapel of St Augustine, looking away from the great Roman walls to the misty flats and the sea; to northward the power-station's towers loom up at Ebbsfleet: here or hereabouts, successive waves of invaders have come and landed, bringing, often, the latest type of civilisation with them. Neolithic men, Bronze Age Celts, Iron Age Celts; here at Richborough in 43, the Romans came, bringing the most advanced, the most stable and the most widespread form of civilisation the world had ever known; there at Ebbsfleet, the Jutes, more advanced than their Anglo-Saxon cousins but centuries behind the Romans. At Ebbsfleet Augustine and his monks landed, and to Richborough, perhaps, they came on their way to Canterbury, bringing with them the ideas which, since their beginning, have replaced the dark doubts in men's minds with certainties, founded on faith. Kent has been in the forefront of many subsequent developments, and is likely, for the same geographical reasons, to be in the same position in the future: many modern people put their trust for the future, believing in man's own abilities, in some political creed; others, with similar faith, in technological progress; some, doubting all, have no faith and can only prophesy doom, and some, tremulous, can only cling to the past, deprecate the present and fear the future. Kent, in line still to be the channel for communications with Europe, might do well to remember the faith which brought St Augustine to Ebbsfleet, which built the great cathedral church of Canterbury and gave peace of mind to generations of its people, and pass it on to be the foundation of new ages.

Index

243

Index

Index

Index

Index